French Defence Policy Since the End of the Cold War

This book describes the evolution of French defence policy since the end of the Cold War.

For the past 30 years, there have been significant changes to French defence policy as a result of several contextual evolutions. Changes include shifts in the global balance of power, new understandings of the notion of international security, economic downturns, and developments in European integration. Yet despite these changes, the purpose of France's grand strategy and its main principles have remained remarkably stable over time. This book identifies the incentives, representations, and objectives of French defence policy. The authors examine the general mechanisms that influence policy change and military transformation in democracies, the importance of status-seeking in international relations, the processes of strategy-making by a middle power, and the dilemmas and challenges of security cooperation. By doing so, the book raises a number of questions related to the ways states adjust (or not) their security policies in a transformed international system. This book makes French-language sources available to non-French-speaking readers and contributes to a better understanding of a country that is at the forefront of Europe's external action.

This book will be of great interest to students of defence studies, French politics, military studies, security studies, and International Relations.

Alice Pannier is Research Fellow and head of the Geopolitics of Technologies programme at the the French Institute of International Relations (IFRI).

Olivier Schmitt is Professor of Political Science at the Center for War Studies, University of Southern Denmark, and currently Head of Research and Studies at the French Institute of Higher National Defence Studies (IHEDN).

Cass Military Studies

Countering Insurgencies and Violent Extremism in Asia
Edited by Shanthie Mariet D'Souza

Commercial Insurgencies in the Networked Era
The revolutionary armed forces of Colombia
Oscar Palma

The Politics of Military Families
State, work organizations, and the rise of the negotiation household
Edited by René Moelker, Manon Andres, and Nina Rones

Organisational Learning and the Modern Army
A new model for lessons-learned processes
Tom Dyson

Civil–Military Relations in International Interventions
A new analytical framework
Karsten Friis

Defence Diplomacy
Strategic engagement and interstate conflict
Daniel H. Katz

Management and Military Studies
Classical and current foundations
Joseph Soeters

Understanding Insurgent Resilience
Organizational structures and the implications for counterinsurgency
Andrew D. Henshaw

Military Strategy of Middle Powers
Competing for security, influence and status in the 21st century
Håkan Edström and Jacob Westberg

Military Mission Formations and Hybrid Wars
New sociological perspectives
Edited by Thomas Vladimir Brond, Uzi Ben-Shalom and Eyal Ben-Ari

French Defence Policy Since the End of the Cold War
Alice Pannier and Olivier Schmitt

For more information about this series, please visit: https://www.routledge.com/
Cass-Military-Studies/book-series/CMS

French Defence Policy Since the End of the Cold War

Alice Pannier and Olivier Schmitt

LONDON AND NEW YORK

First published 2021
by Routledge
2 Park Square, Milton Park, Abingdon, Oxon OX14 4RN

and by Routledge
52 Vanderbilt Avenue, New York, NY 10017

Routledge is an imprint of the Taylor & Francis Group, an informa business

© 2021 Alice Pannier and Olivier Schmitt

The right of Alice Pannier and Olivier Schmitt to be identified as authors of this work has been asserted by them in accordance with sections 77 and 78 of the Copyright, Designs and Patents Act 1988.

All rights reserved. No part of this book may be reprinted or reproduced or utilised in any form or by any electronic, mechanical, or other means, now known or hereafter invented, including photocopying and recording, or in any information storage or retrieval system, without permission in writing from the publishers.

Trademark notice: Product or corporate names may be trademarks or registered trademarks, and are used only for identification and explanation without intent to infringe.

British Library Cataloguing-in-Publication Data
A catalogue record for this book is available from the British Library

Library of Congress Cataloging-in-Publication Data
A catalog record has been requested for this book

ISBN: 978-1-138-08462-9 (hbk)
ISBN: 978-1-315-11171-1 (ebk)

Typeset in Times New Roman
by Deanta Global Publishing Services, Chennai, India

Contents

List of figures		vi
List of tables		vii
Acknowledgements		viii
Introduction: The sources of French defence policy		1
1	Defence institutions and civil–military relations	13
2	Transforming the French armed forces	33
3	Nuclear deterrence: capabilities and doctrine	54
4	Defence industry and procurement	80
5	At war: French military operations since 1991	107
6	France and its partners	130
	Conclusion	156
	Index	165

Figures

1.1	Women active duty military personnel in the armed forces of NATO member states in 2017. (Source: NATO)	23
2.1	French defence budgets (Constant USD 2017. Source: SIPRI)	38
4.1	Change in total spending, day-to-day spending, and equipment spending	83
4.2	French equipment expenditure and share of European collaborative procurement, 2005–2017	96

Tables

2.1	Scenarios in the 1994 white paper	34
2.2	Size of the French armed forces	36
2.3	Format reduction in the Military Programming Law 2009–2014 (Sample)	39
4.1	Main French defence companies	86
5.1	List of major French military interventions in Africa since the end of the Cold War	124

Acknowledgements

Olivier Schmitt gratefully acknowledges funding from the Gerda-Henkel Stiftung (grant AZ 12/KF/17), the Independent Research Fund Denmark (grant 95-556-25107), and the Carlsberg Foundation (grant CF17-0148). The views expressed herein are those of the authors and do not necessarily represent the views of the Gerda-Henkel Stiftung, the Independent Research Fund Denmark, or the Carlsberg Foundation.

The authors would like to thank Julien Malizard and Quentin Lopinot for comments on earlier versions of this book. This book is the result of the authors' several years of research on French defence policy, and we are grateful to the many individuals we interviewed or with whom we have discussed this topic.

Introduction

The sources of French defence policy

> As every time we are faced with historic challenges, our reaction must be the same: renewed ambition and audacity. We must shoulder our responsibilities. We have the choice of either taking back control of our destiny or aligning ourselves with any power whatsoever, thereby abandoning the idea of any strategies of our own. An awakening is needed. Overhauling the world order to further peace is the course we must follow, and France and Europe have a historic role to play.
>
> Emmanuel Macron, speech at the *École de Guerre* (official translation), 7 February 2020

As Emmanuel Macron was giving his awaited speech on defence and deterrence strategy in February 2020, at the *École de Guerre*, where no president had spoken since De Gaulle, the French defence apparatus was mobilised in full swing on French territory and across the globe: French troops were deployed in a combat operation in the Sahel and in defensive missions under British command in Estonia; ballistic missile submarines patrolled the oceans to guarantee the credibility of the French nuclear deterrent; soldiers from the Foreign Legion protected the European spaceport in Kourou, French Guiana; and the Minister for the Armed Forces Florence Parly was negotiating with her German counterpart to unlock the funds necessary for the development of the next-generation fighter aircraft that will replace the Rafale. Soon after, French troops were mobilised in response to the COVID-19 pandemic as part of Operation Resilience: they helped transport and distribute medical equipment and patients; a field hospital was deployed to ease the burden on the public health system; and the air force sent aircraft to repatriate French nationals from Wuhan, China.

Despite, or because of the centrality of the military in France's foreign and security policy – and even its industrial policy – tensions abound in the French defence model. Most recently, questions about civil–military relations resurfaced when a chief of the general staff (*Chef d'État-Major des Armées* – CEMA) was forced to resign in 2017. There have been gaps between strategic ambitions and available resources. The Defence and National Security Strategic Review, published that same year, indicated that "the current situation exceeds [the armed forces'] operational contracts and leads to serious difficulties in terms of training

2 Introduction

and support" (Strategic Review, 2017, English, p. 27). Indeed, the French armed forces were reduced so much in the two decades following the end of the Cold War that some feared the French army would soon fit in a football stadium (De Durand, 2011). At the same time, successive French governments chose to allocate more than 22% of its defence budget to the maintenance and modernisation of its nuclear deterrent. How has France ended up in this state of affairs, in 2020, where it maintains a global ambition and multifaceted defence commitments, but is also increasingly dependent on partners for achieving its missions and developing its new equipment? This contrasted situation calls for an assessment of French contemporary defence policy. What are its guiding principles, its strategic priorities, and its instruments? How has France's defence policy adapted to successive changes in the security environment (with which the country has been confronted) since its very principles, priorities, and instruments were spelt out by General de Gaulle in the context of the Cold War?

There is a lack of recent full-fledged monographs on this topic: while sector-specific analyses of aspects of French defence policy exist (for example, in recent years, see Fortmann et al., 2010; Tandler, 2014; Von Hlatky, 2014; Schmitt, 2017; Pannier, 2017; Talmor and Selden, 2017; Ostermann, 2019; Daho, 2019; Pannier and Schmitt, 2019), the most comprehensive English-speaking analyses available (Gregory, 2000; Utley, 2000) need updating. Our book fills this gap. By offering an in-depth analysis of the evolutions of France's defence policy, it helps illuminate the ways a middle power adjusts its strategies in a transformed international system. In this book, we explain the making and evolution of contemporary French defence policy in successive thematic chapters covering all instruments of France's hard power: defence institutions and civil–military relations; armed forces structure and doctrine; the nuclear deterrent; defence industry and procurement; military interventions; and alliances and partnerships.

Besides, this book makes French-language sources available to non-French-speaking readers and contributes to a better understanding of a country that is at the forefront of Europe's external action. Through a study of the instruments of France's hard power, we identify the competing incentives, varied representations, and shifting objectives of France's defence policy. While we look at France, we raise a number of questions related to the ways states adjust (or not) their security policies in a transformed international system. Through the French example, we examine the mechanisms influencing policy change and military transformation in democracies, the importance of status-seeking in international relations, the processes of strategy-making by a middle power, and the dilemmas and challenges of security cooperation.

We argue that, over the course of three decades, changes to French defence policies have been big in all areas of defence. These have resulted from contextual evolutions: from shifts in the global balance of power, to new understandings of the notion of international security, to economic downturns, and to progress in European integration. There has been an adaptation in the means of France's defence policy. Yet, the purpose of the country's grand strategy and its main principles, which we present in this introduction, have remained remarkably stable over

Introduction 3

time: the principles guiding actions have been accommodated to face new threats or new economic conditions and, most of the time, adaptation has been progressive and piecemeal rather than abrupt. Our book thus argues that French grand strategy, and the narratives that sustain it, are strikingly resilient – to the point where its principles and ambitions sometimes risk being unfit for contemporary realities. In this introduction, we explain the historical sources of French defence policy, and the conceptual underpinning of grand strategy, on which this book relies.

The symbolic and material foundations of French defence policy during the Cold War

The French foreign and defence policy is often framed in terms of "exceptionality", which has its roots in Gaullist policies pursued during the Cold War. On 3 December 1959, the then President de Gaulle gave a major speech at the war college, which captures his views on French defence policy:

> The defence of France must be French. It is a necessity that may have been forgotten in recent years. I know that. It is indispensable that it is French again. A country like France, if it is at war, it must be its war. The effort must be its effort. Should it not be the case, our country would contradict everything it ever was since its origins, its role, its self-esteem, its soul. Naturally, French defence policy could be, as appropriate, combined with those of other countries. It is in the order of things. But it is indispensable that our defence is our own; that France defends itself, for itself, in its own ways (…).

> The system called 'integration', which was inaugurated and to some degree implemented after the challenges we went through, while we could think that the free world was facing an imminent and unlimited threat and while we hadn't yet recovered our national personality, this integration system is over. Of course, our defence, the establishment of our means, the conception of the conduct of war, must be combined with other countries. Our strategy must be coordinated with the strategy of others. On the battlefield, it is extremely likely that we will be side by side with allies. But each must get its own part!
>
> (De Gaulle, 1989, pp. 71–74)

This is a particularly interesting speech because it highlights the continuous attempts since the Cold War to square the circle: balancing a desire for independence in the defence realm with the need for cooperation with allies, in particular, military integration within NATO. Indeed,

> in establishing, ahead of time, a supreme commander and plans for the integration of national war machines, the allies hoped they could prevent a third world war. Integration, also, was the essential means by which German rearmament had been made palatable to the citizens and states of Europe.
>
> (Sayle, 2019, p. 101)

4   *Introduction*

However, military integration was always politically problematic for De Gaulle, who had greater ambitions for his country, which is summarised by the famous line in the opening of his *Mémoires de Guerre:* "France cannot be France without greatness" (De Gaulle, 1954, p. 5). In fact, De Gaulle had a grand strategic vision and identified the means to achieve it. The grand strategic design was to ensure the return of France's presence everywhere in the world, create an autonomous Europe open to Africa, decrease the tensions with the Eastern bloc, and establish relations with China (Vaïsse, 1998). The mechanism designed to achieve this grand strategic objective was to maximise French autonomy through the obtention of adequate means. It is easy to confuse the means (autonomy) with the ends (grand strategy) when assessing De Gaulle's foreign policy, but "autonomy was never an objective per se, it was a means to accomplish a foreign policy aimed at overcoming the bipolarity of the Cold War, and the somehow mechanical polarization of alliances that came with it" (Schmitt, 2017, p. 464).

One of the instruments designed to achieve autonomy was the establishment of an independent nuclear force. In a speech in Strasbourg on 23 November 1961, De Gaulle started establishing the foundations of the French nuclear doctrine (De Gaulle, 1961). The timing and location were anything but random: it was the 17th anniversary of the liberation of Strasbourg from Nazi Germany by General Leclerc's troops. Strasbourg was highly significant in the Free French's mythology since after the victory of Kufra in 1941, General Leclerc and his troops had sworn an oath to fight until "our flag flies over the cathedral of Strasbourg" (Notin, 2005). The context of De Gaulle's speech was also important since he had announced the French withdrawal from Algeria and successfully thwarted a putsch attempt that same year. For the French president, the French armed forces were to have three core functions. First, they were to be equipped with modern equipment including nuclear weapons. Second, because of the gradual globalisation of conflicts, French troops should not be limited to fighting in the (former) colonial empire but should ready themselves for worldwide deployments. Third, they should ensure the "immediate defence" of the national territory. The speech is significant because it lays out the foundations for the three pillars of French defence policy that would later be developed: nuclear capabilities as a strategic deterrent, military interventions, and territorial defence. However, according to the former Gaullist Minister of the Armed Forces Pierre Messmer (1992), the armed forces did not welcome the announcement: there was a sense that the defeat in Algeria was compensated by shiny new nuclear weapons that could only be used at De Gaulle's discretion, ultimately reducing the importance of the military. The idea of a national deterrent also sparked a so-called "great debate" in the strategic community, opposing General Pierre-Marie Gallois (a proponent of national deterrence) and Raymond Aron (who feared it would weaken the Atlantic Alliance) (Malis, 2018). Because Gallois' conceptions dovetailed neatly with De Gaulle's foreign policy ambitions, it won the strategic debate and was ultimately implemented.

The second instrument to increase France's autonomy was the withdrawal from NATO's integrated command structure in 1966. The rationale was not so much based on a lack of trust in the US security guarantees, but rather in a reading of the international system according to which a relatively independent policy between the two "blocs" was now possible: "De Gaulle's policy of withdrawal from the alliance in the 1960s was premised not on a belief that France *could* not rely on the United States, but that war was so unlikely it *need* not" (Sayle, 2019, p. 121). Indeed, a few months after leaving the integrated command structure, De Gaulle visited the USSR (30 June to 1 July 1966) in an attempt to establish the foundations of a new European security order (Soutou, 2018), thus initiating a long series of French presidents attempting (and failing) to create closer ties with Moscow in the hope of overcoming the structural dynamics of great power competition. De Gaulle's confrontation with NATO was not universally popular at home. For example, the former French ambassador to Berlin (1931–1938), member of the *Académie Française* and President of the French Red Cross André François-Poncet was a public proponent of the French participation in NATO as a way to counter the USSR. According to Georges Pompidou (who was prime minister at the time), only three members of the government were informed of the decision to withdraw from NATO before its official announcement, and civil servants critical of the policy were gradually ostracised, which illustrates the sensitivity of the topic (Cohen, 1986). Pundits' reactions were largely negative: *L'Aurore* described the decision as a "muck-up", *Le Monde* criticised it as "nonsensical", *Le Figaro* described a "return to obsolete formulas from the past", and *L'Express* called it an "attack against Europe" (Schmitt, 2018, p. 625). Of course, French forces were never entirely disconnected from NATO after 1966: as early as 1967, an agreement between the French chief of staff (General Ailleret) and the Supreme Allied Commander Europe (SACEUR – General Lemnitzer) established the modalities of cooperation in case of a conflict with the Soviet Union. According to this agreement, the French forces in Germany would participate in the conflict as part of the Central Army Group (CENTAG). The volume of the French contribution within CENTAG remained unchanged before and after the withdrawal from the integrated military structure (amounting to one corps); in other words, in operational terms, France invented a pragmatic and efficient way to cooperate with its allies perfectly compatible with the NATO alliance's logic (Bozo, 1992), as we further explain in chapter 6. However, the gap between the realities of a pragmatic cooperation with the alliance framework and a sometimes-inflammatory French discourse on NATO was also established early on and would remain during the Cold War and beyond (Cogan, 1997). In fact:

> French policy was often internally contradictory. On the surface at least, it would appear that France actually achieved very little through its policy of Alliance without integration and its resolute pursuit of national independence. Paris failed either to bring about a reform of NATO which increased its own influence within the organisation or to achieve the creation of alternative, European structures more to its liking.
>
> (Menon, 2000, p. 29)

6 *Introduction*

The third instrument designed to ensure a policy of autonomy was the French military presence in the former colonial empire. From 1960 onwards, France capitalised on its former colonial domination and developed new means to exert influence in Africa. Several mechanisms of technical, economical, and cultural cooperation were established with former colonies, and the military was an important tool providing leverage and influence in the region. The spectrum of activities ranges from influence (notably through the diffusion of the French military culture and practices) to plain coercion, in order to shape the political trajectories of nominally independent countries (Evrard, 2016). Training the newly independent states' armed forces proved to be an important tool of influence for Paris. For example, after its independence in 1960, the Ivory Coast's armed forces lacked officers in sufficient numbers, and it was only in the 1970s that Ivoirian officers replaced the French ones, after they were taught French military procedures and routines (Banga, 2014). In the early years following decolonisation, Gabon became a centrepiece of the African policy defined in Paris, which led France to intervene in 1964 in order to restore Léon M'Ba, who had been ousted by a coup. The signal was clear: France would not hesitate to use military force in order to protect allied regimes (Smith, 2017). Chad was also an important partner for Paris, which intervened as early as 1969 with Operations Limousin (1969–1971) and Bison (1970–1972), followed by operation Tacaud (1978–1980) and Operation Manta (1983–1984), which ended up being the largest troops deployment since the end of the Algerian War (Debos and Powell, 2017). Between 1955 and 1970, France also participated in the civil war in Cameroon through a "secret war", fighting the independentist movement *Union des Populations du Cameroun* (UPC), thus being partly responsible for the thousands of Cameroonian citizens killed during the conflict. This war was barely covered in France, and also faded from the collective memory of decolonisation, but was a stark example of Paris' willingness to use force in order to protect strategic interests in Africa (Deltombe et al., 2011). In the 1970s and due to the changing Cold War context, the USSR attempted to forge bilateral relationships with African countries. As a response, France mobilised its military, including its navy (that performed missions related to naval diplomacy), in order to counter the communist influence on the continent (Le Hunsec, 2016). Like many other countries, France was thus able to couch the defence of its strategic interests in the language of the Cold War, thus securing support (or benevolent indifference) from the NATO allies, notably the United States. François Mitterrand's election in 1981 did not change these dynamics since the socialist president very quickly reproduced his predecessors' rhetoric and practices. One of those practices was the widespread use of covert operations, secret services, or mercenaries in order to support France's policy in Africa (Bat, 2012). Such operators were found in Katanga, Angola, Biafra, Gabon, Central African Republic, and Chad conducting activities that ranged from advising to fighting (including mentorship and corruption). In fact, a real epistemic community of specialists dedicated to covert action in Africa gradually emerged, including spies, soldiers, and business people (especially related to the oil company Elf's networks).

Introduction 7

Those three instruments supported the policy of autonomy during the Cold War, which was, all considered, a comfortable period for French foreign policy. Indeed, Paris "gained a US peacetime engagement in Europe it was looking for since 1919 and gained (this is how policy-makers perceived it) the division of Germany" (Soutou, 2018, p. 21). As such,

> France was quite comfortable with the bipolar world, as the opposition between the US and the USSR meant that there was room for an ambitious actor to try to find a third way beyond the bipolarization of the international system. It also meant that France could develop genuinely autonomous ways to act abroad, in particular through military interventions in former colonies and the acquisition of nuclear capabilities. This allowed France to keep behaving as a great power, by adopting practices (in particular nuclear practices) similar to those of the major powers, thus mitigating the objective loss of geopolitical importance that France suffered after the Second World War.
>
> (Schmitt, 2017, p. 468)

The end of the Cold War drastically altered this status quo, yet the past three decades could do nothing but build a contemporary defence policy on the legacies of De Gaulle and the Cold War.

Adapting to a new world order

France's defence policy during the Cold War was based on core foundations (autonomy, nuclear deterrence, military interventionism) that had to be adapted after the collapse of the USSR. The core fundamentals on which French foreign and security policy was based were significantly shattered with the end of the Cold War. The first major transformation was the unravelling of Europe's strategic landscape, which posed a number of problems for France. First, the collapse of the USSR meant the disappearance of the main enemy, which was structuring the volume (and the mission) of the French armed forces. Therefore, French policy-makers had to once again ask themselves the classic question "To What Ends Military Power?" (Art, 1980), with no answer easily available in a fluctuating strategic environment. Second, French security during the Cold War was actually based on the principle of "double security", meaning obtaining security guarantees against the Soviet Union, but also against a (potentially revanchist) Germany (Soutou, 1996). Several Franco-German defence cooperation attempts during the Cold War were thus designed as tethering mechanisms supposed to restrain Germany (Weitsman, 2004; Pressman, 2008). This fear of a reunified Germany, epitomised by François Mauriac's famous joke "I like Germany so much that I am delighted that there are two of them", explains François Mitterrand's cautious (but not outright hostile) approach during the negotiations leading to the post-Cold-War security architecture (Bozo, 2005; Sarotte, 2014). Considering that a divided Germany was overwhelmingly considered to be in France's interest, the reunification was bound to be perceived

8 *Introduction*

as a major strategic shift by policy-makers. Third, France had to rethink the European security institutions, and important parts of the French strategic community called for the dissolution of NATO after the Cold War (Heuser, 1998). For more than a decade, French policy-makers hoped for a reshuffling of European security institutions in favour of more "European" solutions, through a pillar within NATO or through independent European institutions (Hofmann, 2013).

In addition to the dramatic transformation of the European strategic landscape, France also had to adapt to the new international order that emerged at the end of the Cold War, characterised by a unipolar system in favour of the United States (Brooks and Wholforth, 2008; Monteiro, 2013; Reich and Lebow, 2014; Brands, 2016; Beckley, 2018). This situation made many French observers uncomfortable since they had been used to navigating between two blocs: complaints about the US "hyperpower" (Védrine, 2003) and calls for a "multipolar world" were frequent in French policy circles after the end of the Cold War. While actively disliking the configuration of the international system, French policy-makers were nevertheless forced to adjust to it, in particular redefining their relationship to the US and to NATO and the means through which to act in the world (Charillon, 2010). According to Thierry Balzacq (2019), a shift in French grand strategy occurred at the end of the Cold War: from a grand strategy of "grandeur", France adjusted to a grand strategy of "liberal engagement". This strategy of liberal engagement has several tenets:

> France should primarily focus on entrenching powerful states within the constraining structure of world politics rather than pursuing unilateral options. Military power should only be employed prudently when the utility of other instruments have been exhausted. Furthermore, liberal engagement substitutes multilateral Western leadership for American primacy, enhancing the prospect of stability and peace among states. Finally, while Grandeur lauded French exceptionalism, liberal engagement aims to present France as a power whose strength derives from its ability to muster two main levers. The first is France's commitment to Western values. (…) The second is the capacity of France to "soft balance" contenders for influence within the framework of international organizations.
>
> (Balzacq, 2019, p. 100)

While Balzacq observes a change in the French grand strategy, Pernille Rieker (2017) identifies strong continuities. She argues that "grandeur" is still the foundation of French foreign policy, and that four "status indicators" inherited from the Fifth Republic still operate as anchoring practices in the post-Cold-War era: historical legitimacy for the role of France, strong national institutions (especially the executive), strong instruments for power projection, and core representation in key global institutions. Of course, the specific mechanisms through which these status indicators are implemented change over time, but Rieker leans towards a stable core of representations and practices.

Introduction 9

So, to what extent did France adjust its grand strategy after the end of the Cold War? Maybe an answer lies in the fact that while pragmatically adjusting its activities to a changed international system, French policy-makers failed to change the narratives underpinning their actions. In fact, since the end of the Cold War, it is possible to observe a

> growing disconnect between, on the one hand, a narrative of *grandeur* inherited from De Gaulle and still pushed forward by French politicians, and, on the other, the disappearance of the objective this narrative was designed to serve. In a new context, the coping strategy had involved sticking to a narrative unfit for the evolutions of the international system, effectively functioning as a form of rhetorical entrapment, which is partly the cause of the current French gloominess.
>
> (Schmitt, 2020, p. 117)

Being a core sovereign task, defence policy is a good entry point to analyse the degree to which France adapted its grand strategy, and the instruments of this grand strategy, to a new international order.

The first chapter discusses civil–military relations in France. It shows how the importance of the executive in the French decision-making system influences the conduct of defence policy, but it also illustrates the changes in the social make-up of the armed forces and their perception in French society at large. This civil–military context shapes the ways the French armed forces are perceived and used as a policy instrument. The second chapter details the transformation of the French armed forces since 1991, notably the professionalisation and the downsizing of the armed forces. It explains how those changes were made based on strategic assessments of the (mis)fit between the armed forces and their operational environment, and how changing political conditions shaped the 2020 format of the armed forces. The third chapter details the evolution of France's nuclear deterrence capabilities and strategy. A cornerstone of the policy of *grandeur*, French nuclear deterrence was adjusted to fit the transformations of the international system. Zooming in on nuclear policy thus illustrates the continuities and changes of narratives and practices in French security policy-making. Chapter four analyses the role of the arms industry in French defence policy, as well as defence procurement practices. France has pursued an autonomous capability to produce advanced weapons systems as a requirement for any ambitious foreign policy. However, the transformations of the global arms trade that followed the end of the Cold War (moving from a producer-centric to a consumer-centric market) forced some adjustments and raises questions about the shape of France's desired strategic autonomy. Chapter five analyses the evolution of French military operations, an uneasy combination of "legacy practices" (notably in Africa) and adjustments to the changing character of war (peacekeeping operations followed by coalition warfare). The willingness to use military force is consistently seen in Paris as a status indicator, but it has produced mixed results on the ground. Finally, chapter six tackles the important question of reconciling autonomous

10   *Introduction*

ambitions and cooperation with allies. Finally, in the book's the conclusion, we discuss the nature of France's power and the future challenges for French defence policy.

References

Art, R. (1980), "To What Ends Military Power?", *International Security*, 4/4, 3–35.

Balzacq, T. (2019), "France", in Balzacq, T., Dombrowski, P. and Reich, S. (eds.), *Comparative Grand Strategy. A Framework and Cases*. Oxford: Oxford University Press, 99–122.

Banga, A. (2014), "Le Rôle des Conseillers Militaires Français dans l'Élaboration de l'Outil de Défense Ivoirien", in Bruyère-Ostells, W. and Dumasy, F. (eds.), *Pratiques Militaires et Globalisation*. Paris: Bernard Giovanangeli, 298–310.

Bat, J.P. (2012), *La Fabrique des 'Barbouzes'. Histoire des Réseaux Foccart en Afrique*. Paris: Nouveau Monde.

Beckley, M. (2018), *Unrivaled. Why America Will Remain the World's Sole Superpower*. Ithaca: Cornell University Press.

Bozo, F. (1992), *La France et l'OTAN. De la Guerre Froide au Nouvel Ordre Européen*. Paris: IFRI.

Bozo, F. (2005), *Mitterrand, la Fin de la Guerre Froide et l'Unification Allemande: de Yalta à Maastricht*. Paris: Odile Jacob.

Brands, H. (2016), *Making the Unipolar Moment: U.S. Foreign Policy and the Rise of the Post-Cold War Order*. Ithaca: Cornell University Press.

Brooks, S.G. and Wholforth, W.C. (2008), *World Out of Balance: International Relations and the Challenge of American Primacy*. Princeton: Princeton University Press.

Charillon, F. (2010), *La France Peut-Elle Encore Agir sur le Monde?* Paris: Armand Colin.

Cogan, C. (1997), *Forced to Choose: France, Atlantic Alliance and NATO – Then and Now*. Westport: Prager.

Cohen, S. (1986), *La Monarchie Nucléaire*. Paris: Hachette.

Daho, G. (2019), "A Revenge of the Generals. The Rebalancing of the Civil-Military Relations in France", *Journal of Intervention and Statebuilding*, 13/3, 304–322.

Debos, M. and Powell, N. (2017), "L'Autre Pays des 'Guerres Sans Fin'. Une Histoire Militaire de la France au Tchad", *Les Temps Modernes*, 693–694, 221–266.

De Durand, E. (2011), "L'Europe en voie de clochardisation militaire", *Atlantico*, 20 April.

De Gaulle, C. (1954), *Mémoires de Guerre. Tome 1*. Paris: Plon.

De Gaulle, C. (1961), *Discours du 23 novembre 1961, Strasbourg*, INA.

De Gaulle, C. (1989), "Allocution du 3 novembre 1959, Ecole Militaire", in David, Dominique (ed.), *La Politique de Défense de la France*. Paris: FEDN, 70–78.

Deltombe, T., Domergue, M. and Tatsitsa, J. (2011), Kamerun! Une Guerre Cachée aux Origines de la Françafrique, 1948–1971. Paris: La Découverte.

Evrard, C. (2016), "Retour sur la Construction des Relations Militaires Franco-Africaines", *Relations Internationales*, 165, 23–42.

Fortmann, M., Haglund, D. and Von Hlatky, S. (2010), "France's 'Return' to NATO: Implications for Transatlantic Relations", *European Security*, 19/1, 1–10.

Gregory, S. (2000), *French Defence Policy into the Twenty-First Century*. Basingstoke: Palgrave.

Heuser, B. (1998), *Strategic Mentalities? Strategies and Beliefs in Britain, France and the FRG*. Basingstoke: Palgrave.

Hofmann, S. (2013), *European Security in NATO's Shadow. Party Ideologies and Institution Building*. Cambridge: Cambridge University Press.

Le Hunsec, M. (2016), "Lier la France à l'Afrique: la Marine Nationale au Service de la Politique d'Influence (1960–1990)", *Relations Internationales*, 165, 57–80.

Malis, C. (2018), "Raymond Aron, War and Nuclear Weapons: the Primacy of Politics Paradox", in Schmitt, O. (ed.), *Raymond Aron and International Relations*. Abingdon: Routledge, 93–110.

Menon, A. (2000), *France, NATO and the Limits of Independence 1981–97. The Politics of Ambivalence*. Basingstoke: Palgrave.

Messmer, P. (1992), *Après Tant de Batailles: Mémoires*. Paris: Albin Michel.

Monteiro, N. (2013), *Theory of Unipolar Politics*. Cambridge: Cambridge University Press.

Notin, J.-C. (2005), *Leclerc*. Paris: Perrin.

Ostermann, F. (2019), *Security, Defense Discourse and Identity in NATO and Europe. How France Changed Foreign Policy*. Abingdon: Routledge.

Pannier, A. (2017), "From One Exceptionalism to Another: France's Strategic Relations with the United States and the United Kingdom in the Post-Cold War Era", *Journal of Strategic Studies*, 40/4, 475–504.

Pannier, A. and Schmitt, O. (2019), "To Fight Another Day: France between the Fight Against Terrorism and Future Warfare", *International Affairs*, 95/4, 897–916.

Pressman, J. (2008), *Warring Friends. Alliance Restraint in International Politics*. Ithaca: Cornell University Press.

Reich, S. and Lebow, R.N. (2014), *Good-Bye Hegemony! Power and Influence in the Global System*. Princeton: Princeton University Press.

Rieker, P. (2017), *French Foreign Policy in a Changing World. Practising Grandeur*. Basingstoke: Palgrave MacMillan.

Sarotte, M.E. (2014), 1989. *The Struggle to Create Post-Cold War Europe*. Princeton: Princeton University Press.

Sayle, T. (2019), *Enduring Alliance. A History of NATO and the Postwar Global Order*. Ithaca: Cornell University Press.

Schmitt, O. (2017), "The Reluctant Atlanticist: France's Security and Defence Policy in a Transatlantic Context", *Journal of Strategic Studies*, 40/4, 463–474.

Schmitt, O. (2018), "Accompagner les Mutations de la Puissance Française de 1962 à nos Jours", in Drévillon, Hervé and Wieviorka, Olivier (eds.), *Histoire Militaire de la France. Tome II: de 1870 à nos Jours*. Paris: Perrin, 589–668.

Schmitt, O. (2020), "Decline in Denial: France Since 1945", in Mérand, F. (ed.), *Coping with Geopolitical Decline*. Montréal: McGill-Queen's University Press, 107–126.

Smith, E. (2017), "Sous l'Empire des Armées. Les Guerres Africaines de la France", *Les Temps Modernes*, 693–694, 4–27.

Soutou, G.-H. (1996), L'Alliance Incertaine. *Les Rapports Politico-Stratégiques Franco-Allemands, 1954–1996*. Paris: Fayard.

Soutou, G.-H. (2018), *La Guerre Froide de la France, 1941–1990*. Paris: Tallandier.

Strategic Review of Defence and National Security (2017). Paris: Ministry of Armed Forces.

Talmor, A. and Selden, Z. (2017), "Is French Defence Policy Becoming More Atlanticist?", *Cambridge Review of International Affairs*, 30/2–3, 160–176.

Tandler, J. (2014), "French Nuclear Diplomacy. Grand Failure?", *The Nonproliferation Review*, 21/2, 125–148.

Utley, R.E. (2000), *The French Defence Debate. Consensus and Continuity in the Mitterrand Era*. Basingstoke: Palgrave.

12 *Introduction*

Vaïsse, M. (1998), *La Grandeur. Politique Étrangère du Général de Gaulle*. Paris: Fayard.
Védrine, H. (2003), *Face à l'Hyperpuissance*. Paris: Fayard.
Von Hlatky, S. (2014), "Revisiting France's Nuclear Exception After its 'Return' to NATO", *Journal of Transatlantic Studies*, 12/4, 392–404.
Weitsman, P. (2004), *Dangerous Alliances. Proponents of Peace, Weapons of War*. Palo Alto: Stanford University Press.

1 Defence institutions and civil–military relations

Understanding the relations between French society and its armed forces is necessary in order to properly grasp how the armed forces have transformed since 1991 (chapter 2), the centrality of nuclear deterrence in French strategy (chapter 3), the relationship with the arms industry (chapter 4), and the support for military interventions (chapter 5).

The first dimension that will be addressed in this chapter is the institutions involved in defence decision-making in the Fifth Republic. Born out of a coup and initially led by a general turned politician, the Fifth Republic is heavily defined by the tumultuous relations between the civilian and military powers (Roussellier, 2015), and is largely an effort to redefine civil–military interactions following the Algerian war (1954–1962). This redefinition of civil–military relations is characterised by a centralisation of decision-making within the executive branch, particularly the president, which is reinforced by the importance granted to the presidency in the development of the nuclear deterrent capability. However, the end of the Cold War and the beginning of the "intervention era" facilitated a comeback of the military power in decision-making, raising new questions about proper civil–military interactions.

The second dimension is the importance of Jacques Chirac's 1996 decision to move from a "mixed model" (combining conscripts and professional forces) to an all-volunteer force in redefining the social make-up of the armed forces. In 2019, the French forces had more women members and were more ethnically diverse than ever, but these changes have yet to be reflected in the power structure of the armed forces with regards to the officer corps.

Finally, the last section will explore French society's perception of its armed forces, in particular the phenomenon of an overall positive, but misunderstood image.

Defence decision-making in the Fifth Republic

The establishment of the Fifth Republic led to a redefinition of civil–military relations, which was necessary considering the multiple political interventions of military officers in the context of the war in Algeria: they massively supported a retired general's return to power in 1958 (De Gaulle), only for a disappointed

14   *Defence institutions*

fraction of the armed forces to turn on the executive in a putsch attempt in 1961, followed by attempts to assassinate De Gaulle conducted by disfranchised military personnel that regrouped in the terrorist organisation OAS (*Organisation Armée Secrète*). This blurring of civil–military interactions contributed to the "civil war in France" (Anderson, 2018) that unfolded between 1958 and 1962. The key issue was that the armed forces claimed that they were speaking on behalf of the entire country. The "military society" thought itself as the ultimate line of defence guaranteeing the protection of French interests, and conceived its relationship to the political sphere as conditional obedience:

> everything seems to happen as if the armed forces thought of themselves as holding, on a political level, some sort of arbitrary power, or veto. The armed forces think they are authorized to use this arbitrary power or veto against a transformation of the civilian power which would threaten, in their own eyes, the requirements of the national destiny.
>
> (Girardet, 1960, p. 3)

The end of the Algerian crisis and the consolidation of the Fifth Republic from 1962 onwards restored the primacy of civilian power through several mechanisms: a constitutional setting establishing the president as the "commander of the armed forces"; the removal of the generals suspected of disloyalty (particularly after the failed 1961 putsch attempt); and the reorientation of defence policy towards nuclear deterrence, which reinforced the president's authority.

One of the classical problems of civil–military relations is the asymmetry in expertise between the civilian authorities and the military leaders, in favour of the latter. This asymmetry can lead to behaviours such as attempts to manipulate information or presenting options in such a way that the seemingly most reasonable course of action is the one chosen by the military (Feaver and Kohn, 2001). The institutions of the Fifth Republic minimise this risk because the system is designed so as to quickly inform the president. The Élysée is at the top of the intelligence chain on all topics of strategic interest: it receives daily telegrams from the French defence attachés abroad as well as analyses from the different intelligence services, the Ministry of Defence, and the Ministry of Foreign Affairs. The president also chairs the defence councils, which define the main orientations and policies, and a member of the president's private military staff (*état-major particulier*) participates in every meeting organised by the prime minister on arms exports since any export of sensitive material must be approved by the head of state.

In addition to centralising at the Élysée all the information and analysis channels available in the administration, the president is also the uncontested master of nuclear deterrence, the cornerstone of the system (see chapter 3). The president approves equipment projects and strike plans, and decides on the alert levels and on eventual strikes:

> the presidential function is made sacred by the capacity to push the "red button". The entire organisation of the State is determined by this exclusive

function. The Bomb imposes respect towards he who is his master. Deterrence is at the very heart of the French political regime.

(Guisnel and Tertrais, 2016, p. 162)

Indeed, France is the only nuclear democratic country in which the commander of the armed forces is also a head of state elected through direct universal suffrage: the latter role being devoted to the Queen in the United Kingdom and the US president being elected through indirect suffrage. The relationship between the political regime, the strategic posture, and the institutional settings thus establishes the president as the cornerstone of French defence policy.

The institutional configuration of French defence policy is then de facto dominated by the primacy of the president, which in practice validates presidentialism, while the constitutional text looks more like a dyarchy, that is, the government is supposed to determine and conduct national policies, decide on the use of armed forces, and the prime minister is responsible for national defence (Cohen, 1986).

Within the government, the minister of defence (renamed in 2017 minister of the armed forces) plays an important role of interface between the armed forces, the president, and the government. The minister must make governmental decisions acceptable to the armed forces (usually unpopular decisions such as budgetary cuts) while explaining to the president and the government (usually without military experience) the needs and requirements of the services. This role as an interface often leads military officers to assume that a good minister is someone able to obtain a good defence budget. Military leaders are often aware that the minister is their best ally and one of the very few political actors able to carry their demands: there is then a strong institutional incentive to establish an at least decent relationship with the minister, regardless of how she is perceived. The minister has at her disposal both a civilian and military cabinet. The former plays an important role in the organisation of the ministry, because of its role in centralisation and public policy oversight (Eymeri-Douzans et al., 2015):

aware of their responsibility to contribute to the civilian control of the military, usually not liked by the military hierarchy which judges them incompetent and irresponsible, (the) members [of the civilian cabinet], usually smart minds and hard workers, become a disturbing factor for the pride of the military headquarters.

(Cohen, 2008, p. 25)

The prime minister is constitutionally tasked with coordinating the government's action in the field of security and defence, as well as overseeing the implementation of the decisions made in the Defence and Security Council (which regroups the president, the prime minister, the ministers of armed forces, foreign affairs and interior, and other qualified politicians or civil servants depending on the agenda). In order to fulfil this coordination role between the different ministries in charge of France's defence and security policy, the prime minister can rely on the *Secrétariat Général à la Défense et la Sécurité Nationale* (SGDSN), an

16 Defence institutions

office dedicated to the coordination and centralisation of the state's activities in the defence and security realms.

In this context of a strong executive, the parliament's role is more limited than in other liberal democracies. The parliament's main power comes from the fact that it votes on the state's budget. It is thus mostly through the voting and the oversight of the military programming laws that MPs participate in public debates on defence policies. Indeed, the role of the two chambers (national assembly and senate, making up the parliament) is reduced through several mechanisms. First, the French constitution distinguishes between the regulatory and legislative domains, and the parliament can only influence the latter: everything that falls under the reglementary domain (and this can be large in the field of defence, including senior appointments in the MoD) is organised by the executive. Second, the two constitutional articles (35 and 36) that would grant parliament extra oversight powers only deal with exceptional situations: war or siege. However, states no longer declare war (Fazal, 2012), which means that all military interventions in the Fifth Republic have been decided by the executive, and nobody seriously expects that France will soon be under siege. Even during the Gulf War,[1] which was probably the closest to a high-intensity conflict that French forces have encountered since 1958, François Mitterrand called two exceptional parliamentary sessions (27 August 1990 and 16 January 1991), but article 35 was not mobilised, since the government argued that it was not a war, but a "collective security operation" under chapter VII of the Charter of the United Nations. The session on 27 August 1990 was a debate without a vote, and the session of 16 January 1991 was a confidence vote, based on article 49 of the constitution. Article 35 was revised during the constitutional update of 2008, and the parliament must be consulted four months after the deployment of French troops. However, since the 2000 reform that reduced the presidential mandate to five years in order to match the parliament's term, the presidential and parliamentary elections now take place only one month apart: the parliamentary majority is then most likely to come from the same party as the president. This political proximity leads the parliament to validate almost automatically military decisions, even more so because they are still perceived as as belonging to the president's "reserved domain" (Ostermann, 2017).

The decision-making apparatus under the Fifth Republic is then largely stacked in favour of the executive branch and civilian authorities, which has led some scholars to note a "defeat of the generals" (Cohen, 1994). It is true that the Cold War context facilitated this domination of civilian over military actors, since it was structuring the international system around nuclear deterrence (and thus civilian strategic decision-making), and was coupled in France with the internationalisation of a taboo regarding military involvement in politics that followed the end of the Algerian war. France was then close to the "unified" model described by Avant (1996–1997), in which the mandates from the executive and the legislative come from the same electorate.

However, the end of the Cold War, which has been coupled with a higher number of military interventions (see chapter 5), has led to a gradual erosion of the "Algerian taboo" and a redefinition of civil–military relations (Daho, 2014).

The multiplication of military interventions allowed the armed forces to claim an expertise that only they possess within the state: the use of violence in support of a political goal outside of French territory. While nuclear deterrence deprived the military of their authority on defence issues, or at least did not give them a significant advantage compared with civilians,[2] military interventions allowed them re-establish a monopoly of expertise on the legitimate use of armed force.

This dynamic of consolidation of military authority is paradoxical because it is a result of political decisions (military interventions) that have regularly been criticised by members of the armed forces. As early as the mid-1990s, General Fricaud-Chagnaud was lamenting the "drift that makes us move from a logic of global deterrence to a quasi-automatic intervention in crisis management", as a result of the "interventionist impulses of our Presidents" pointed by Colonel Jean-Louis Dufour (Pascallon, 1997). This phenomenon is far from being specifically French: US generals are usually much more reluctant towards military interventions than their civilian masters (Recchia, 2015). Ironically, while the military intervention in Afghanistan has been criticised by several highly visible members of the armed forces, because of its duration, this military operation has initiated a rebalancing towards military authorities.

It is true that tensions can always exist between the civilian and military elites within the MoD, especially because, unlike in the United Kingdom, the socialisation and the standard career paths between civilian and military roles are starkly separated in France. But military authorities have gradually gained more influence on decision-making since the end of the Cold War. This dynamic is institutionally illustrated by the gradual reinforcement of the powers granted to the chief of the joint staff (*Chef d'État-Major des Armées* – CEMA). Following the Gulf War, the French armed forces developed joint capabilities (see chapter 2). As a consequence, a 2005 decree made the CEMA the second most important person in the ministry, after the minister himself. As part of his expanded responsibilities, the CEMA was commanding the three services and was responsible for the preparation, the cohesiveness, and the use of the armed forces, on top of having diplomatic duties as a French military representative. As such, "the 2005 reform has definitely established the pre-eminence of the CEMA, not only over the services, but also in the ministry and the administration at large" (Gautier, 2009, p. 360). The powers of the joint staff were even further extended in a 2009 decree, which raised important issues of civil–military relations since the CEMA was effectively in charge of military policy within the MoD. A former chief of the joint staff, General Georgelin, provocatively summarised the situation by saying "the minister must give me the means to execute the orders I receive from the President" (Merchet, 2013).

When the socialist François Hollande was elected in 2012, his government was explicit in wanting to return more powers to the defence minister. The first major shift was instituting a practice during the Operation Serval intervention in Mali to have a daily meeting with the military chiefs in the office of the head of the civilian cabinet. This was done in order to symbolically mark the domination of the civilian over the military leadership. The practice was enshrined in law

18 *Defence institutions*

with a new decree adopted in September 2013, which re-established the prerogatives of the minister: the joint staff is then supposed to "assist" the minister in the use of armed forces and is "responsible for their operational use". This emphasis on civilian control also had an organisational dimension for the MoD. After the 2005 decree firmly established the joint chief of staff as a superior authority to the chiefs of the three services, the joint staff started to expand its structures. A 2011 report from the ministry's control authority noticed that the joint staff tended to create positions that were going beyond the need of establishing authority over the three services, in effect duplicating structures within the MoD (Guibert, 2018). Reducing the authority of the joint chief was also a way to streamline the MoD's structure, and some functions under the joint staff's authority (international relations, human resources, support) were transferred to the civilian branch of the ministry (*Secrétariat Général pour l'Administration* – SGA). Of course, this move was resented by some in the military who denounced a loss of power and a gradual "civilianisation" of the ministry. A former CEMA, General Bentégeat, denounced in an op-ed in *Le Figaro* a "mistrust, in principle, of the military officers' loyalty" (Bentégeat, 2013). This was probably a reaction to the words attributed to Cédric Lewandowski, chief of the civilian cabinet for Defence Minister Le Drian, who supported the new decree by mentioning that "we should put the putsch of the Generals to an end" (Guibert, 2018, p. 138).

These terms may reveal a deeper misunderstanding between officers and politicians, which De Gaulle (who was then still a military officer but would soon become a politician) had theorised in *Le Fil de l'Épée*:

> politicians seek to please public opinion and soldiers are bound by rules; soldiers are subordinated to functions rather than to people, while politicians primarily value personal loyalty; soldiers find politicians unreliable, fast-changing and seeking attention while politicians dislike the taste for systems, the rigidity, the absolutist mindset and the confidence of the soldier.
>
> (De Gaulle, 1932, p. 74)

Some of these tensions still clearly exist in post-Cold-War civil–military relations. Following the erosion of the "Algerian taboo" described by Daho (2014), a number of officers have embraced the writings of General Lyautey, a 19th-century military commander and author of a book widely read among the armed forces: *The Social Role of the Officer* (*Le Rôle Social de l'Officier*). In this book, Lyautey adopts a paternalistic perspective in which the officer is supposed to become the educator of the entire nation in a post-1870 context of intellectual and moral crisis within the French elite (Digeon, 1959). This is, of course, a reassuring vision for many 21st-century officers (on average more conservative and more Catholic than the French population) who see themselves as the "moral" backbone of a French nation they perceive as being on the verge of disintegration. This explains the political engagement of some retired senior officers, such as General Dary (former military governor of Paris) who became one of the main organisers of the "*Manif Pour Tous*" (a conservative Catholic movement campaigning against the same-sex marriage law adopted in France in 2013), but it is also revelatory of a feeling among the military community of gradual disappointments towards politicians, triggered by the unfulfilled promises of the professionalisation (see chapter 2) and the constant reduction of the format of the armed forces since 1991.

Granted, military officers may have more influence on decision-making now than during the Cold War, but "the rebalancing of the relations between political authorities and high-ranking officers is probably less the result of advances voluntarily made by the officers than retreats unconsciously conceded by the politicians" (Daho, 2014, pp. 77–78). The crisis of July 2017, in which the newly elected Emmanuel Macron forced the CEMA, General Pierre de Villiers, to resign after the latter had criticised potential further cuts in defence spending is an illustration of another adjustment of the relationship between civilian and military authorities in the Fifth Republic.

A new "military society"?

In 1953, the French historian Raoul Girardet published his influential book *La Société Militaire dans la France Contemporaine (1815–1939)* ("The Military Society in Contemporary France (1815–1939)"), which traced the social make-up of the French armed forces and their interaction with civil society in the 19th and early 20th century. Girardet was arguing that the perception of the armed forces within French society drastically evolved over time: after 1815, the monarchist elites thought that the armed forces were a bastion of revolutionary sentiments. This perception changed after the short-lived revolutions of 1830 and 1848, during which the armed forces saved the bourgeoisie. The Second Empire cemented this alliance between the dominating classes and the armed forces, at the liberals' expense (the latter favoured armed forces based on conscription, purely focused on national defence and not engaged in foreign operations such as the expedition in Mexico in 1861–1867). National unity was briefly achieved after the 1870 defeat: adopting a model of universal conscription, the armed forces were briefly perceived as the great teacher of a French nation in search of itself in the wake of defeat. Twenty years later, the Dreyfus affair made the armed forces a target of the left, while World War I recreated a sense of unity that quickly dissipated between the two World Wars.

Continuing Girardet's analysis, it is easy to argue that the relations between the armed forces and French society strongly evolved after World War II. An important factor was obviously the Algerian War. Not only did it upset civil–military relations, but it also affected interactions with society, since conscripts were sent to fight a widely unpopular war. The newly established Fifth Republic started adapting this framework by creating the category of "conscientious objectors" in 1963, and transforming the "military service" into a "national service" in 1965: instead of serving in the armed forces, conscripts could alternatively be assigned to civilian institutions or to international cooperation services in postcolonial states that maintained strong relations with France. The post-May 1968 societal transformations, that called for more liberal societal norms, also affected

20 *Defence institutions*

society/armed forces interactions, and important demonstrations against a reform of the national service occurred in 1973. These tensions further rose because of the project to extend the military camp of Larzac (in central France) by expropriating local peasants. Although some regulatory changes were introduced in the 1970s to relax military discipline a bit, the interactions between the two sides were still marked by two widely different imaginaries and perceptions. On the one hand, the military was still obsessed with the fear of "subversive" activities, because of the lasting influence of the *"guerre révolutionnaire"* theories that had been developed in the context of the wars in Indochina and Algeria (Tenenbaum, 2018). Social movements were naturally interpreted according to the frame of an "internal enemy" undermining the unity of the nation in collaboration with foreign adversaries. Some political leaders, including De Gaulle himself in 1968 and Defence Minister Yvon Bourges in the 1970s, supported the military, and they were quick to denounce alleged conspiracies against the armed forces. On the other hand, the left-wing imaginary was still marked by a very strong antimilitarism that was translated into popular culture: popular singer Maxime le Forestier released in 1972 a song equating paratroopers (who had become the iconic representation of the Battle of Algiers, and of the use of torture) with fascists[3] while Serge Gainsbourg sang a reggae version of the French national anthem which infuriated veterans associations.

The tensions were less intense in the 1980s, the main transformation being the abolition of peacetime military justice, which was both a privilege for officers (who were supposed to be judged by their peers in criminal cases) but mostly an instrument of control over society since most cases were actually dealing with resistance to military service (desertion or insubordination in one form or another). The abolition of peacetime military justice was another step in normalising the military's status within French society, but the main mechanism of civil-military interaction was still, obviously, conscription, which ensured that most French males had a degree of military experience. The suspension of the national service in 1996, which de facto abolished conscription, was then a major change in the interaction between the armed forces and society.

While the strategic reasons justifying the end of conscription by President Chirac in 1996 will be examined in chapter 2, it is worth detailing its symbolic importance in French republican mythology. France was, until the end of conscription, usually considered a model of the "nation in arms" (Challener, 1955; for a critique, see Gresle, 1998). This is intimately tied with a republican myth according to which the soldier is also a citizen (or vice versa), and is illustrated by some symbolic battles: Valmy (1792), Sedan (1870), and Verdun (1916). Those battles have their heroes (Kellermann and Dumouriez for Valmy, Gambetta in 1870, and Clemenceau, Joffre, Foch, and Pétain during World War I), and this symbolic material contributes to forging the political myth of the nation in arms: the idea that in times of extreme duress, France is saved by the bravery and courage of its citizens. Therefore, this myth strongly associated the notions of "national defence" and "military service" during the 20th century. Two other ideological constructions helped cement the myth: first, the "citizen-soldier" was constructed by the French revolutionaries as the counter-model of the "mercenary soldier" serving European monarchies. Second, the socialists historically tended to contrast the "proletarian soldier" with the "career officer" as illustrated in Jaurès' book *L'Armée Nouvelle* (1911), in which he pleaded for armed forces that would be an exact reflection of society, including in the commanding echelons. For Jaurès, such a social composition of the armed forces would be intrinsically pacifist: since wars were, in the socialist conception, a consequence of capitalism through territorial and economic expansion, a citizen-army would not be tempted by aggressions as this would run against the workers' interests. Together, these three imaginaries (nation in arms, citizen-solder, proletarian soldier) were cemented to create a powerful myth of the social importance of conscription.

Of course, these are political myths, since the actual history of conscription in France is more complex (Cochet, 2013). The 1789 Assembly originally rejected conscription as too constraining for civil liberties, and the new French Republics originally called upon voluntary troops: the 52,000 troops that fought against the Prusso-Austrian troops at Valmy in 1792 were volunteer forces in which professional soldiers were dominating. It was in 1793 that the Convention, under enormous military pressure, introduced mandatory conscription and the concept of *levée en masse*. However, those mobilisations were supposed to be temporary in order to face exceptional situations. The 1798 "Loi Jourdan" introduced a mechanism of conscription, which was maintained under the Consulate and the Empire, and was thus the primary (and unpopular) means through which the Napoleonic armies were formed. Conscription was abolished with the Restoration, as one of the first decisions by the new King Louis XVIII. For most of the 19th century, conscription was widely unpopular among the French population, and different means to man the armed forces were tested (volunteer forces, random selection, etc.). It is towards the end of the Second Empire that the issue of conscription was once again discussed, through an attempt to emulate the Prussian model. The Battle of Sadowa (1866) illustrated how the comparatively small Prussia could defeat the Austro-Hungarian empire, notably through the use of conscription, and inspired several initiatives between 1866 and 1870 (notably the "Loi Niel" in 1868). However, the Assembly always defeated attempts to introduce a real conscription system until the collapse of the Second Empire after the Franco-Prussian War, in which French troops could not match the number of the Prussian army (Crépin, 2005). The Third Republic, therefore, established the principles of conscription in 1872, which were confirmed in 1905. For the republicans, military service was becoming part of a "republican package" that would make sure that all French citizens would share a minimum educational (through the introduction of mandatory schooling), cultural, and ideological background in order to cement the Republic (Duclert, 2014), although this was more an ideology than a reality since conscription helped maintain social hierarchies (in particular between officers and soldiers) (Marly, 2019). Cemented in 1905, conscription was then never seriously challenged before the 1995 elections during which Jacques Chirac campaigned on its abolition (decided in 1996).

22 *Defence institutions*

It must be noted that the majority of military actors were opposed to the ending of conscription since it was perceived as an effective way to connect society with the armed forces. In his book detailing the end of conscription, Bastien Irondelle has illustrated how the military (and sometimes civilian) leadership had an emotional connection to conscription. The former chief of staff of the navy, Admiral Lefebvre, for example, declared that "we were living in quite a surprising 'French model', consensual (less than 5% of conscientious objectors and 1% of deserters), socially well-installed, culturally accepted, ingrained in national memory". Another senior officer declared "the moral balance sheet of the national service was overall very positive … or it would have exploded a long time ago" (both quoted in Irondelle, 2011, pp. 254–255). However, the underlying tone of this "link" with civil society was that the connection could only be conceived as a form of subordination: the civilian had to be put under military command, in practice putting the military in the role of "educator", a paternalistic view that can be traced to the writings of Lyautey (see above). The journalist Jean Guisnel noticed, for example, that "when knowing the institution, one sometimes has the impression that – for the military – the only good civilians are the conscripts doing their national service and the reserve officers" (Guisnel, 1990, p. 281).

New soldiers for a new era

In this context, it is then unsurprising that the end of conscription drastically transformed the relations between the armed forces and French society. The first major change was brought by a transformation of the structure of the armed forces themselves, which evolved in different ways.

First, the end of conscription automatically raised the proportion of officers and non-commissioned officers compared to soldiers. This evolution is a reflection of the increase in technical skills required by modern warfare.

Second, the French armed forces now include more women. From 1998 onwards, the quota on women in the forces has been lifted, and since 2015, all jobs within the French armed forces have been theoretically open to female applicants. Women constituted 6.5% of the armed forces before the end of conscription, increasing to 15.5% in 2019 (Guibert, 2019) (Figure 1.1).

However, while the French MoD regularly claims that the French armed forces are among those with the greatest proportion of women in the world, only 7.8% of officers are women at the time of writing. There are also important differences between the services: in 2019, the French army had 10% women in its ranks, while they constituted 23% of the air force. Moreover, at major career steps, women tend to be victims of the "leaking pipe" phenomenon: for example, there were very few female officers being accepted for the war college course per year until 2017, although it is an important career milestone in the French armed forces (Guibert, 2019).

Thus, in 2019, Minister for the Armed Forces Florence Parly – one of only two female defence ministers in French history (excluding Sylvie Goulard who held the office for only one month in 2017) – introduced a number of policies designed

Defence institutions 23

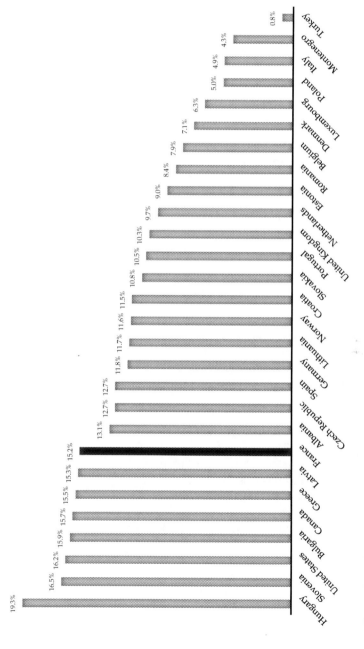

Figure 1.1 Women active duty military personnel in the armed forces of NATO member states in 2017. (Source: NATO).

24 *Defence institutions*

to retain and facilitate the career of women in the French armed forces. The challenges women have to face in the French armed forces go beyond the limitations of professional opportunities. Several journalists have documented the humiliations and physical assaults that women have had to go through, for example at the army officer school *Saint-Cyr* but also in the special undergraduate programs preparing for the entrance exam (*Classes Préparatoires aux Grandes Écoles* in French) (Lecaplain and Moran, 2018). These assaults are perpetrated by groups of self-proclaimed "traditionalists" (usually coming from a conservative Catholic background) who claim that women should not be tolerated in the armed forces. As the armed forces are heavily gendered institutions that usually associate masculinity with the profession of arms, women in the French armed forces are caught in a "status contradiction": their male counterparts struggle to reconcile their gender with their function, which in turn tends to construct the presence of female soldiers in the armed forces as a "problem". Women are thus expected to become "honorary males" and not disturb the expressions of virility and masculinity that constitute basic socialisation within the military organisation (Prévot, 2010). As such, the challenges for women in the French armed forces are eerily similar to those found in other military organisations worldwide (Egnell and Alam, 2019).

The third major change has been the relationship of populations with an immigrant background and persons of colour within the French armed forces. It must first be noted that the "republican myth" is very strong in the armed forces, which praises themselves for strong practices of merit-based promotions. When a French sociologist conducted his research on second- and third-generation immigrants in the French armed forces, he encountered many reactions such as officers claiming that there were "no French soldiers with an immigrant background. There are only French soldiers, period" (Settoul, 2015, p. 33). He also attended an international conference on recruitment in the armed forces worldwide in which a US general's claims that the US armed forces should be more proactive in targeting African American and Latinx communities bewildered French generals who openly questioned: "how can you talk about African-American and Latinx-American communities? Aren't they all Americans?" (Settoul, 2015, p. 35). Such reactions are typical of the large acceptance within the French armed forces of the French republican notion of a community based on political, instead of ethnic/cultural, citizenship.

The gap between this claim and the actual practices within French society at large has been documented on many occasions, but the myth is still immensely evocative among the soldiers and the officers. This myth has mobilised because the end of conscription has introduced a massive change in the social make-up of the armed forces. Before the end of conscription, France had established a number of partnerships with other countries (including Algeria and Tunisia) according to which conscripts with dual citizenship could conduct their national service in the armed forces of the country of their other citizenship if they wished so. Thus, the vast majority of Franco-Algerians and Franco-Tunisians (who are the majority of dual citizens in France) used to decide to conduct their service in either Algeria or Tunisia instead of France (because of emotional attachment to the country of origin and/or familial pressure).

Moreover, in the 1980s and the 1990s, among the 20,000 French citizens of Maghrebi heritage theoretically subjected to the national service, only 5,600 (one in four) actually accomplished it. This means that French citizens of Maghrebi heritage constituted only 2% of the 260,000 French citizens mobilised for military service. This can probably be explained by the fact that military leaders wanted to limit the arrival of populations they identified as "problematic", especially in a context where the amount of potentially mobilisable candidates exceeded the needs of the armed forces (Settoul, 2017). In 1990, a report signed by Colonel Yves Biville and entitled "Armed Forces and Population with Integration Issues" explicitly addressed the case of citizens with a Maghrebi heritage in the armed forces. The report noticed that this population suffered from several institutional difficulties. First, unlike the Catholic, Protestant, and Jewish faiths, the Muslim faith did not have any chaplaincy within the armed forces, and their specific religious requirements (fasting during Ramadan, meals without pork, etc.) were not properly integrated within daily military practices, which was experienced as a social relegation. The report highlighted the frustrations experienced by this population which, despite initial high expectations, felt they did not have a place in the armed forces.

The end of conscription changed this logic because the armed forces now had to convince young French citizens to willingly join the services: they had to manage the shift from a logic of selection (in order to manage the overflow of conscripts) to a logic of incitement (in order to manage the scarcity of qualified candidates). In that sense, the French armed forces had to appeal to all populations, including those of Maghrebi heritage and of Muslim background. This population has an ambivalent relationship with the armed forces, caught between a perception of a colonial debt and compliance with the ethos and values of the military. On the one hand, a discourse exists in which the armed forces are the extension of colonial troops and should not be joined for two reasons. First, populations of Maghrebi (and Sub-Saharan) heritage would have already "paid their debt" by serving alongside the metropolitan troops, in particular, during World War I and World War II. The movie *Indigènes* (2006) is illustrative of the perception that this population was forced to fight for France, and then forgotten. Second, the Algerian War looms large in the perception of the armed forces among the populations with Maghrebi heritage, and enlisting can be perceived as a collaboration with the former oppressor: the term "harki" (Maghrebi troops fighting alongside French troops against the National Liberation Front (FLN) during the Algerian war) is still used in a derogatory way by some of the population with Maghrebi heritage in order to castigate those willingly deciding to serve the French state.

On the other hand, this population with Maghrebi heritage is attracted to the values they perceive as being constitutive of the military ethos: virility, cohesion, and mutual support. Moreover, unlike other public institutions, the armed forces are perceived as being "truly" meritocratic, in the sense that promotion would be exclusively based on good performance. The armed forces also constitute an attractive career option for members of this population with less access to higher education, as they can, instead, invest in physical performance as a means of

26   *Defence institutions*

distinction: they can then identify careers that reward physical fitness (Settoul, 2017). The French armed forces have attempted to capitalise on this perception (by creating recruitment campaigns with persons of colour and emphasising the "colour-blindness" of the institution), which was easily accommodated within the "republican" ethos discussed earlier. The main institutional change in the past two decades was the creation of a Muslim chaplain in 2005, as a pragmatic response to the growing diversification of the armed forces. One of the first actions initiated by the Muslim chaplain was to campaign for the reintroduction of the halal combat rations, which had been introduced in the forces in the early 1990s but had disappeared without official justification by the end of the decade (Bertossi, 2017). These steps towards institutional recognition have been largely positively accepted within the armed forces and in wider society. In total, French soldiers self-identifying as Muslims composed 10% to 12% of the armed forces in 2019.

However, just like in the case of women, these changes are largely limited to the ranks of soldiers and NCOs. The officer corps was still predominantly white, Catholic, and male in 2019 (Jonnet, 2017), which has largely to do with modes of selection that rewards academic performance for junior officers and thus favours social reproduction (Coton, 2017).

It is clear that the end of conscription has changed French "military society", which is now more diverse in terms of ethnic background, faith, and gender, but this change has only marginally affected the upper command, which illustrates the ways power relations are maintained within the armed forces. However, the move from conscript-based to professional armed forces not only affected the social composition of the latter: it also changed the ways they are perceived within French society at large.

Support the troops? The armed forces within contemporary French society

A tourist going through Paris in 2019 would be forgiven for thinking that the military is very present in French society: metro stations are named after famous battles (Bir Hakeim, Iéna, Wagram, Austerlitz, Sébastopol, etc.) or famous officers (La Motte Piquet, D'Estienne d'Orves, Cambronne, Foch, Hoche, etc.); one can stroll from the Eiffel Tower to the massive campus of the *École Militaire* (which hosts many institutions such as the war college or the joint doctrine centre) and from there to the *Invalides* and their memorial to Napoleon; and if around for Bastille day (14 July), one can attend the annual military parade, which apparently prompted the US President Donald Trump's desire to organise one in Washington, DC. Or one could simply encounter one of the military patrols deployed within the framework of the Sentinelle counter-terrorism operation (see chapter 5) and wonder whether the military is routinely integrated within the daily functioning of society.

According to polls, eight to nine out of ten French citizens have a good opinion of their armed forces, in stark contrast to the wave of antimilitarism that existed

Defence institutions   27

in the 1970s (Jankowski, 2017). This positive perception is consistent across time since the late 1990s. However, the media coverage regarding the armed forces regularly mentions low morale, linked to the fact that the military perceives that their job is not acknowledged in society. There is then a paradox: the French population loves its armed forces but doesn't know what they are doing. The French soldier is a "misknown soldier" (Chéron, 2018).

Part of this misperception is related to a gradual disappearance of what constitutes the cornerstone of the military profession: a collective organisation with the aim of delivering organised violence for political goals. In short, being a soldier is primarily about fighting. However, this objective of fighting was gradually forgotten during the Cold War, since the conscripts were preparing for a war against the Soviet Union that never happened, and postcolonial military interventions were reserved for the small number of professional troops. Therefore, the national service became increasingly gradually disconnected from the activity of fighting in the collective memory. Meanwhile, the civil (and military) discussion about the "military values" (discipline, courage, sacrifice, etc.) has increasingly tended to consider them as autonomous and disconnected from operational purposes. This tendency to overlook the core of the military's work was reinforced by the professionalisation of the French armed forces, which triggered a sociological debate about the alleged "normalisation" of the military profession (Bardiès, 2011): if the soldiers were no longer drafted and had to willingly join the forces, did it mean that the military was becoming a profession like any other? The armed forces themselves seemed to reinforce this notion by developing targeted recruitment ads emphasising the "normality" of the military profession. Just after the end of conscription, the armed forces promoted a campaign highlighting the "400 jobs" that recruits could be trained in if they joined. For example, a picture of combat boots was subtitled "with these shoes, you can become a hairdresser", while the drawing of a helmet promised that "with this helmet, you can become an accountant" (Chéron, 2018). The core message was thus that there was no substantial difference between civilian and military life except for the uniform, and a career in the military could be training for a civilian career. The following recruitment campaign (in 2007) kept a similar messaging: it showed actors reconciling the daily military job on the field with a "normal" civilian life by going bowling or being a caretaker for a child. Here again, the combat dimension was totally overlooked by the recruitment campaign. It was only in 2010, after the 2008 Uzbin valley ambush in Afghanistan (in which a section of French paratroopers was outmanoeuvred and almost wiped out by the Taliban), that the recruitment campaigns started re-emphasising the purpose of the armed forces – fighting – and became much more explicit about French participation in foreign interventions.

In the 1990s, most French military interventions were conducted in a UN framework, in particular, in the Balkans. The media narrative around these interventions created two effects: first, it gave the impression that local fighters were the only ones with agency and influence in the course of the conflicts, thus implicitly raising questions about the role of the "blue helmets". Second, it emphasised a discourse organised around the notion of "peace soldiers" (a discourse also promoted

28 *Defence institutions*

by the armed forces' communication), thus confusing the role of soldiers with humanitarian actors. Two other interventions defined the French armed forces in the 1990s: in Iraq (for Operation Desert Storm) and in Rwanda. However, French participation in Desert Storm was too small (Schmitt, 2018) to give any other impression than being a cog in a very large multinational, US-led, machinery, and the intervention in Rwanda, marked by intense controversies about the role of the French troops in the genocide (Piton, 2018), mostly evoked an image of soldiers as executioners. The perception of French soldiers in the French population in the 1990s was thus defined by those three poles: "humanitarian peace-maker", "cog in the multinational machine", or "murderer". This trend continued in the 2000s since French engagement in Afghanistan was limited until 2008, and the other interventions in Sub-Saharan Africa did not lead to major combat actions. Therefore, when soldiers were killed in the Uzbin ambush, the surprise was intense amongst the French population, which had not been exposed to the fact that French soldiers were actually fighting and at the risk of losing their lives.

With an official communication confused about the fundamental purpose and the armed forces, it is no surprise that the French population has a blurred image of their soldiers. Opinion polls regularly illustrate that the French population globally supports military interventions. In 2017, 88% of French citizens approved of operations against Islamic State in Syria and in Iraq, and 61% supported the Barkhane operation in the Sahel. This support can fluctuate over time. For example, 66% of the French population approved of the Enduring Freedom operation in Afghanistan in 2001. In 2008, the proportion of the population *opposing* the intervention was 62%, which increased up to 76% in 2011. Similarly, the "Harmattan" operation in Libya (2011) was supported by 66% of the population at its beginning, and only 54% one month later (Jankowski, 2017). The French population thus usually leans towards support for military interventions, but not overwhelmingly so. It should, however, be noted that since 2015 and the Islamist attacks in Paris (Charlie Hebdo and 13 November), military interventions explicitly mobilising the "frame of the fight against terrorism" (Pannier and Schmitt, 2019) enjoyed a higher degree of popular support. Here again, the media framing of French military interventions since the end of the Cold War has contributed to this disappearance, and gradual rediscovery, of the "fighting" dimension of the armed forces (Chéron, 2018).

This phenomenon was part of a larger issue regarding military identity in France:

> the military specificity being based on defending the country, the meaning of the engagement of those wearing the uniform cannot be understood by their fellow citizens if the fighting dimension is hidden. The armed forces need an epic identity which is not a bellicose and idealistic exaltation of the fight, but a recognition of the deep driver of sacrifice to which agree those who are enlisted.
>
> (Chéron, 2018, p. 89)

However, this "epic identity" has been frustrated both by the evolution of the character of warfare and the media narrative around the interventions. The first trend has been the increase in peacekeeping missions, in which the French armed forces are regularly engaged. The main difficulty in those types of operations is how to explain the mission to the French population? The French armed forces are not legally "at war", they are in a peacekeeping operation designed to separate fighting groups and (usually) stop atrocities. Therefore, the vocabulary used by the military actors and the media mostly revolve around notions of civil unrest or accidents: when asked to explain the mission in the Central African Republic launched in 2013, a French general declared that the opponents were "outlaws and bandits". Similarly, in 2003, two French soldiers on patrol were killed in the Ivory Coast, and the general commanding the operation declared that it was a "regrettable accident" (Chéron, 2018). This vocabulary borrowed from the semantic field of crime and policing is not meant to deceive, as it reflects the complexity of modern military interventions, but it also has the consequence of de-politicising the context of the intervention while giving the impression that French forces only serve as an international police force, not as a political tool mobilised against an enemy, a trend not specific to France (Olsson, 2019). This narrative of French soldiers as police officers started to evolve in media representations because of Afghanistan: between 2008 and 2011, there were regular segments on national TV highlighting fighting activities, and the trend continued briefly during the initial phase of the intervention in Mali (Operation Serval) in 2013, before receding in the public sphere (the Barkhane operation, which is a follow-up to Operation Serval, barely ever gets media coverage). In 2019, after the death of 13 French soldiers in a helicopter crash during Operation Barkhane, the media coverage (and the official communication from the armed forces) also highlighted that they were engaged in a difficult combat operation, continuing the trend initiated in Afghanistan. An evolution towards more acknowledgement of the fighting dimension of military activities is then noticeable, especially for the land forces, which is a reflection of the overall trend of greater lethality on the battlefield.

But a second evolution of the character of warfare in the post-Cold-War era has contributed to this difficulty in creating an "epic identity" for the French military: how to explain and communicate about air operations? Modern military interventions have an important aerial component, and the French Air Force has been engaged in three major air operations since the end of the Cold War: in Kosovo in 1999, in Libya in 2011, and in Syria/Iraq since 2014. However, these types of operations are difficult to fit into a media narrative because of the stereotyped and limited imagery they rely on. A typical segment dedicated to air operations will usually show pictures of the base from which the planes depart, maybe some plane camera recording of a target being hit (pictures usually hard to understand and interpret for the untrained eye), and the presentation of an after-action report listing the number of targets being hit. It is thus extremely difficult to convey the feeling and meaning of modern air operations since even a pilot explaining "what it is like" in the cockpit would have difficulties making her experience relatable in the absence of obvious visual support. The "epic identity" is then difficult to create because of the nature of an experience most people will have difficulty relating to and making sense of, but also because, in an operational environment in which

30 *Defence institutions*

Western armed forces have an uncontested air superiority, modern pilots are much more "bombers" than "fighters" and cannot capitalise on the iconic imagery of the "knights of the sky". Finally, the decision to launch the Sentinelle operation on French territory following the 2015 terrorist attacks further contributed to the blurring of the perception of French soldiers, which were relegated to conducting patrolling tasks similar to those of the police. The initial media narrative surrounding the intervention highlighted how the soldiers contributed to daily tasks, from giving directions to lost tourists to performing CPR procedures on citizens having a heart attack. While the perception was positive, the media coverage of the operation further contributed to blurring the specificity of the military profession in public discourse, the soldiers becoming something in-between police officers, firefighters, and emergency medical responders.

Conclusion

These difficulties in establishing an "epic identity" and a stable narrative about the armed forces are revelatory of the ambiguous place soldiers occupy in post-Cold-War French society: constantly deployed but for unclear missions, well-perceived but also little known by the population. It is nevertheless clear that the relationship between the armed forces and society has been importantly transformed since the end of the Cold War, in particular, because of the 1996 decision to end conscription (see chapter 2). This led to both a deep transformation of the social make-up of the armed forces (although this transformation is much more limited for the officer corps) but also forced the armed forces to try to attract candidates instead of relying on a guaranteed workforce. This necessity to become appealing in a competitive jobs market led to an attempt to "normalise" the perception of the armed forces which, coupled with the difficulty in establishing clear narratives about modern interventions, challenged the "epic identity" of the soldiers and, in turn, their perception by French society. Because of this blurred image, French society is characterised by a support bordering on indifference regarding French military interventions, which thus plays into the centrality of the executive in military decision-making.

Notes

1 Throughout the volume, "Gulf War" refers to the "first Gulf War" (August 1990 to February 1991).
2 In the United States, the civilian Alain C. Enthoven, one of McNamara's "whiz kids", is famous for having declared "General, I have fought just as many nuclear wars as you have", thus illustrating that military officers could not claim any particular expertise in nuclear strategy.
3 In French, the word for "paratrooper" (*parachutiste*) rhymes with "fascist".

References

Anderson, G. (2018), *La Guerre Civile en France (1958–1962)*. Paris: La Fabrique.

Avant, D. (1996–1997), "US Military Reluctance to Respond to Post-Cold War Low Level Threats", *Security Studies*, 6/2, 51–90.

Bardiès, L. (2011), "Du Concept de Spécificité Militaire", *L'Année Sociologique*, 61, 273–295.

Bentégeat, H. (2013), "Métier des Armes: Une Porte se Ferme", *Le Figaro*, 12 September.

Bertossi, C. (2017), "Raisonnements Publics et Appartenance à une Institution: les Musulmans dans les Armées Françaises", *Migrations Société*, 169, 81–102.

Challener, R.D. (1955), *The French Theory of the Nation in Arms, 1888–1939*. New York: Columbia University Press.

Chéron, B. (2018), *Le Soldat Méconnu. Les Français et Leurs Armées: État des Lieux*. Paris: Armand Colin.

Cochet, F. (2013), *Être Soldat en France, de la Révolution à nos Jours*. Paris: Armand Colin.

Cohen, S. (1986), "Monarchie Nucléaire, Dyarchie Conventionnelle", *Pouvoirs*, 38, 13–20.

Cohen, S. (1994), *La Défaite des Généraux. Le Pouvoir Politique et l'Armée sous la Ve République*. Paris: Fayard.

Cohen, S. (2008), "Le Pouvoir Politique et l'Armée", *Pouvoirs*, 125, 19–28.

Coton, C. (2017), *Officiers. Des Classes en Lutte Sous l'Uniforme*. Marseille: Agone.

Crépin, A. (2005), *Défendre la France. Les Français, La Guerre et le Service Militaire de la Guerre de Sept Ans à Verdun*. Rennes: Presses Universitaires de Rennes.

Daho, G. (2014), "L'Érosion des Tabous Algériens. Une Autre Explication de la Transformation des Organisations Militaires en France", *Revue Française de Science Politique*, 64/1, 57–78.

De Gaulle, C. (1932), *Le Fil de l'Épée*. Paris: Plon.

Digeon, C. (1959), *La Crise Allemande de la Pensée Française*. Paris: Presses Universitaires de France.

Duclert, V. (2014), *La République Imaginée, 1870–1914*. Paris: Belin.

Egnell, R. and Alam, M. (eds.) (2019), *Women and Gender Perspectives in the Military: An International Comparison*. Washington, DC: Georgetown University Press.

Eymeri-Douzans, J.-M., Bioy, X. and Mouton, S. (eds.) (2015), *Le Règne des Entourages. Cabinets et Conseillers de l'Exécutif*. Paris: Presses de Sciences Po.

Fazal, T. (2012), "Why States No Longer Declare War", *Security Studies*, 21/4, 557–593.

Feaver, P.D. and Kohn, R.H. (eds.) (2001), *Soldiers and Civilians. The Civil-Military Gap and American National Security*. Cambridge: MIT Press.

Gautier, L. (2009), *La Défense de la France Après La Guerre Froide*. Paris: Presses Universitaires de France.

Girardet, R. (1953), *La Société Militaire dans la France Contemporaine (1815–1939)*. Paris: Plon.

Girardet, R. (1960), "Pouvoir Civil et Pouvoir Militaire dans la France Contemporaine", *Revue Française de Science Politique*, 10/1, 5–38.

Gresle, F. (1996), "Le Citoyen-Soldat Garant du Pacte Républicain? A Propos des Origines et de la Persistance d'une Idée Reçue", in Thomas, J.-P. and Cailleteau, F. (eds.), *Retour à l'Armée de Métier*. Paris: Economica, 29–50.

Guibert, N. (2018), *Qui C'est le Chef?*. Paris: Robert Laffont.

Guibert, N. (2019), "La Trop Lente Féminisation de l'Armée Française", *Le Monde*, 7 March.

Guisnel, J. (1990), *Les Généraux. Enquête sur le Pouvoir Militaire en France*. Paris: La Découverte.

32 Defence institutions

Guisnel, J. and Tertrais, B. (2016), *Le Président et la Bombe. Jupiter à l'Élysée*. Paris: Odile Jacob.

Irondelle, B. (2011), *La Réforme des Armées en France. Sociologie de la Décision*. Paris: Presses de Sciences Po.

Jankowski, B. (2017), "L'Opinion des Francais sur leurs Armés", in Letonturier, Éric (ed.), *Guerres, Armées et Communication*. Paris: CNRS Éditions, 81–98.

Jaurès, J. (1911), *L'Armée Nouvelle. L'Organisation Socialiste de la France*. Paris: Éditions Socialistes.

Jonnet, F. (2017), "Diversifier les Élites Militaires: Réalités et Défis", *Migrations Société*, 169, 53–68.

Lecaplain, G. and Moran, A. (2018), "Lycée Saint-Cyr: Une Machine à Broyer les Femmes", *Libération*, 22 March.

Marly, M. (2019), *Distinguer et Soumettre. Une Histoire Sociale de l'Armée Française (1872–1914)*. Rennes: Presses Universitaires de Rennes.

Merchet, J.-D. (2013), "Le Ministre de la Défense Redevient celui de la Guerre", *Secret Défense*, 13 September.

Olsson, C. (2019), "Can't Live with Them, Can't Live without Them: 'The Enemy' as Object of Controversy in Contemporary Western Wars", *Critical Military Studies*, 5/4, 359–377.

Ostermann, F. (2017), "France's Reluctant Parliamentarization of Military Deployments. The 2008 Constitutional Reform in Practice", *West European Politics*, 40/1, 101–118.

Pannier, A. and Schmitt, O. (2019), "To Fight Another Day: France between the Fight against Terrorism and Future Warfare", *International Affairs*, 95/4, 897–916.

Pascallon, P. (ed.) (1997), *Les Interventions Extérieures de l'Armée Française*. Bruxelles: Bruylant.

Piton, F. (2018), *Le Génocide des Tutsi du Rwanda*. Paris: La Découverte.

Prévot, E. (2010), "Féminisation de l'Armée de Terre et Virilité du Métier des Armes", *Cahiers du Genre*, 48, 81–101.

Recchia, S. (2015), *Reassuring the Reluctant Warrior. U.S. Civil-Military Relations and Multilateral Intervention*. Ithaca: Cornell University Press.

Rousselier, N. (2015), *La Force de Gouverner. Le Pouvoir Exécutif en France, XIXe-XXIe Siècles*. Paris: Gallimard.

Schmitt, O. (2018), *Allies that Count. Junior Partners in Coalition Warfare*. Washington, DC: Georgetown University Press.

Settoul, E. (2015), "Analyser l'Immigration Postcoloniale en Milieu Militaire: Retour sur les Enseignements d'une Enquête Ethnographique", *Les Champs de Mars*, 27, 31–41.

Settoul, E. (2017), "L'Armée Vue par les 'Héritiers de l'Immigration': Entre Rhétorique de la Dette et Vecteur d'Intégration", *Migrations Société*, 169, 69–80.

Tenenbaum, E. (2018), *Partisans et Centurions. Une Histoire de la Guerre Irrégulière au XX° Siècle*. Paris: Perrin.

2 Transforming the French armed forces

As already described, the end of the Cold War led to a "crisis of the fundamentals" (Poirier, 1994) for French defence policy because of the combination of three mechanisms. First, the disappearance of the enemy on the Eastern flank shook the three fundamental pillars of the French military: military conscription, deterrence, and autonomy. Second, transnational threats that started emerging were not easily tackled by traditional military organisations. Finally, the French choice to support European integration, but also a relative normalisation within NATO (Schmitt, 2017a; see chapter 6) led to greater integration of the French forces with those of their partners. In that sense, the French armed forces have also experienced the dual process of concentration and transnationalisation described by Anthony King (2011). More professional and more technological, the French armed forces have encountered an expanded set of missions, with the integration of new domains of fighting (such as cyber), and remain an important element of France's great power ambitions. As such, their transformation illustrates the (limited) redefinition of the French international profile in the post-Cold War era.

Adjusting to the end of the Cold War

A number of transformations in the French defence apparatus began in 1991 because of the combination of three events: the Gulf War revealed some structural issues in the French defence capabilities, the fall of the USSR removed the core assumptions of French defence policy, and the beginning of the Balkan conflicts suggested a change in the character of warfare (from high intensity to protracted conflicts involving non-state actors), which would later be called "war amongst the people" (Smith, 2005).

Overall, in the late Mitterrand era, two main dynamics triggered an incremental change in the French armed forces. First, the discourse of "peace dividends" had an important political and psychological impact: the perception that defence budgets could now be reduced legitimised policies designed to minimise spending on the armed forces. Between 1990 and 1995, the French armed forces lost about 100,000 personnel and the defence budget was reduced from 3.5% to 3% of GDP.

Second, the lessons from the Gulf War (encapsulated in a November 1991 report) triggered a number of limited internal reforms, but which nevertheless

34 *Transforming the French armed forces*

paved the way for the process of concentration. The most important reform was the establishment of major joint institutions. The powers of the joint chief of staff (CEMA) were reinforced as he acquired planning responsibilities that were previously devolved to single services (they previously had a lot of latitude in designing their own force structure) and the creation of truly joint institutions supporting the CEMA: a joint planning staff (*État-Major Inter-armées*), a joint command and control unit (*Centre Opérationnel Interarmées*), a joint military intelligence service (*Direction du Renseignement Militaire*), a joint command for special operations (*Commandement des Opérations Spéciales*) and a joint war college (*Collège Interarmées de Défense*). Jointness in the French armed forces was therefore initiated after the Gulf War.

Some adjustments were initiated as early as 1991: reduction of the duration of compulsory military service to ten months, removal of 9,000 French troops from Germany, and early professionalisation of the army regiments tasked with intervention duties. However, those changes were mere short-term adaptations and did not reflect an overall vision for the French armed forces. Tellingly, the 1989 "Military Programming Law" (*Loi de Programmation Militaire – LPM*) was recognised as outdated in 1991, but there was a lack of legislative efforts to provide new frameworks to the decisions made by the executive: the legal project drafted after the Gulf War for the 1992–1994 period was never discussed in parliament as the Bérégovoy government never put it on the agenda, and the 1994 LPM prepared by the Balladur government for the 1995–2000 period was discarded after Jacques Chirac's election to the presidency in 1995 (Gautier, 1999). In 1994, a new white paper on defence policy was adopted, which can clearly be read as an attempt to maintain the Cold War paradigms while taking into account some emerging challenges and mitigating the left–right tensions related to the cohabitation between François Mitterrand and the Balladur government: "The White Paper sought, in the spirit of cohabitation, to combine continuity with change and ended up somewhere in-between" (Rynning, 2002, p. 139). The main doctrinal innovation in the white paper was the abandonment of the logic of "concentric circles" (France, Europe, and the world) defining security priorities and which had guided French defence policy since Charles de Gaulle's terms as president. They were replaced by different "scenarios" that would involve different combinations (and degrees) of intervention and deterrence (Table 2.1).

Table 2.1 Scenarios in the 1994 white paper

Scenario 1	A regional conflict that does not affect vital French interests
Scenario 2	A regional conflict that could affect vital French interests
Scenario 3	Threats to national territory outside of metropolitan France (overseas territories)
Scenario 4	Obligations from bilateral defence agreements (notably in Africa)
Scenario 5	Operations to support peace and international law
Scenario 6	Resurgence of a major threat to Western Europe

The white paper noted the emergence of some of the transnational threats that would define the 1990s and the 2000s (notably international terrorism and transnational crime) but had difficulty articulating those observations with a cohesive posture for the French armed forces (Forget, 2016). Another issue addressed in the white paper was the professionalisation of the French armed forces: the white paper embraced a mixed model, basically continuing the limited professionalisation of the troops earmarked for intervention purposes, but without addressing the main difficulties in terms of costs (differentiated procurement, training), military readiness, and morale, coming with such a model. However, this mixed model clearly had the support of the political-military elites, since it was perceived as a good combination of the republican tradition of the "citizen in arms" and the need to professionalise the armed forces to increase their effectiveness in a changing conflict environment.

The immediate post-Cold-War period was then marked by limited and incremental change in the armed forces (Gautier, 1999), which can probably be explained by a combination of uneasiness in front of the "crisis of the fundamentals" and the relative undecidedness of the political authorities in a context of "cohabitation" in the *Assemblée Nationale* (1993–1995): changes were certainly more important in the nuclear than in the conventional domains (see chapter 3). This would change with Jacques Chirac's election in 1995.

Professionalising the armed forces

Very early in his presidency (as soon as autumn/winter 1995), Jacques Chirac announced that military reform would be a defining aspect of his term. In his speech on 26 December 1995, Chirac announced that 1996 would be an important year for the armed forces, with "new directions" being given to "organisation and procurement" (Irondelle, 2011a). On 22 February 1996, in a televised interview, Chirac declared that the French model of armed forces was wholly unfit for purpose and announced a number of major reforms, most notably the gradual end of the conscription system, but also a reduction in the format of the armed forces, further cuts in defence spending and a restructuring of the defence industry (Chirac, 1996). The decision to professionalise the armed forces is particularly important as the administrative-military elite opposed it and instead favoured a "mixed model". The 1995 presidential election was thus a window of opportunity that allowed Jacques Chirac to play the role of a policy entrepreneur. Chirac had strong preferences for the professionalisation as he considered that the main role of the armed forces in the post-Cold-War era would be military interventions (as opposed to territorial defence) and that a mixed model maintaining conscription would hinder military effectiveness. The reform was then quietly prepared between July and December 1995 (which eventually led the administrative-military consensus on the mixed model to fracture), before being announced in 1996 (Irondelle, 2011a). It must be noted that the draft, in legal terms, had not been suppressed but merely "suspended" and could theoretically be re-instituted in case of need but, for all intended purposes, the 1996

36 *Transforming the French armed forces*

decision is fundamentally a professionalisation. The process was emblematic of the importance of the executive in the French system, with the president being able to drastically shape the agenda and impose strong strategic re-orientations when using the right window of opportunity and through careful agenda-setting. All things considered, the imposition of the professionalisation of the armed forces upon a reluctant ministry and armed forces is akin to De Gaulle's 1963 strategic decision to refocus French defence policy towards nuclear deterrence, a move resented at the time by the armed forces, which were still obsessed with the recently terminated Algerian War.

In March 1996, the French Ministry of Defence (MoD) released a document announcing a new format for the armed forces by 2015, and the draft of the new Military Programming Law for the 1997–2002 period was sent to parliament in June 1996. The "model 2015" announced a radical transformation of the format of the French armed forces, which had to go from 525,000 to 396,000 troops. In order to partially compensate for such a drastic reduction, reserves were planned to be reorganised, more integrated with the forces, but also cut from 500,000 to 100,000 reservists. The army was supposed to receive the most important cuts, going from 239,000 to 136,000 soldiers, and had to close 44 regiments (going from 129 to 85 regiments), which would have unforeseen consequences on the socio-political balances of the cities near which they were deployed, and in which soldiers and their families were living (Droff and Malizard, 2019). This also had consequences for the overall force structure: the "Rapid Action Force" and the "Armoured Army Corps" were dissolved as organisational structures and reorganised into a "Land Action Force" whose headquarters were to command a total of 11 brigades. Logistics was also regrouped in a "Land Logistic Force". The navy and the air force also had to reduce their format, but with fewer consequences for their organisational structures, as they could reduce in size without transforming their overall structure.

As important as they were, these reductions were far from being the last ones, as will be detailed below (Table 2.2).

The professionalisation of the armed forces, officially launched after it was voted by the parliament in 1997, was accomplished without major issues and completed in 2001, one year before the originally scheduled deadline. The irony of the Chirac presidency is that the main reform he initiated was actually voted and implemented by a left-wing government led by Prime Minister Lionel Jospin after the socialist party won the legislative elections in 1997 (following a tactical mistake by Chirac to dissolve the National Assembly). That the socialist

Table 2.2 Size of the French armed forces

	1995	*"Model 2015" (as envisioned in 1996)*	*2015*
Army	239,100	136,000	111,628
Navy	63,800	45,500	36,044
Air Force	89,200	63,000	43,597

Transforming the French armed forces 37

government did not try to reverse the decision to professionalise (while as little as three years earlier, a socialist President – François Mitterrand – was still heavily in favour of a mixed model) illustrates the redefined national consensus on the role of the armed forces in the intervention era, but also an accepted division of labour between the president and the prime minister (see chapter 1). Lionel Jospin decided not to contest the decisions enshrined in the 1997–2002 Military Programming Law because it would have immediately initiated a very hostile cohabitation, but also because he considered, following constitutional practice, that the president was the head of the armed forces and that the decision to professionalise had legitimately been made. However, he did not hesitate to intervene in the areas where the government had constitutional authority, notably in budgetary decisions regarding the professionalisation.

After Chirac was re-elected in 2002, the impulse for reform slowed down because of major budgetary issues. After the Jospin government had gradually decreased defence spending (the technical term is that the 1997–2002 Military Programming Law vas "voted but not executed"), Jacques Chirac vowed to restore the budget, which was the objective of the 2003–2008 Military Programming Law. This followed the 9/11 attacks, which had created a new sense of vulnerability, but it was also a way for the right-wing Chirac to differentiate himself from the socialist government (Irondelle, 2011b). However, the costs of professionalisation had been underestimated, and the long-term financing of the "Model 2015" was put into question, in particular, because no clear choice was made between the different procurement programs: the MoD ended up cancelling some purchases of equipment, which led unitary costs of production to explode and the French armed forces to receive less equipment for the same price as originally envisioned (Foucault, 2012). Moreover, the increasingly demanding foreign interventions consumed important parts of the extra resources (see chapter 5), thus slowing down the reform of the armed forces and of the MoD. It is clear that the budget of the French MoD increased between 2003 and 2008, but this increase was insufficient to fully cover the costs of the transformation towards the "Model 2015", which then had to be questioned (Figure 2.1).

As soon as Nicolas Sarkozy was elected in 2007, he initiated three major converging initiatives related to French defence policy: the writing of a new white paper (published in 2008) to replace the obsolete 1994 one, a new Military Programming Law for 2009–2014 and the application to the French MoD of the "General Review of Public Policies" (*Révision Générale des Politiques Publiques* – RGPP), a reform inspired by the new public management ideology and designed to reduce public spending by improving the efficiency of the state (Lafarge and Le Clainche, 2010). Combined with the decision to fully reintegrate the NATO structures and to increase the French contribution to the intervention in Afghanistan (see chapters 5 and 6), these decisions contributed to Sarkozy's initial self-presentation as a radical reformist.

Initiated in 2007, the discussions about the new white paper were organised around seven working groups, which auditioned 52 key French and foreign personalities in October–November 2007. Moreover, a website was created to collect

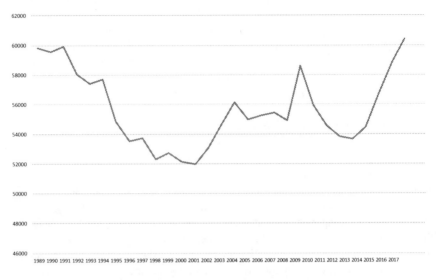

Figure 2.1 French defence budgets (Constant USD 2017. Source: SIPRI).

contributions from the public and support the work of the working groups. This apparent effort of inclusiveness and relative openness was nevertheless short-lived: the journalist Jean Guisnel revealed that beyond the official seven working groups, a "dark cabinet" of eight close collaborators was working for the president of the commission for the white paper, Jean-Claude Mallet, and orientated the writing process. Claiming that what was supposed to be a collaborative process was turning into rubber-stamping, three members of the commission decided to publicly resign: the attorney François Sureau, the socialist Senator Didier Boulaud, and the socialist MP Patricia Adam (Guisnel, 2008). The white paper was eventually published in 2008 and introduced a number of novelties. First, it established a continuum between security and defence (the full title is "The French White Paper on Defence and National Security"), proof of the gradual concerns with terrorism (particularly jihadism) since 9/11: the white paper considered that the traditional distinction between internal and external security was no longer relevant, and that new integrated strategies must be devised. Second, the authors identified five core strategic "functions" to which the French armed forces should contribute: knowledge and anticipation (with announcements of the development of the French intelligence capabilities), prevention, deterrence, protection of the national territory (with the introduction of the concept of "resilience" of the population as a guide for public policy) and force projection. Finally, the white paper described an "arc of crises", vaguely defined as an area comprising four or five "critical zones": Sub-Saharan Africa, Middle East and North Africa (MENA), the Gulf, and the Afghanistan/Pakistan zone. Again, such an identification of the "arc of crises" is revelatory of a post-9/11 mindset focused on the fight against terrorism (Foucher, 2012).

Coupled with the 2009–2014 Military Programming Law, the 2008 white paper abandoned the "Model 2015", which had been the official goal since the decision to professionalise the armed forces a decade earlier. The army's "operational contract" (meaning the number of troops the army is supposed to be able to deploy at all times) was reduced from 50,000 to 35,000 troops, thus acknowledging that the previous model was unrealistic given the constrained budgetary environment. Similarly, the MoD had to cut 54,000 positions: 18,000 of those cuts were related to the reduced ambition for the armed forces as laid out in the white paper, and 36,000 were part of the "General Review of Public Policies". This led to two processes of concentration, at the operational and policy levels. First, the logistics of the fundamental tactical units (regiments, air bases, flotillas) was centralised in newly created "defence bases" in order to cut costs and redundancies. This had a disruptive effect on the training and readiness of many of those units that all of a sudden had to ask authorisation and request funding for even the simplest tasks such as repainting walls and forced them to invent new bureaucratic practices. Sixty of those "defence bases" were created between 2009 and 2011. Second, it was decided that the core functional units (joint staff, defence procurement agency, centralised services of the ministry) would be regrouped in a common, modernised building established in Balard, in the south-west of Paris (and nicknamed the "French Pentagon" or "balardgon"). This concentration was designed to reduce the functioning costs of the ministry, with the hope that the selling of a large, historical building (the Ministry of Defence was located at Rue Saint-Dominique, in the heart of Paris) would also provide short-term incomes.

However, the objective of the Military Programming Law was to reduce the overall ambitions, without sacrificing the major procurement programs, such as the Rafale multirole fighter jet, the A400M strategic airlift plane, the FREMM destroyer, the new Barracuda submarines, and the Tigre and NH90 helicopters. The procurement goals were thus reduced, but without fundamentally altering the overall force structure and with an eye towards protecting the French defence industrial base (see chapter 4). This led, once again, to an increase in the nominal costs of the various weapon systems, and the French forces now had fewer capabilities but for the same original price. The table below summarises some of the key reductions in procurement from the 2009–2014 Military Programming Law (Table 2.3).

Table 2.3 Format reduction in the Military Programming Law 2009–2014 (Sample)

Navy	Air Force	Army
From 17 to 8 FREMM (frigates)	From 50 to 66 Rafales (multirole fighter jet) From 5 to 0 Mirage 2000D (air superiority fighter jet) From 18 to 8 A400M (strategic airlift plane)	From 22,230 to 17,884 Felin (infantry combat system) From 69 to 67 Caesar (artillery system) From 500 to 287 Porteur Polyvalent Terrestre (logistics system) From 23 to 21 NH90 (helicopter)

40   *Transforming the French armed forces*

Unlike the decision to professionalise the armed forces, which had been overall well-received (despite the associated budget cuts) and implemented, the 2008 reforms created a large degree of frustration. Shortly after the white paper was published, a group of anonymous senior officers published an op-ed in the daily *Le Figaro* under the pen name "Surcouf" (a 19th-century French corsair famous for numerous naval victories over British forces) (Groupe Surcouf, 2008). The op-ed was highly critical of the white paper, questioning the security assumptions (the white paper seemed unable to prioritise between the risks of high-intensity warfare and global pandemics especially when Russia had just invaded Georgia), the reduction of the armed forces without establishing priorities in the different procurement programs, and policy choices influenced by industrial rather than military considerations. This op-ed allegedly infuriated President Nicolas Sarkozy, who ordered an internal inquiry in order to identify the authors. No sanctions were given, but the op-ed was a sign of a gradual unease in the armed forces.

Sarkozy's presidency was also marked by an increased contribution to the war in Afghanistan, the decision to intervene in Libya in 2011, and a reformist ambition that had an important impact on the structure of the French armed forces. Following the structural change that was professionalisation, the increased operational tempo combined with a further reduction in format led to a feeling of "permanent reform" among the troops.

Stabilising the professional military?

When François Hollande was elected in 2012, little was known about his priorities for defence, except his campaign pledge to withdraw "French combat troops" from Afghanistan by the end of 2012. One of his first decisions was to order the writing of a new white paper to take stock of the major changes in the international environment since 2008: the consequences of the financial crises, the Arab Spring, and the perceived shifts in US strategy towards Europe in the context of an alleged "pivot to Asia". While work on the white paper was being completed, François Hollande decided to launch the Operation Serval intervention in Mali (January 2013) in order to protect the capital Bamako from being taken over by jihadist forces. The situation in Mali had drastically deteriorated in 2012, the country was clearly on the mind of French decision-makers and the imminent risk precipitated the intervention. From a military standpoint, French forces capitalised on the tactical skills gained from the Afghanistan intervention and showed that they were capable of audacious operations, including long-range helicopter interventions and an airborne assault on Timbuktu. This operational success allegedly had consequences for some choices made in the 2013 white paper in terms of the format of the armed forces (for example by preserving airborne assault capabilities and the regiments able to do so), but the format was even further reduced compared with the 2008 white paper, amounting to about a "15 percent cut, on average, of several major capabilities such as ground combat forces, destroyers, and fighter-bombers" (Tertrais, 2013, p. 55). The "operational contract" was also reduced when compared with 2008, since the ambition was to be able to deploy a maximum of two joint brigades (15,000 troops) in high-intensity operations.

Furthermore, extra personnel reductions amounting to a cut of 34,000 people were also registered in the 2014–2019 Military Programming Law. The yearly budget was supposed to remain constant at €31.4 billion for 2013, 2014, and 2015 (thus amounting to a yearly reduction of 1%–2% because of inflation) and to remain stable in real terms in 2016 and 2017, before increasing again in 2018 and 2019. A major justification for these budget cuts was the alleged need to balance the armed forces' requirements with the protection of France's financial sovereignty (as of 2013, France's debt was 60% owned by foreign actors). The 2015 jihadist attacks in Paris changed this rationale, and Hollande shifted gear on two counts. First, he agreed to "reduce staff cuts from 28,500 to 18,300 personnel up to 2019. Thus 7,500 positions were saved, including 1,500 in 2015" (Rynning and Schmitt, 2018, p. 809). Second, he started to reverse the shift in defence spending by increasing the budget instead of maintaining it. Coupled with the Russian aggression against Ukraine, which sent a shockwave among NATO countries, the second half of Hollande's mandate was marked by a clear realisation that the post-Cold-War security comfort was over. Hollande's presidency also initiated the framing of a French "war on terrorism" (Pannier and Schmitt, 2019), which was continued under President Macron.

Once Emmanuel Macron was elected in May 2017, he decided to avoid the lengthy committee process that had led to the two previous white papers and instead tasked Arnaud Danjean, a member of the European parliament widely respected for his expertise on defence issues, to author (with the support of staff from the Ministry of Defence) a "Strategic Review of Defence and National Security". Published in 2017, the Review defines the French threat perception and provides a guideline for the transformation of the armed forces. In military terms, the Review notes the increasing intensity of conflicts in the whole spectrum of warfare and identifies a number of threats. First, jihadi terrorism is identified as "the most immediate and enduring threat" because of its direct challenge to the safety of French citizens on French territory. The jihadi threat is understood as a long-term threat as none of the factors underpinning its development (social inequalities and ideologisation) are receding. It is unsurprising that Islamist terrorism is a key issue for French policy-makers: the 2013 Operation Serval intervention in Mali (which was later turned into operation Barkhane in the Sahel) was justified by the imminent threat of jihadist groups aiming at taking control of Bamako, and the 2015 attacks in Paris (against the newspaper *Charlie Hebdo* and the "Hyper Cacher" shop in January, and at several places including the "Bataclan" concert hall in November) were stark reminders of the reality of the jihadist threat. The French armed forces have then been engaged on several fronts under the framing of the fight against terrorism: in the Sahel, in Iraq/Syria (in support of the anti-ISIS coalition), but also at home under the framework of Operation Sentinelle to patrol and secure public areas (see chapter 5).

42   *Transforming the French armed forces*

Second, the Review is concerned with proliferation in all domains:

- Conventional, with the spread of advanced equipment (such as artillery or missiles) to an increasing number of actors, including non-state actors, which allows them to compete on almost equal terms with Western forces. This relates to the challenges of "techno-guerrilla" identified by some actors of the French strategic debate but also to a general realisation that the future battlefield will be characterised by increased speed and lethality
- Chemical and biological, particularly because of the conflict in Syria in which "the violations have not been followed by sanctions commensurate with the taboo that had been broken"
- Nuclear, with concerns about the sustainability of the nuclear agreement with Iran, the North-Korean proliferation, the mass acquisition of tactical nuclear capabilities by Pakistan, and the gradual erosion of the main arms limitation treaties. The Review coins the term "nuclear multipolarity" to describe an environment in which nuclear postures are less well-known and deterrence becomes more difficult to maintain

Third, the Review notes the return of the use of military power in world politics (notably by Russia and China) and the gradual competition in most domains: sea and air, but also the exosphere (perceived as very lightly regulated and in fast militarisation), and cyberspace (which is the object of intense competition). Therefore, the operational environment is marked by a gradual "ambiguity" since actors have more and more opportunities (and technological capabilities) to conduct aggressive actions with a veneer of plausible deniability and are thus able to craft integrated strategies of coercion. Combined with the gradual hardening ("*durcissement*") of warfare, the Review concludes that escalation risks have now increased in an international system marked by its gradual fragmentation. This return of strategic competition and the heightened risk of high-intensity conflict is taken very seriously by high-ranking military actors such as the CEMA, General Lecointre, who, for example, stated: "we need to be ready to engage in a potential 'conflict of survival', alone or in coalition, quickly and in the long term" (Lagneau, 2019). Compounding these two main strategic trends, the Review identifies a number of "challenges", notably a migration crisis, persistent vulnerability in the Sahel-Sahara region, and enduring destabilisation in the Middle East. This combination is perceived as challenging the cohesiveness of the European Union and thus destabilising the French security environment. All these developments took place in the context of a gradual disaffection, at the global level, towards multilateral mechanisms, which follows a gradual redistribution of power in the international system, leading some countries to be much more assertive (for example, Russia gradually dismantling the European security architecture). Finally, France is also concerned with rising tensions in Asia, which could challenge established diplomatic partnerships and freedom of navigation.

The perception of an increasingly dangerous international environment has triggered a modernisation of the French armed forces. The first element is a gradual increase in the defence budget since Emmanuel Macron was elected in 2017. The latest Military Programming Law was adopted for the 2019–2025 period and aims to reach a 2% share of GDP spent on defence by 2025. Funding for defence between 2019 and 2025 will amount to €295 billion, of which €198 billion are secured until 2023. Unless reductions are announced, the defence budget will amount to 1.91% of GDP in 2023 and 2% in 2025. However, the lack of secured funding for the 2023–2025 period means that an important share of the financial effort (€97 billion) will be put on the last two years of the LPM, and not-so-coincidentally after the 2022 presidential elections: a change in political priorities could then affect the French defence effort. The budgetary debate is related to the financial cost of the necessary modernisation of the French nuclear arsenal which, according to estimates, will increase from €3.9 billion in 2017 to €6 billion per year between 2020 and 2025, and decrease afterwards (see chapter 3). Therefore, it is possible that this financial effort will come at the expense of the conventional forces, particularly the purchase of new equipment and weapons systems, but the upwards trajectory has been welcomed by the forces after almost 30 years of uninterrupted cuts in defence spending. France has been in a recapitalisation phase since 2014, when defence budgets start increasing for the first time since the 2008 financial crisis, and it was only in 2017 that pre-crisis funding levels were once again reached (in constant 2010 US$). According to NATO figures (2017), France consistently spends about 47% of its defence budget on personnel costs (salaries and pensions), but the share devoted to equipment fell from 30% in 2010 to 24% in 2017; the upward trajectory since 2014 was then necessary to ensure the cohesiveness of the French armed forces and needs to continue in order to fund the modernisation efforts. According to General Lecointre, in 2025, the French armed forces will "no longer be exhausted", but they will still be geared for "peaceful times" and more efforts will be necessary to create resilient armed forces in case of a high-intensity conflict (cited by Guibert, 2018).

The COVID-19 crisis once again raises the issue of the French military model's sustainability. The French GDP is expected to decline by 11% in 2020, which will certainly have an impact on the armed forces' budget. At the time of writing, a debate was emerging about the proper budgetary goal: should it still be a firm 2% of GDP for the armed forces (implying less funding in a context of contracting GDP) or should the "absolute" pre-COVID numbers be maintained? Regardless of the decision that will be made, the COVID-19 crisis will have a strong impact on the French armed forces' modernisation process.

Thirty years after the end of the Cold War, French defence priorities have attempted to balance the reduction in defence spending, the modernisation of the forces, and adaptation to the security environment. The fluctuations between these incentives have had important consequences on the format and shape of the services: the armed forces of 2019 are drastically different from those of 1989. It is to the study of this evolution that we now turn.

44 *Transforming the French armed forces*

New armed forces for a new era?

The combination of professionalising the armed forces and reducing defence budgets led to a process of concentration of the French armed forces between 1990 and 2019. This process of concentration was accompanied by different degrees of internationalisation. First, from the mid-1990s onwards, there has been a process of "Europeanisation without the European Union" (Irondelle, 2003; Hoeffler and Faure, 2015). French political-military elites started to compare the French experience with other countries and adopted new cognitive frames regarding European integration. The "European horizon of French defence policy" (Gautier, 2009) was thus a motivation, but also a rhetorical resource, to drive the reforms. The rhetorical resource started to be matched with relevant instruments from the mid-2010s onwards, when the European Union started to develop cooperative armament programs such as PESCO (Permanent Structured Cooperation) or a European Defence Fund. From 2008 onwards, a different international mechanism started to play an important role in the transformation of the French armed forces, namely a "selective emulation" (Schmitt, 2015; 2017b) of other military practices observed within a NATO framework, in the context of the French participation in NATO operations in Afghanistan. Finally, since 2017, a combination of perceived international threats and a desire to remain technologically relevant within a NATO framework have led to a declared process of "innovation" within the French MoD. These different mechanisms provide the broader international context in which the transformation of the French armed forces is conducted.

The French army

The French army was at the centre of the debates on professionalisation through the 1990s, because the army represented the "nation in arms" that had become both a legacy of the 1789 Revolution and a bulwark against the insurrectionism that characterised parts of the professional army in the early 1960s (see chapter 1). Concerned that France could not pull its weight in the Atlantic Alliance and not back claims of enhanced "European" influence, President Chirac in 1996–1997 opted for full professionalisation. The key organisational challenge for the French army in the late 1990s/early 2000s was then to integrate and digest the consequences of professionalisation, including changes in its relationship with authority that it triggered within the forces (Jakubowski, 2007). Some years later, when the United States drove the new wave of "transformation", the French army was again put to the test: it had to integrate into a "joint" information technology architecture and simultaneously define its own distinct service footprint in the shape of an expeditionary warfighting capacity (Farrell et al., 2013, pp. 192–282).

The decade of "transformation" that followed put brigades front and centre of the army because they were versatile (compared to divisions) and had real punch (compared to battalions). In that sense, the French army's transformation was very similar to what was observed in other European countries (King, 2011). Moreover, among the brigades, the onus fell on the "medium" heavy brigades equipped with armoured vehicles that had greater speed compared to heavy brigades with main battle tanks and greater firepower and protection compared to infantry brigades. In this, the French army matched that of the United States, whose land force transformation effort likewise focused on integrating information technology, networked vehicles, and standoff firepower in expeditionary brigade structures that in the United States were labelled Stryker and in France Scorpion (*Synergie du contact renforcée par la polyvalence et l'infovalorisation*), which involves acquiring a new generation of land vehicles and involves a massive networking and digitalisation effort aimed at facilitating platform and unit integration. In other words, it is network-centric warfare for the 21st century, with a French flavour. It will be different from the American model in light of the fact that French forces will be considerably smaller and will emphasise the "robustness" of the platforms in their ability to fight even when networks fail.

At the height of the transformation wave, the French army had eight regular brigades and then three special brigades, and Scorpion defined a horizon of development. Since then, battle experience and battle lab testing and development in cooperation with the armament industry have made Scorpion a reality. The program is organised around the progressive acquisition of new equipment, particularly a new generation of armoured personnel carriers (APCs), Griffons, and Serval, as well as the ongoing acquisition of a new armoured reconnaissance and combat vehicles, the Jaguar, which started being delivered in 2019–2020. The ambition is to procure 1,872 Griffons, 978 Servals, and 300 Jaguars, half of which should be delivered by 2025. The goal is to be able to deploy the first joint battlegroups of 4,000 soldiers with enhanced networking capabilities and new ground vehicles by 2021. The French army then expects that, with four years of "lessons learned" from this initial deployment, it will be in good shape to fully integrate these new capabilities by 2025, when half of the equipment will have been delivered. An additional program goal is to be able to conduct joint operations at the tactical level, notably through the development of a tactical data link connecting the army, the air force, and the navy by 2023. The French military's ambition is to better integrate and concentrate fire regardless of the delivering platform, while also facilitating the adoption of "swarming" tactics as part of its plans for manoeuvre warfare. It will also enable better integration with like-minded, similarly equipped allies (such as the United States) in joint operations.

In mid-2016, the army consolidated its brigades into a division structure and a slimmed-down command structure, in part to take the greatest possible advantage of Scorpion technologies, but also in part to respond to a punishing tempo of expeditionary operations and to strengthen the army's contribution to homeland security (King, 2019). Today, the main land forces are thus organised into two Scorpion divisions of three brigades each: the first division headquartered in Besançon and the third division headquartered in Marseille. In addition, the army has opened a new homeland security command headquartered in Paris, which has 10,000 troops assigned to it in addition to army reserves. The latter took form as a consequence of professionalisation and is thus relatively new, and the aim is to build the reserve force up to a level of 40,000.

46 *Transforming the French armed forces*

The future army's range of main equipment, from Leclerc battle tanks to Griffon and Jaguar armoured vehicles and to new drones, will thus be connected to improve infantry gear and communication systems, generating an integrated Scorpion land force. It is a slimmer force compared to 2010, for instance, when its combat size was 110,000 personnel; its level of ambition is now 77,000. However, this is an improvement compared to the 2013–2014 plans, which would have cut the army to 66,000. The game-changer, the reason for the increase in force size, was the terrorist attacks on French soil in 2015 and the ensuing deployment of 10,000 army personnel for the purpose of homeland security, which severely stretched the army.

Besides contributing to homeland security at the level of 10,000 troops, the army's operational level of ambition remains that of the 2013 white paper: to maintain a national emergency force of 4,000 of a total of 5,000 troops, which includes an immediate reaction force of 2,300, of which the army will deliver 1,500. In addition, the army must have a capacity to deploy and sustain 6,000–7,000 troops for each of three simultaneous crisis management operations, or, the capacity to pull together a force of 15,000 troops to a major combat operation in coalition (or NATO) format (Rynning and Schmitt, 2018). The army has in recent years consistently had a high tempo of deployments, which includes not only an extensive presence in homeland protection but also participation in eight combat theatres (in 2018) – more than any time in recent French history. Counting the forces dedicated to homeland protection and crisis management operations, the army will have up to 30,000 troops engaged at any one point in time.

The sum total is a land force that remains coherent and operational and is also modernising. It is stretched, though, even as it pulls in reserves. Force modernisation (Scorpion) will continue to be costly, as will operations. However, the French land capacity for and experience in operations along the periphery of Europe will continue to be significant and will bolster French foreign policy in an era of declining US engagement.

The French navy

Like the other services, the French navy has been reduced since 1991. However, it is still a "blue water" navy capable of worldwide intervention, despite a diminishing trend in capabilities and the necessity to operate within a multinational framework in the case of high-intensity coercion operations. The reduction of the navy's format has been homothetic, without questioning (so far) the organisational model and strategic conceptions around which the French navy was built.

Historically, France has a complicated relationship with its navy and has struggled to balance being both a naval and land power, a geopolitical incentive derived from France's particular geographic position of simultaneously being open to the Atlantic Ocean, the Mediterranean Sea, and the English Channel while bordering the landmass of Germany (Taillemite, 2010). Yet, because of its overseas possessions (*Départements et Territoires d'Outre-Mer*), notably in Guyana, New Caledonia, or the Indian Ocean, France maintains naval forces contributing to the affirmation of French sovereignty. Unlike the United States, France does not have a coastguard capability. Therefore, the navy (alongside other services such as customs and *gendarmerie*) contributes to the protection of the French naval domain from risks such as pollution, accidents, trafficking, and smuggling. This mission covers 20% of the navy's activities.

The navy is organised around four main commands: naval action force (*Force d'Action Navale*, FAN), submarine forces (*Forces Sous-Marines*, FSM), naval aviation (*Aéronautique Navale*, ALAVIA), and the commando and marine force (*Force Maritime des Fusiliers Marins et Commandos*, FORFUSCO). As of 2019, the main capability at the disposal of the French navy is the carrier strike group, organised around the aircraft carrier *Charles de Gaulle* and comprising (beyond the aircraft carrier itself) one attack submarine, four destroyers (two specialised in air defence, two specialised in submarine defence) and one frigate acting as a scout. The French navy can also mount an amphibious group organised around one of the three landing helicopter dock ships of the Mistral class. The navy contributes to the French deterrence mission in two ways. First, ALAVIA has developed a squadron of 43 Rafale and 9 Super-Etendard jets, which can be equipped with an ASMP-A nuclear missile. But mostly the French navy operates four ballistic missile submarines that constitute the heart of the French nuclear deterrence capability.

With a total of about 300 ships (10 submarines, 90 combat ships, and 200 support ships), the French navy can be considered a "second-rank" navy with worldwide capabilities. Yet, the gradual reductions in combat ships because of budget pressures (notably reducing the number of new destroyers being available to the navy) raises questions regarding the resilience of the navy in the case of high-intensity coercive operations; in such a situation, the French navy would be comparable to a powerful rifle, but with only one bullet (Rynning and Schmitt, 2018). The navy is in the process of modernising key elements of the fleet as well. A new class of nuclear-powered attack submarines (SSNs), the Barracuda, is gradually replacing the Saphirs. (In 2015, a Saphir was responsible for the "virtual" sinking of the *USS Roosevelt* during a bilateral US–France naval training exercise.) In addition, the French navy will be adding a new class of "multi-mission frigates" (FREMMs). From 2021 onwards, the FREMMs will be equipped with enhanced networking capabilities comparable to the French Army's Scorpion. One of the main topics of discussion in the coming years will be the size and features of the aircraft carrier replacing the *Charles de Gaulle*, which will be decommissioned between 2030 and 2040. Plans for its replacement have started, but the final design and program decisions have not been made.

The French Air Force

Since the end of the Cold War, the French Air Force (FAF) has had to reconcile a need for technological upgrade with a reduction in its overall format. The FAF began the new Cold War era with a shock. The Gulf War demonstrated the limits of its capabilities and doctrine. As Anrig explains: "Desert Storm proved too big,

48   *Transforming the French armed forces*

too technologically advanced and too Anglo-Saxon for the FAF" (Anrig, 2011, p. 103). The tactical skills of the French pilots were appreciated by their partners in the coalition. Nevertheless, the contribution was limited by material problems. The FAF lacked compatible Identification Friend or Foe (IFF) equipment and was poorly equipped in night-vision capabilities. This realisation led to an active policy of upgrading the FAF's capabilities, notably through the acquisition of precision-guided munitions and capabilities necessary to operate within a multinational framework (Forget, 2013). Yet, this has not led to sustained doctrinal work on par with the efforts conducted by the United States Air Force or the Royal Air Force. Historically, the FAF has not developed the institutional setting necessary to produce a sophisticated doctrine of force employment and has relied on a "learning by doing approach" (Irondelle and de Durand, 2006). Two attempts were made in 1997 and 2003 to establish a cohesive doctrine of force employment, both unsuccessful as fighter pilots (who hold most of the commanding positions in the FAF) felt it would question the heart of their professional identity: air-to-air combat (Vennesson, 1997; Dubey and Moricot, 2016).

The main capability upgrade for the FAF was the introduction of the multirole Rafale aircraft from 2006 onwards. A technological success, and combat-proven in Afghanistan, Libya, and Iraq, the Rafale increased the fighting power of the FAF while being praised for its modularity. Yet, capability gaps still exist, notably in two fields: suppression of enemy air defences (SEAD) and strategic airlift. Beyond military interventions and the protection of the French airspace, the FAF is also part of the French nuclear deterrence capability by providing two squadrons (Rafale F3 and Mirage 2000-N) equipped with ASMP-A missiles. Introduced in 1964, this capability remains very important for the FAF.

Like the other services, the FAF was hit by budget and format reductions, with 200 fighter planes available in 2020 (380 in 2000). The drastic reduction is partly compensated by the increase in the overall quality of the planes (with the Rafale gradually replacing older models) and the acquisition of unmanned combat aerial vehicles (UCAVs) (12–16 Reapers). Nevertheless, it is hard to escape the fact that, just like for the navy, the format reduction implies a reduction of resilience and flexibility. For the FAF, the key program is the Future Combat Air System (SCAF – *Système de Combat Aérien du Futur*) being developed in partnership with Germany and Spain. The SCAF is conceived as a system enabling "networked collaborative air combat". The system will consist of a core platform (a jet fighter with stealth features), working in combination with secondary platforms (such as drones) that could serve as sensors or logistics airframes. In an increasingly contested environment – through the development of advanced anti-access, area-denial (A2/AD) defence systems by potential adversaries – these secondary platforms could help conduct tasks such as electronic warfare or precision targeting. The FAF is particularly interested in the development of artificial intelligence (AI) to help pilots effectively utilise the various platforms and avoid cognitive overload from the large amounts of data constantly being fed into the cockpit by onboard and network sensors. An AI-assisted "virtual assistant" would act as an "analyst", fusing data in order to provide the pilot with a tactical overview; an "advisor", suggesting solutions to flight or combat situations; a "delegate", handling logistical or less pressing tasks; and, as a "guardian angel", taking over from the pilot in life-threatening situations, such as when a pilot is incapacitated. Some of the technologies necessary for the system are being developed and should be in place in the next Rafale upgrades.

Tactical airlift is also in transition with the introduction of the A400M and the gradual decommissioning of the venerable (more than 50 years old) C-160 Transalls. The fleet also consists of a number of C-130 Hercules. With the procurement of the A400Ms, French tactical airlift capability will certainly be improved. However, the timing of the C-160's decommissioning and of the gradual introduction of the A400M may lead to short-term gaps in capabilities. Moreover, more broadly, the French military's airlift capability is insufficient to fully meet current and potential deployment requirements, making France dependent for lift either on allies or on leasing from private companies.

The new domains: space and cyberspace

Although France has been a space power since the early 1960s, a formal military space strategy was not released until 2019. Previously, discussions of space assets having military utility were minimal. This was true even when, in 1984, France put its first communication satellite (Télécom 1A) into orbit, a satellite equipped with military capability. Strategic thinking about space really began with a reaction to President Reagan's Strategic Defence Initiative, which made French decision-makers realise that space assets might become vulnerable to attack. In the 1980s, France initiated a number of diplomatic initiatives to prevent the deployment of anti-satellite (ASAT) weapons. With the publication of the defence white paper in 1994 and the launch of the first French reconnaissance satellite, *Helios 1*, in 1995, the utility of space for surveillance and the possibility of an arms race in space was recognised as a possibility down the road. However, the threat of an arms race was not perceived as particularly imminent and, after having been active on the arms control front diplomatically, French diplomacy became relatively silent on the issue from the mid-1990s onwards.

The real game-changing shock was the Chinese ASAT test in 2007, which had an impact on how space was treated in subsequent defence white papers and which culminated in the 2019 Defence Space Strategy (Ministry of Armed Forces, 2019a). In substance,

> the space strategy sets a two-fold ambition. The first is to provide better space situational awareness in support of national decision-making. The second is to improve the protection of national and key European space assets, including the possible provision of onboard lasers for satellite defence. Underpinning both is the intent to sustain and support national and European space industrial bases.
>
> (Laudrain, 2019a)

50 *Transforming the French armed forces*

Space-based assets are now seen as a critical supporting element in France's nuclear deterrent capability.

Other aspects of the strategy include a rebranding of the FAF, which will now be called the Air and Space Force. This includes the establishment of a space command in charge of all military space-related units as of 1 September 2019. This reflects the changing perception of space as an operational domain. France is particularly interested in developing measures to protect its satellites, including onboard cameras and greater manoeuvrability in space. France is also looking at the development of nano-satellites to serve as a redundant capability to provide resilience in case of a successful attack on major satellite assets. These initiatives are understood as staying within the bounds of self-defence as France is adamant on emphasising its compliance with international law. In total, France is allocating US $800 million from 2019 to 2025 in support of its space ambitions.

The first National Strategy for Cyber Defence was issued in 2018 by the *Secrétariat Général à la Défense et la Sécurité Nationale* (SGDSN, 2018). The French approach to cybersecurity differs from the United States and the United Kingdom in the sense that

> France assumes a clear separation between offensive and defensive cyber operations and actors. This means that, contrary to the National Security Agency or the United Kingdom's Government Communications Headquarters, France's leading agency for cyber security is not part of the intelligence community.
>
> (Laudrain, 2019b)

The rationale for keeping offensive and defensive cyber operations separate is that private companies and government bodies not associated with national security are more willing to cooperate with the agency (*Agence Nationale de la Sécurité des Systèmes d'Information*, ANSSI) tasked with network protection and cyber defence if they are not associated with the "militarised" use of cyberspace. Keeping the two realms separate lessens the perceived reputational costs of working with the military.

In January 2019, France released a doctrine for offensive cyber operations and established a Cyber Defence Command aimed at coordinating cyber activities within the armed forces (Ministry of Armed Forces, 2019b). The government's acknowledgement of an offensive cyber doctrine is part of a declaratory posture aimed at establishing deterrence in cyberspace. Minister for the Armed Forces Parly stated that France has the means to identify perpetrators and would not refrain from retaliating if needed (Parly, 2019). Unlike some allies, France has been publicly reluctant to attribute cyber-attacks to particular state actors and seems more inclined to address these issues bilaterally and in closed discussions (Delerue et al., 2019). From the French perspective, cyber capabilities can have a tremendous "multiplier effect" on the conduct of military operations, with offensive cyber operations having three main goals: intelligence gathering, neutralisation of an adversary's capabilities, and deception (Taillat, 2019).

The publication of the doctrine signals the growing maturity of the French cybersecurity architecture. This domain is clearly important for the defence ministry as illustrated by the Military Programming Law 2019–2025, which dedicates an extra €1.6 billion to cyber operations and authorises an additional 1,500 additional personnel in order to reach a total of 4,000 cyber-combatants by 2025.

Conclusion

French ambitions on the global stage remain so far intact. Paris intends to keep acting as a middle power with a global reach. There is a consensus among France's political parties that it should maintain an independent foreign policy and that an essential instrument for doing so is the military.

The upward trend in defence spending observed in recent years is a welcome improvement and a reflection of France's perception of a degraded security environment. But this trend will strongly depend on the country's future economic performances. While the government has put forward reforms to improve the efficiency of the labour market and of public spending, another major recession could derail France's defence plans as government resources fall flat or decline. Yet even if a more optimistic economic future were to unfold, France will still face the strategic problem of maintaining its global aspirations with middle power resources – and do so in a security environment that has grown significantly more complex and difficult.

References

Anrig, C. (2011), *The Quest for Relevant Air Power. Continental European Responses to the Air Power Challenges of the Post-Cold War Era.* Maxwell: Air University Press.

Chirac, J. (1996), *Allocution sur TF1 et FR2.* 22 February.

Delerue, F. et al. (2019), "A Close Look at France's New Military Cyber Strategy", *War on the Rocks*, 23 April.

Droff, J. and Malizard, J. (2019), "Quand l'Armée s'en va! Analyse Empirique de la Cohérence de l'Accompagnement des Territoires par le Ministère des Armées", *Revue d'Economie Régionale & Urbaine*, 19, 97–123.

Dubey, G. and Moricot, C. (2016), *Dans la Peau d'un Pilote de Chasse. Le Blues de l'Homme-Machine.* Paris: PUF.

Farrell, T., Rynning, S. and Terriff, T. (2013), *Transforming Military Power Since the Cold War.* Cambridge: Cambridge University Press.

Forget, G. (2013), *Nos Forces Aériennes en OPEX. Un demi-siècle d'Interventions Extérieures.* Paris: Economica.

Forget, G. (2016), *Nos Armées au Temps de la Ve République.* Paris: Economica.

Foucault, M. (2012), *Les Budgets de Défense en France, entre Déni et Déclin, Focus Stratégique N° 36.* Paris: IFRI.

Foucher, M. (2012), "L'Arc de Crise, Approche Française des Conflits", *Bulletin de l'Association des Géographes Français*, 89/1, 6–17.

Gautier, L. (1999), *Mitterrand et son Armée: 1990–1995.* Paris: Grasset.

Groupe Surcouf (2008), "Livre Blanc sur la Défense. Une Espérance Déçue", *Le Figaro*, 19 June.

52 *Transforming the French armed forces*

Guibert, N. (2018), "Le Général Lecointre: 'Nous Resterons une Armée de Temps de Paix'", *Le Monde*, 7 September.

Guisnel, J. (2008), "Dans le Plus Grand Secret, un Groupe Occulte a Épaulé la Commission du Livre Blanc", *Le Point*, 18 July.

Hoeffler, C. and Faure, S. (2015), "L'Européanisation sans l'Union Européenne. Penser le Changement des Politiques Militaires", *Politique Européenne*, 48, 8–27.

Irondelle, B. (2003), "Europeanization without the European Union? French Military Reforms 1991–96", *Journal of European Public Policy*, 10/2, 208–226.

Irondelle, B. (2011a), *La Réforme des Armées en France. Sociologie de la Décision*. Paris: Presses de Sciences Po.

Irondelle, B. (2011b), "Qui Contrôle le Nerf de la Guerre? Financement et Politique de Défense", in Siné, A. (ed.), *Gouverner (par) les Finances Publiques*. Paris: Presses de Sciences Po, 491–523.

Irondelle, B. and de Durand, E. (2006), *Stratégie Aérienne Comparée : France, Etats-Unis, Royaume-Uni*. Paris : C2SD.

Jakubowski, S. (2007), *La Professionalisation de l'Armée Française. Conséquences sur l'Autorité*. Paris : L'Harmattan.

King, A. (2019), *Command. The 21st Century General*. Cambridge: Cambridge University Press.

King, A. (2011), *The Transformation of Europe's Armed Forces*. Cambridge: Cambridge University Press.

Lafarge, F. and Le Clainche, M. (2010), "La Révision Générale des Politiques Publiques", *Revue Française d'Administration Publique*, 136, 751–754.

Lagneau, L. (2019), "Général Lecointre: 'Il faut être prêt à s'engager pour un conflit de survie", *Opex 360*, 26 July.

Laudrain, A. (2019a), "France's 'Strategic Autonomy' Takes to Space", *Military Balance Blog*, 14 August.

Laudrain, A. (2019b), "France's New Offensive Cyber Doctrine", *Lawfare*, 26 February.

Ministry of Armed Forces (2019a), Stratégie Spatiale de Défense. Available at: https://www.defense.gouv.fr/actualites/articles/florence-parly-devoile-la-strategie-spatiale-francaise-de-defense (last access: 17 September 2019).

Ministry of Armed Forces (2019b), Éléments Publics de Doctrine Militaire de Lutte Informatique Offensive. Available at: https://www.defense.gouv.fr/salle-de-presse/dossiers-de-presse/dossier-de-presse_elements-publics-de-doctrine-militaire-de-lutte-informatique-offensive (last access, 17 September 2019).

NATO, *Defence Expenditure of NATO Countries 2010–2017*. Available at: https://www.nato.int/nato_static_fl2014/assets/pdf/pdf_2017_06/20170629_170629-pr2017-111-en.pdf

Secrétariat Général à la Défense et la Sécurité Nationale (2018), *Revue Stratégique de Cyberdéfense*. Available at: http://www.sgdsn.gouv.fr/evenement/revue-strategique-de-cyberdefense/ (last access: 17 September 2019).

Pannier, A. and Schmitt, O. (2019), "To Fight Another Day: France between the Fight against Terrorism and Future Warfare", *International Affairs*, 95/4, 897–916.

Parly, F. (2019), *Speech*. 18 January. Available at: https://www.defense.gouv.fr/salle-de-presse/discours/discours-de-florence-parly/discour-de-florence-parly-ministre-des-armees-strategie-cyber-des-armees (last access, 17 September 2019).

Poirier, L. (1994), *La Crise des Fondements*. Paris: Economica.

Rynning, S. (2002), *Changing Military Doctrine: Presidents and Military Power in Fifth Republic France, 1958–2000*. Westport: Praeger.

Rynning, S. and Schmitt, O. (2018), "France", in Meijer, Hugo and Wyss, Marco (eds.), *The Oxford Handbook of European Defence Policies and Armed Forces*. Oxford: Oxford University Press, 35–51.

Schmitt, O. (2015), "Européanisation ou Otanisation? Le Royaume-Uni, la France et l'Allemagne en Afghanistan", *Politique Européenne*, 48, 150–177.

Schmitt, O. (2017a), "The Reluctant Atlanticist: France's Security and Defence Policy in a Transatlantic Context", *Journal of Strategic Studies*, 40/4, 463–474.

Schmitt, O. (2017b), "French Military Adaptation in the Afghan War: Looking Inward or Outward?", *Journal of Strategic Studies*, 40/4, 577–599.

Smith, R. (2005), *The Utility of Force. The Art of War in the Modern World*. London: Allen Lane.

Taillat, S. (2019), "Signaling, Victory, and Strategy in France's Military Cyber Doctrine", *War on the Rocks*, 8 May.

Taillemite, E. (2010), *Histoire Ignorée de la Marine Française*. Paris: Perrin.

Tertrais, B. (2013), "Leading on the Cheap? French Security Policy in Austerity", *The Washington Quarterly*, 36/3, 47–61.

Vennesson, P. (1997), *Les Chevaliers de l'Air. Aviation et Conflits au XXIe Siècle*. Paris: Presses de Sciences Po.

3 Nuclear deterrence: capabilities and doctrine

At its inception, nuclear deterrence was conceived as the cornerstone of French defence policy under the Fifth Republic. It had its "thirty glorious years" between 1960 and 1990, to use Louis Gautier's words (Gautier, 2009, p. 150) and remains today deeply marked by the circumstances and the concepts that presided over its birth. In the decade following the Fall of the Berlin Wall, however, French nuclear deterrence was re-scaled, and its doctrines and equipment were revisited to account for geopolitical changes. If, in the 1990s and 2000s, nuclear deterrence no longer "overdetermine[d] the security equation" for France (Gautier, 2009, p. 150), the decade of the 2010s has marked the return of nuclear military issues to the forefront of international affairs, and an increase in instability and strategic risk. In the context of the Ukraine crisis initiated in 2014, Russia did not hesitate to simulate attacks against allied countries and to deploy nuclear-capable systems of various ranges, thus causing alarm among the members of the Atlantic Alliance. Russia, in particular, deployed nuclear-capable missiles to the Kaliningrad exclave in 2018, and on a permanent basis in early 2019 (Axe, 2019). Across the globe, it is estimated that more than 30 countries possess ballistic missile systems capable of carrying nuclear warheads (Berger and Lasconjarias, 2019, p. 220). North Korea, which since 2003 has not respected the terms of the Non-Proliferation Treaty (NPT) and is not a party to the Comprehensive Nuclear Test Ban Treaty (CTBT) started conducting increasingly successful nuclear tests from 2006 onwards. In July 2017, it tested its first intercontinental ballistic missile (ICBM), and in September 2017, it conducted a test of what it claimed was a thermonuclear weapon (Nuclear Threat Initiative, 2019). Meanwhile, the United States announced in May 2018 its withdrawal from the Joint Comprehensive Plan of Action (JCPOA, known as the Iran nuclear deal) signed in July 2015 between Iran, the United States, China, Russia, France, the United Kingdom, Germany, and the European Union. At that same moment, the Treaty on the Prohibition of Nuclear Weapons, prepared in 2007 by the International Campaign to Abolish Nuclear Weapons (ICAN), opened for signature at the United Nations. The treaty was signed by 70 members of the UN and ICAN received the Nobel Peace Prize in 2017.

How have successive French presidents, from François Mitterrand to Emmanuel Macron, adapted France's nuclear capabilities and doctrine, and with what relations to partners and allies in Europe and across the Atlantic? What positions has France taken on those key international dossiers, and how has it contributed to shaping the international nuclear order? In this chapter, we start by briefly reviewing the development of France's nuclear deterrent in the context of the Cold War, before examining how the country adapted both its capabilities and doctrine from the 1990s onward. We then cover the institutional aspects of France's deterrence, explaining what actors are involved in its decision-making and implementation. Finally, we move on to discuss France's role in international non-proliferation and arms control efforts, before highlighting some of the contemporary debates surrounding nuclear weapons today, between calls for global disarmament and needs for system modernisation.

Origins of France's nuclear deterrence

France's military nuclear program was developed in the greatest secrecy at the Liberation, building on networks created by common experience in the French Resistance (Mongin, 2018a). Fifteen years later, with its successful nuclear test in February 1960 in the Algerian desert (*"Gerboise Bleue"*), France became the fourth country to acquire the bomb after the United States, the Soviet Union, and the United Kingdom. The objectives of the French program were broad and multiple, with deep and lasting ramifications (Guisnel and Tertrais, 2016, pp. 19–20). First, its purpose was to ensure national self-defence, based on the lessons learned from the defeat of 1940. Later, as the Cold War unfolded, the deterrent served to protect the national territory against the existential threat posed by the Soviet Union. Yet, beyond this direct threat, nuclear deterrence aimed at making up for the limits of alliances, as experienced during the Suez crisis of 1956, and responded to the desire for an independent defence policy. Finally, nuclear weapons made France both a part of the circle of great powers and an alternative to the dominance of the United States and the USSR. Indeed, they were an element of affirmation of France's diplomatic and military power in between the two blocs, as the country used its status of autonomous nuclear power to generate political room to manoeuvre (Gautier, 2009, pp. 149–153). For the following three decades, the decision to endow France with a completely autonomous nuclear arsenal was the priority of all governments and the centrepiece of France's defence.

The development of the French independent nuclear deterrent came together with means for autonomous research and manufacturing. France produced fissile materials for military purposes (plutonium and highly enriched uranium) in the plants at Pierrelates and Marcoules. National industry and agencies – Aérospatiale, Thomson, Dassault, the *Commissariat à l'Énergie Atomique* (Commission for Atomic Energy, CEA), and the *Direction Générale de l'Armement* (Directorate General of Armaments, DGA) – ensured the development and manufacture of equipment. Finally, the atolls of Mururoa and Fangataufa (in French Polynesia) provided experimental sites.

56 *Nuclear deterrence*

While France sought to ensure its national defence through nuclear deterrence, the goal was never to match those of the two great powers, and both the equipment and doctrine reflected France's specific ambitions. During the Cold War, the doctrine of "counter-city strikes", which could cause dozens of millions of deaths, served to ensure that the gains of any Soviet attempt at seizing French territory would be extremely limited. The counter-city doctrine and the accompanying principle of intolerable damage were logical compensation for the small size of the French arsenal. As Brustlein puts it,

> for a medium-sized power such as France, it [was] not a matter of systematically attempting to rival the USSR; the aim instead [was] to develop an arsenal [...] sufficient to deter even one of the superpowers from directly striking against its vital interests.
>
> (Brustlein, 2017, p. III)

Indeed, there was – and remains – in France an understanding that the use of nuclear weapons, regardless of their yield, would change the nature of the conflict, and that escalation into the nuclear domain would imply the mobilisation of the whole of its nuclear arsenal (Gautier, 2009, p. 176). To French strategists, Hiroshima and Nagasaki had indeed shown that nuclear weapons possessed a power so tragic that they were necessarily a weapon of deterrence rather than a weapon of use, and a weapon of self-defence rather than offence.

During the Cold War decades, France possessed a triad of land, maritime, and airborne nuclear weapons. The operationalisation of the air component was completed in 1968, with the coming into service of the 62 aircraft of the Strategic Air Force (*Force Aérienne Stratégique*, FAS) (Tertrais, 2017, p. 82). France also deployed land-based intermediate-range ballistic missiles on the Albion Plateau aimed at the Soviet Union, from 1971 onwards. The silo-based S3 missiles possessed a range of 3500 kilometres and a yield of approximately one megaton (Tertrais, 2017, p. 84). Thirdly, the first nuclear submarine (SSBN), *Le Redoutable*, came into service in 1972. That same year, the first French defence white paper came out and placed a significant emphasis on the doctrine of nuclear deterrence. Finally, after its withdrawal from NATO's integrated military structures, France launched its first independent tactical weapons program, and the ground-launched Pluton missiles came to equip the French army from 1974 onwards. Similar tactical systems equipped the French Air Force and aeronaval forces. Tactical nuclear weapons were an essential link in the "*force de frappe*" (literaly: strike force), to protect French territory. In 1966 doctrinal documents, tactical weapons were considered for use between conventional forces and strategic nuclear forces (Baille, 2019, p. 61). French authorities were never content with the notion of "tactical nuclear weapons" or the concept of nuclear weapons as battlefield weapons but envisaged such weapons – called "pre-strategic" weapons from Mitterrand onwards – to be used as an ultimatum should its vital interests be at stake. In the midst of the Euromissile crisis, President Mitterrand took measures in 1982 to authorise the launch of the Hadès program, which replaced the Pluton missiles.

Hadès was a 400-kilometre-range ballistic nuclear weapon system. The first qualifying fire took place in 1988, and the first units (six missiles) were delivered in 1991. In total, France possessed 250 warheads in 1970 and 500 by 1990, when the budget and military resources devoted to nuclear deterrence were at their highest in French history (Gautier, 2009, p. 153).

Changes to France's nuclear capabilities at the turn of the 1990s

The Fall of the Berlin Wall and the broader geopolitical changes that accompanied it led to a revision of France's nuclear deterrence capabilities and doctrines. On the one hand, nuclear weapons lost centrality in the international system and democratic governments needed to provide renewed justifications for the possession of a nuclear deterrent. On the other hand, the types of challenges to international security posed by nuclear weapons evolved. The maintenance of France's nuclear deterrent, however, was never seriously questioned. In 1991, François Mitterrand justified the maintenance of deterrence at the heart of France's defence strategy on the ground that new global uncertainty renewed the justification for nuclear weapons: "Given the uncertainties surrounding the future evolution of Europe and the world in general, France considers it necessary to maintain a credible deterrence while encouraging the balanced reduction of nuclear weapons of the United States and the USSR" (Mitterrand, 1991).

Nonetheless, the president decided to lower the readiness level of French nuclear forces in May 1992 (Présidence de la République, 1992). More importantly, from Mitterrand onwards, successive governments undertook four changes to France's nuclear capabilities: France reduced the number of its warheads and abandoned the land-based and pre-strategic components of its arsenal, ceased the production of fissile materials, joined the Nuclear Non-Proliferation Treaty, and ceased nuclear field tests, which were replaced by a simulation program.

In the 1990s, France abandoned its land component, dissolved the nuclear artillery regiments, closed the base of the Albion Plateau where the silo-based missiles were located, and reduced the number of SSBNs from six to four. The Albion Plateau's purpose was conceived as a sanctuary for the national territory, and lost its purpose when the end of the USSR removed the direct threat against French territory. When it comes to pre-strategic weapons, Chirac, after consulting with Germany, announced the definitive withdrawal of the Hadès system in February 1996 (Chirac, 1996). Overall, France reduced the number of its warheads from over 500 to 320 by the end of the Chirac presidency in 2007, and down to "under 300" during the Sarkozy presidency (Gautier, 2019, p. 183; Tertrais, 2017, p. 83). The budget allocated to deterrence was consequently cut in half between 1991 and 1998.

Another significant set of decisions related to the interruption of nuclear tests. On 8 April 1992, Mitterrand announced a unilateral French moratorium on nuclear testing, following Russian and American commitments to ban nuclear tests. In September 1992, US Congress passed an amendment setting strict conditions on any further US testing and requiring the start of global test ban negotiations. The

58 Nuclear deterrence

US moratorium was further extended in July 1993 (Arms Control Association, 2019). As an alternative to field tests, the Mitterrand government initiated an ambitious simulation program, considered essential to ensure the safety, security, reliability, and technical credibility of French systems (Yost, 1996, p. 110). However, more nuclear field tests appeared necessary. Mitterrand's 1992 moratorium had been taken by the president himself against the advice of the CEA, the DGA, and the defence minister (Tranchez, 2019, p. 6). Indeed, developing the simulation capability took several years, and the CEA then was not yet in a position to set up a credible program. Now, in the context of French strategic posture, it was vital for French policy-makers that the simulation program be developed nationally, rather than engaging in close cooperation with the United States, which, it was feared, could have drawn France into a technical dependence (Yost, 1996, pp. 110–111). When he came to power in 1995, Jacques Chirac thus had two priorities for France's defence policy: to abolish military service, as discussed in Chapter 1, and to resume nuclear tests.

With the first test in French Polynesia in September 1996, France broke the three-year-old moratorium that had been observed by the other recognised nuclear powers except for China. This caused international outrage, in particular from South Pacific countries. The test was one of a series of six that France completed before it signed the CTBT later that year. Chirac was determined to complete these tests, which would serve to develop a new nuclear warhead that could withstand future technological developments without requiring new tests (Tranchez, 2019, p. 7). The tests would also provide additional data for the development of simulation capabilities themselves, and thus would enable France to do without field tests in the future (Yost, 1996, p. 108).

Once field tests ceased, France only relied on a program named "Simulation", developed over the course of the period 1996–2010, under the responsibility of the *Direction des Applications Militaires* (Division of Military Applications) of the CEA. The program, aimed at ensuring the safety and reliability of the systems, is composed of three highly technological tools: supercomputers, the Laser Mégajoule, and x-ray radiographic facilities. Concretely speaking, the Simulation program includes physical modelling, digital simulation, and experimental validation. The nuclear warheads that today constitute France's submarine and airborne deterrents, the airborne nuclear warhead (*tête nucléaire aéroportée*, TNA) and the oceanic nuclear warhead (*tête nucléaire océanique*, TNO) were both developed on the basis of the results of the 1996 campaign of nuclear tests, and conceived through the Simulation program, and therefore did not need to be field-tested (Tranchez, 2019, p. 3). In addition to those capabilities, France launched in 1991 the imagery intelligence satellite *Helios*. Coming into service in summer 1995, it provided France with an exceptional capacity of strategic intelligence, which has since become essential for targeting, but also providing the precise coordinates and altitude of any geographical point on Earth (Guisnel and Tertrais, 2016, p. 135). Besides, it has helped devise ground models that are included in the computers on French aircraft and are also integrated into the ASMPA strategic missiles (Ibid.).

In a parallel set of measures, France in the 1990s ended its production of fissile material, dismantled its production facilities, adhered to the NPT and the 1997 additional protocol, and engaged in new efforts to support international arms control and non-proliferation efforts, as we examine later in this chapter. With the disappearance of the Soviet threat, France was not alone in reducing its arsenal and abandoning some components and adapting its posture to the new context. The United Kingdom also reduced its arsenal, choosing in 1998 to abandon its airborne component and dissolve its eight bomber squadrons, maintaining only its submarine component (Berger and Lasconjarias, 2019, p. 211). As a result of these post-Cold-War adaptations, as of 2019, France possesses less than 300 nuclear warheads (Sarkozy, 2008), and maintains two different types of systems: one submarine-launched and one airborne. France's nuclear submarines (SSBNs, which compose the Strategic Oceanic Force), can carry 16 M51 missiles with multiple warheads, for a total estimated power of about 100 kilotons and a range of about 10,000 kilometres. This invulnerable capacity offers France a second-strike capability. The airborne component (the Strategic Air Force and the Naval Nuclear Force) is composed of Rafale (B and M types) and Mirage 2000N aircraft, equipped with supersonic cruise missiles, ASMPA, with a power of 300 kilotons and a potential range of over 600 kilometres (Tertrais, 2017, pp. 84 and 150).

France's nuclear doctrine

France's nuclear doctrine is expressed and regularly updated by means of a presidential speech, which normally occurs once during a president's mandate. Aside from presidential speeches, the principles of the nuclear doctrine are also expressed in defence white papers (1972, 1994, 2008, 2013, and 2017). Changes to the language are subtle, and over the last 50 years, French deterrence doctrine has been characterised by continuity. To use Louis Gautier's words, successive governments have adopted an "orthodox approach which preserves the bases on which the consensus on deterrence has gradually been established" (Gautier, 2009, p. 161).

French nuclear deterrence doctrine today rests on the following principles:

- First, nuclear weapons are conceived as weapons of deterrence and self-defence. As Mitterrand summed up in 1993, "nuclear weapons have been and must remain thought of in terms of deterrence and the threat of use"[1] (Mitterrand, cited by Irondelle, 2005, p. 10). This is accompanied by the notion of "*tous azimuts*" self-defence, which means that no adversary is *a priori* included in or excluded from France's deterrence. The 2013 defence white paper summarised these combined overarching goals and principles: "strictly defensive, nuclear deterrence protects France from any state-led aggression against its vital interests, of whatever origin and in whatever form" (Présidence de la République, 2013, p. 127). The logic remains that France must be able to inflict "irreparable damage" to an adversary. Irreparable

60 *Nuclear deterrence*

damage was notably defined in the 2008 white paper in the following way: "unacceptable damage to [the opponent], out of proportion to the purpose of an aggression" (Premier Ministre, 2008, p. 65)

- Second, France's nuclear deterrence rests on the principle of "strict sufficiency". While the underlying principles were set out in the 1972 white paper, suggesting that France's level of armament need not be comparable to that of the greater powers (Ministère de la Défense, 1972, p. 5), the concept was institutionalised in subsequent defence white papers. The notion contains three aspects (Assemblée Nationale, 2019, p. 4): an operational aspect, which is to guarantee to the president of the Republic that he or she will be able to inflict unacceptable damage not only today but also in the coming decades. This assumes permanent work to assess the enemy's defences, the reliability and capacity of French systems, and to control the effects to ensure efficiency of deterrence. A second, strategic aspect consists of avoiding an arms race. Even during the Cold War, French authorities considered that France did not need to possess 10,000 warheads like the USSR did: it was deterrence "of the strong by the weak" (*"du faible au fort"*). The logic of counter-city strikes and their associated "unacceptable damage" permitted that. The third aspect is technical, industrial, and financial. Effective national deterrence means controlling the whole of the industrial and technological chain, and to have weapon systems delivered on time, while controlling costs. The financial investment needed to sustain this credibility in the long run must be guaranteed, and therefore acceptable to the public and by successive governments
- Third, nuclear weapons serve to defend France's "vital interests", which are voluntarily unspecified. This is for two reasons. On the one hand, vital interests cannot be defined in advance, as circumstances may change, and each French president may have his or her appreciation of some specific aspects of those interests. That being said, there are undisputed indicators. The defence white papers of 1994 and 2008 provide some elements of what they are necessarily made of: "These vital interests notably comprise the elements constituting our identity and existence as a nation-State, and in particular our territory, our population, and the free exercise of our sovereignty" (Premier Ministre, 2008, pp. 64–65). Ambiguity on the actual extent of France's vital interests is also a way of not tempting the adversary. As the former CEMA Jean-Louis Georgelin explained: "Deterrence thus defers risk taking on the potential adversary by requiring them to assess our determination to protect our vital interests without knowing exactly where this limit lies" (Georgelin, 2010, p. 115). This raises, for example, the question of the potential threshold in terms of the number of casualties that would constitute a threshold for a nuclear response. As we further discuss later in this chapter, it also poses the question of the extension of France's vital interests to, or at least its interdependence with, the vital interests and territory of allies
- Fourth, nuclear deterrence applies to states, and not to non-state actors, such as terrorist groups. It is a dialogue between nations. However, nuclear

weapons can be used whatever the nature of the attack against French interests, even if said attack is not nuclear

- Fifth, France maintains freedom of action in all circumstances. That is to say, that the deterrence posture and the decision to use nuclear weapons, or not, rests on France alone, free from foreign pressures or control
- Sixth, France maintains a threat of final warning. This used to be conceived as the function of pre-strategic weapons (Baille, 2019, p. 78). To signal the proximity of France's vital interests, the president has several options before having to undertake any nuclear strikes, such as visibly deploying nuclear-armed Rafale aircraft when the enemy's satellite passes over French territory or sending a diplomatic cable to express the president's readiness to cross the nuclear threshold. Should vital interests be actually threatened, the president maintains the ability to send a final warning to reestablish deterrence. In French doctrine, this is the only possible use of nuclear weapons before a massive retaliation that would cause unacceptable damage. The president could choose to fire a single shot on a symbolic target without doing phenomenal damage or detonate a nuclear weapon at a very high altitude to generate an electromagnetic pulse that would destroy electronic circuits. In any case, the final warning is and remains an option and not an obligation for the president
- Finally, should a nuclear strike be launched, France would target the adversary's centres of power. This is probably the main evolution of France's nuclear doctrine in the post-Cold-War changes from counter-city strikes (or massive retaliation) to plans for targeting – "in priority" – a state's centres of political, economic, and military power (Premier Ministre, 2008, p. 69). In a 2006 speech, President Chirac explained that change. He described an international context characterised by the post-9/11 concern with "hyperterrorism" and the increased relevance of regional nuclear powers, such as Iran, India, or North Korea. This led him to enact a turn from a "deterrence of the strong by the weak" to a "deterrence of the weak by the strong" (*"dissuasion du fort au faible"*), where France has become the stronger player. In other words, in the post-Cold-War era, the targets of French deterrence were seen as being weaker, but no less potentially dangerous, nuclear powers. The strong-to-weak notion was preferred to another 1990s' concept controversially coined *"du fort au fou"* – *"fou"* meaning crazy – referring to certain authoritarian leaders that could fail to be deterred by the threat of a strike against their population (Dumoulin and Wasinski, 2010). Aside from reflecting the greater diversity of nuclear-armed opponents in the 21st century, the doctrinal turn also served the purpose of making the threat of use more credible, to the extent that France's decision-makers would likely be less hesitant if potential collateral damage was known to be limited

Institutions and decision-making powers

French nuclear doctrine, policy, and decision-making lie in the hands of the president. Unlike in the United States or the United Kingdom, the president's

62 *Nuclear deterrence*

speech on deterrence signals his personal implication in the strategy, the capability development, and the doctrinal principles that accompany French nuclear weapons. The president, as chief of the armed forces, is legally responsible for nuclear deterrence, and his legitimacy derives from his election by universal suffrage (Gautier, 2009, p. 156). In practice, however, the policy is not elaborated by the president himself but through the common work of the nuclear community. The command post "Jupiter", a bunker under the Élysée, is where the *Conseil des Armements Nucléaires* (Nuclear Weapons Council), formally created in 2009, meets. Those meetings involve the president, the prime minister, the defence minister, the CEMP, the CEMA – together with the defence staff's office for nuclear forces (*État-Major des Armées/ Forces Nucléaires*, EMA/FN) – the head of the DGA, and the CEA (Tertrais, 2017, p. 93). On an ad hoc basis, other actors such as the ministry of foreign affairs' directorate for strategic affairs and disarmament, the interior ministry, and the DGSE can be involved. Within the framework of the orientations decided at the council, the president determines by instructions the characteristics of the forces (stocks of fissile materials, number of operational heads, calendars of the patrols of SSBNs, etc.).

More specifically, the prime minister and the defence minister oversee the practical preparation and implementation of the guidance on deterrence (Gautier, 2009, p. 157). According to Decree 2009-1118 of 17 September 2009, which sets out the main principles of the internal organisation of deterrence, the government, under the responsibility of the prime minister, guarantees the readiness of nuclear forces at all times; the compliance of the forces' posture with the president's directives; and the integrity, safety, and security of nuclear weapons and materials (*Journal Officiel de la Republique Française*, 2009). The EMA/FN is in charge of elaborating the doctrine, the planning of nuclear operations, and the technical and financial aspects of procurement. The CEA's division of military applications (*Direction des Applications Militaires*, CEA/DAM) has major responsibilities. It designs nuclear warheads and propulsion systems, produces them, keeps them in operational condition and dismantles them, so it is present at every stage of the warheads' lifecycle. The confidence in the technical credibility of the president's nuclear warheads rests only on the assurance given by the director of the DAM, and he reports only to the president (Tranchez, 2019, p. 8). The DGA, as the procurement agency, deals with the non-nuclear aspects of the weapons system. Finally, the defence industry (especially MBDA, Naval Group, and Dassault) is involved in designing and manufacturing the missiles and the platforms that carry nuclear warheads.

The efficiency of French nuclear weapons ensures the credibility of deterrence. This efficiency is guaranteed by the joint work of all the aforementioned actors; the operational and technical credibility provided by the defence staff, the DGA and the CEA; the president's speech on nuclear deterrence, elaborated with the support of the CEMP; and the international legitimacy provided by France's diplomacy, elaborated by the foreign ministry and the strategy directorate of the defence ministry. The parliament is strictly absent in this framework, except through its vote on the budget and the exercise of parliamentary control. In a judgement passed in 1995 following the scandal of the *Rainbow Warrior* incident, the Conseil d'État declared itself incompetent to examine the presidential decision to resume a series of nuclear tests, judging it "not detachable from the conduct of foreign relations of France", which is under the president's control (Haupais, 2019). What is more, as we mentioned in Chapter 1, the constitution of the Fifth Republic allows the president to take exceptional measures should the nation be attacked or under serious threat, including acquiring additional power (*les pleins pouvoirs*) (Gautier, 2009, pp. 158–159; Haupais, 2019, p. 24).

If a major crisis should indeed occur, the CEMP would provide advice to the president on strategy, and the CEMA would prepare strike plans. As Lewis and Tertrais explain:

> The decision to use nuclear weapons could conceivably be taken in a meeting of the Nuclear Weapons Council, a specialized and more restricted formation of the Defence Council. However, there is no formal requirement for the president to consult anyone before taking the decision. (Lewis and Tertrais, 2019, p. 16)

Since 1996, the CEMA has been the only military authority under the orders of the president in charge of the planning and employment of nuclear forces. If the president gave the order to launch a nuclear strike, it would flow directly to the commanders of the nuclear forces, via the CEMA, without any other human intervention than the verification of the codes. It is retransmitted by the CEMA and the commanders of nuclear forces (Gautier, 2009, pp. 158–159). The commands of the Strategic Air Force and the Strategic Oceanic Force are respectively responsible for the operational implementation of the aircraft and SSBNs placed under their orders. They monitor the missions entrusted to these forces. Should the president ever give an order to launch an SSBN strike, this would require the simultaneous activation of two digital keys in two different zones of the submarine. The same two-man rule applies onboard strategic bombers. Finally, France has at its disposal a "last resort" communications network called SYDEREC (*Système de Dernier Recours*). It is composed of antennas supported by inflatable balloons, carried by mobile vehicles that would be dispersed across French territory in emergency situations, should the military transmission system be unavailable (Tertrais and Lewis, 2019, p. 17).

The alliance dimension

As we explained, France developed its nuclear weapons to rebuild itself economically, politically, and strategically and to ensure its strategic autonomy and national independence after World War II. A decade later, the defeat of Dien Bien Phu in Indochina and the Suez Crisis highlighted the limits of alliances and reinforced the argument for national strategic autonomy (Mongin, 2019, p. 54). Yet this effort was never thought of outside an alliance framework (Ibid., p. 49). The 1972 defence white paper on deterrence reads: "France lives

64 *Nuclear deterrence*

in a fabric of interests that transcends its borders. It is not isolated. As a whole, Western Europe cannot but, indirectly, benefit from the French strategy which constitutes a stable and determining factor of security in Europe" (Ministère de la Défense, 1972, p. 5). What has changed over time since De Gaulle is that subsequent presidents have each slightly reinforced the European dimension of French deterrence.

Nuclear collaboration between the United States and France actually emerged from the early 1970s under the terms of a 1961 agreement (Mélandri, 1994, p. 254; Mohr, 1989). This technical cooperation, however, was not coupled with a political-diplomatic "rapprochement between the United States and France, even if, in a certain manner, [there was] a partial consensus between the two countries on defence issues" (Mélandri, 1994, p. 249). This cooperation was also kept secret so as to not appear inconsistent with the overall Gaullist posture of national independence (Ibid.).

The first links were actually built with the United Kingdom. From the early days of the two countries' nuclear deterrents to the 1990s, French–British attempts at cooperation in the nuclear arena had been misaligned and had produced little. There was a first attempt at cooperation at De Gaulle's initiative in 1962, but the United Kingdom chose to acquire Polaris missile systems from the United States (Duval, 1989, p. 78). There were other attempts to develop cooperation on nuclear deterrence with Britain too in the 1960s and 1970s, apparently from a British initiative, as the British were possibly seeking to "wield some influence over the shape of a French nuclear force" (Harris, 2012, p. 11).

Bilateral exchanges only developed in the early 1990s through the creation of the Franco-British Joint Commission on Nuclear Policy and Doctrine in November 1992, made public in July 1993, and later known simply as the Joint Nuclear Commission (Butcher et al., 1998, §4.3). Under the Commission, ten officials would meet three times a year – more often for those members of the "supporting group" – and discuss nuclear policies, doctrine, disarmament, and non-proliferation (Howorth, 1997, p. 31). The Commission was initially modest in ambition (Tertrais, 2012), and the exchanges centred on comparing approaches to deterrence, nuclear doctrines and concepts, anti-missile defence, arms control, and non-proliferation (Butcher et al., 1998, §4.4). The Commission increasingly dealt with central and concrete issues, as it led to "thorough exchanges on crisis management and principles for nuclear planning (including through the informal consideration of fictitious scenarios), as well as the drafting of common policy papers" (Tertrais, 2012, p. 10). Besides, the Anglo-French Defence Research Group also dealt with nuclear matters in the more technical fields of nuclear, biological, and chemical defence, energetic materials, nuclear blast effects, and directed energy technology (Butcher et al., 1998, §4.5).

The Franco-British rapprochement in the nuclear field was further upheld politically in 1995, following Clinton's nuclear test ban. That year, John Major was one of the few to support Chirac during the French nuclear tests (Butcher et al., 1998, §4.3). The same year, the two heads of state and government signed a common declaration, known as the Chequers Declaration, which read:

We do not see situations arising in which the vital interests of either France or the United Kingdom could be threatened without the vital interests of the other also being threatened. We have decided to pursue and deepen nuclear co-operation between our two countries. Our aim is mutually to strengthen deterrence, while retaining the independence of our nuclear forces. The deepening of co-operation between the two European members of the North Atlantic Alliance who are nuclear powers will therefore strengthen the European contribution to overall deterrence. (Chirac and Major, 1995, cited by Butcher et al., 1998, §4.3)

Cooperation in the nuclear domain also offered opportunities to make savings by sharing the cost of building, using, and maintaining the infrastructure necessary for the testing and stewardship of nuclear warheads, among other things and France and the United Kingdom took significant steps forward in that direction with the signing of the Lancaster House treaties in 2010. The treaty relating to joint radiographic/hydrodynamic facilities provides for significant enhancements of bilateral cooperation through the exchange of (classified) information related to nuclear weapons and the building of shared infrastructures for the simulation of nuclear testing and technology development. In particular, it provided for the construction of radiographic-hydrodynamic facilities as part of the Teutates project. The EPURE facility (*Expérimentations de Physique Utilisant la Radiographie Éclair*[2]) is under construction at the CEA/DAM at Valduc (France), while a complementary technology development centre was commissioned in 2014 and is under construction at the Atomic Weapons Establishment (AWE) at Aldermaston (UK). In 2014, both countries approved national investments in the Teutates program, and further areas of cooperation were identified, including working together on the development of energetic materials for the future and a plan to conduct joint research at their respective laser facilities (AWE Orion and the CEA/DAM Laser Mégajoule) (Cameron and Hollande, 2014). As another sign of the good health of UK–France cooperation in the nuclear domain, the two governments announced in 2018 that they would "develop the Joint Nuclear Commission for [...] strategic discussion on nuclear deterrence policy; nuclear proliferation; and nuclear disarmament" (Macron and May, 2018, §7).

Beyond bilateral exchanges and cooperation, at the multilateral level, France's nuclear role within NATO has remained limited. Despite re-joining the integrated structures of NATO in 2009, France has remained outside of the Nuclear Planning Group (NPG). Indeed, as we explained above, successive French governments have all sought to maintain full independence and control over nuclear strategy ("freedom of action") at all times. These objectives limit France's ability to commit to a nuclear alliance. Yet, while France does not participate in the NPG, French authorities contribute to the wording of NATO's communiqués and negotiate the Alliance's discursive posture in trilateral settings with the United States and the United Kingom, and then in quadrilateral meetings, in which Germany participates. The French nuclear capability indeed contributes to the Alliance's deterrence posture, as is affirmed in NATO's Strategic Concept. The NATO declaration

66 *Nuclear deterrence*

agreed at the Ottawa summit in 1974 specifies that the nuclear weapons of France and the United Kingdom are "capable of playing a deterrent role of their own contributing to the overall strengthening of the deterrence of the Alliance" (NATO, 1974). Then, the Alliance 2010 Strategic Concept, still in force today, describes the "deterrent role" of the "independent strategic nuclear forces of the United Kingdom and France" (NATO, 2010, §18). This statement is included in each NATO summit communiqué. More recently, following the evolution of the security landscape in Eastern Europe, NATO's communiqués stated more forcefully the nuclear dimension of the alliance, in a way more explicit than had been the case since the 1999 Strategic Concept. Paragraph 53 in the 2016 communiqué is a novelty; it adds that "these Allies' separate centres of decision-making contribute to deterrence by complicating the calculations of potential adversaries" (NATO, 2016).

Besides, since the 1990s, all French presidents have included an alliance element in their deterrence doctrine speech. Jacques Chirac, for example, declared in 2006:

> The integrity of our territory, the protection of our population, the free exercise of our sovereignty will always be the heart of our vital interests. But they are not limited to it. The perception of these interests is changing at the pace of the world, a world marked by the growing interdependence of European countries and also by the effects of globalization. For example, the guarantee of our strategic supplies or the defence of allied countries are, among others, interests that should be protected. (Chirac, 2006)

More recently, François Hollande's deterrence speech also underlined the European dimension of France's nuclear deterrent forcefully. The speech was pronounced in January 2015, that is to say shortly after Russia's annexation of Crimea. The president declared:

> By participating in the European project from its outset, France has, with its partners, built a community of destiny. The existence of a French nuclear deterrent has made a strong, essential contribution to Europe. Moreover, France has real, heartfelt solidarity with its European partners. So, who could believe that an aggression threatening Europe's survival would have no consequence? (Hollande, 2015)

After Hollande's speech in Istres, the period 2015–2016 was thus characterised by France clearly showing greater interest in the alliance dimension of its own nuclear deterrent. Meanwhile, other European countries have, since 2014, increasingly considered that the existence of multiple national deterrents could have added value by creating confusion for NATO's adversaries, as was made evident in the 2016 communiqué.

Outside of NATO, when it comes to the European Union, things are less evident. Mitterrand called for discussion of a "European doctrine" for the French and British nuclear forces (Yost, 1996, p. 112). In 1995–1996, the Chirac government even used this European dimension as a justification for a national test campaign. The argument was that "by ensuring its deterrent capabilities, France is performing a service for peace and Europe", which, according to David Yost, "was widely construed throughout Europe as an effort by the French government to dampen the complaints over the tests" (Ibid.). Chirac and Juppé further pushed for the "Europeanisation" of France's deterrent, suggesting opening a dialogue on nuclear issues with Germany and non-nuclear European countries. In any case, a "Europeanisation" of the French deterrent could amount to a "concerted" deterrence with the Europeans, not the American-style deterrence "extended" to the Europeans (Mongin, 2018b). Either way, France was unsuccessful as "Britain and NATO's non-nuclear members made clear their lack of interest in any arrangement that might deprive Western Europe of US nuclear protection and place the NPG in jeopardy" (Yost, 1996, p. 113).

Today, the belief in the French nuclear establishment is that Europeans are not interested in a French nuclear umbrella. This is for two reasons: on the one hand, there are within the European Union, countries which, because they are either neutral or pacifist, take stances against nuclear weapons. This, for example, leads to nuclear deterrence being thoroughly absent from EU discourses and publications. On the other hand, those countries which are not neutral or pacifist trust the US nuclear umbrella better than they would the French. French officials nonetheless consider that the French deterrent contributes to the mobilisation and education of European elites, as they teach them the "grammar of deterrence" (Roche, 2017, p. 516). Indeed, European countries either do not possess nuclear weapons or merely host American warheads under the NATO nuclear sharing agreement. Therefore, they do not necessarily have a tradition of thinking about deterrence strategy or the evolution of doctrine and capabilities. What is more, France's independent nuclear deterrent contributes to the development of high-end technologies in the air, naval, and missile domains, and the maintenance of a strong industry in all those strategic domains. This in turn is thought to contribute to European "strategic autonomy" by reinforcing the European defence industrial and technological base, a theme that (re)emerged in the late 2010s and especially during Macron's presidency, as we further explore in chapter 6. It is in that context that Macron proposed, in his 2020 nuclear deterrence speech:

> I would like strategic dialogue to develop with our European partners, which are ready for it, on the role played by France's nuclear deterrence in our collective security. European partners which are willing to walk that road can be associated with the exercises of French deterrence forces. This strategic dialogue and these exchanges will naturally contribute to developing a true strategic culture among Europeans. (Macron, 2020)

While the rest of the deterrence speech was largely in line with those of previous presidents, Macron's invitation to Europeans was a novelty. We can wonder whether it will have concrete effects as, at the time of writing, reactions from partners have been lukewarm at best. Germany's government announced it was open

68 *Nuclear deterrence*

to dialogue, although Defence Minister Annegret Kramp-Karrenbauer reminded Paris of Germany' participation in NATO nuclear sharing, and suggested that there was not a European solution to replace the transatlantic nuclear alliance (Berghofer, 2020, p. 2). Opinions among German elected officials on nuclear deterrence collaboration with France however in early 2020 were diverse, as they ranged from those who feared a nuclear rapprochement with France would alienate Washington (the socialist party , and some conservatives), to those calling for Germany to reject nuclear weapons altogether (*Die Linke*, The Left) to those arguing for a shared Franco-German or EU nuclear deterrent (Euractiv, 2020; RND, 2020). Some officials or former officials of other European countries have indicated a willingness to have a dialogue with France, but the dominant view – from commentators as well – has been one that puts forward existing NATO arrangement and doubts the credibility of the French proposal (Barbit and Maître, 2020).

France and nuclear non-proliferation

While during the Cold War, France supported nuclear proliferation, the post-Cold-War era marked a shift to a strong emphasis on non-proliferation and arms control activities. France joined the NPT as a nuclear weapon state in 1992. De Gaulle had refused to join in 1968, partly in opposition to the United States (Laval, 2019, p. 89), and partly to denounce a regime that would de jure create an inequality between nuclear- and non-nuclear-weapon states (Guisnel and Tertrais, 2016, p. 123). In that context, France, for instance, helped Israel acquire nuclear weapons from 1956 and into the 1960s (Ibid., pp. 27–28). The tipping point was the Indian nuclear test in 1974 when French authorities realised the potentially destabilising effects of proliferation (Laval, 2019, p. 90). Another significant trigger was the discovery of Iraq's secret nuclear program during the Gulf War. As George-Henri Soutou reported, the French government then also realised that nuclear proliferation would restrain the already relative importance of a medium power like France (Soutou, 2011, p. 7). As Laval explains:

> the 1990s are those that certainly record the most intense normative activity and truly normalise the [French] attachment to the non-proliferation doctrine. Here again, the position of the French authorities remains very strongly marked by the need to maintain a role in world affairs. Unlike previous decades, however, the element of differentiation lies in a scrupulous defence of non-proliferation and in the mobilisation of the multilateral framework. (Laval, 2019, p. 73)

Similarly, according to Pouponneau, the paradigm shift in France in the 1990s was not only due to a re-evaluation of French nuclear ambitions and to the evolution of the threat of proliferation, but also to an adaptation to the international context of the post-Cold-War era: the promotion of multilateral institutions, including in the area of nuclear deterrence and non-proliferation was a way to exist in the context of international American dominance and unilateralism. If France was to have any weight on this political question, multilateralism was the only way (Pouponneau, 2015).

As a result of this shift in the international context and in the analysis of French authorities, France has since the 1990s been one of the "best students" when it comes to upholding and promoting the international nuclear non-proliferation regime. In parallel to joining the NPT in 1992, France began advocating for a policy of arms reduction and campaigning against nuclear tests. It has promoted the CTBT and was the first state, with the United Kingdom, to ratify it in 1998, only two years after the last campaign of field tests that we mentioned earlier. To date, France is also the only nuclear state that has irreversibly dismantled all of its test sites. As a unilateral initiative, France completely dismantled the nuclear experimentation centre of the Pacific. It is today the only country to have committed so far to the irreversible suspension of the test campaigns. France is participating in the work of the CTBT organisation, and especially the establishment of its international monitoring system for nuclear tests, with the setting up of a hydroacoustic station on the Crozet Islands, certified in 2016 (CTBTO, 2017). Besides, France has also granted negative security assurances to all non-nuclear-weapon states party to the NPT and respectful of their commitments to non-proliferation. In the period from 1992 to 1996, France signed several treaties for nuclear-weapon-free zones: Treaty of Tlatelolco (covering Latin America and the Caribbean), Pelindabá (Africa), and Rarotonga (South Pacific). Overall, France is part of a larger number of these treaties than the other endowed states. In addition, France has undertaken not to produce new types of nuclear weapons, it contributes to the IAEA's (International Atomic Energy Agency) budget, and provides experts to the organisation.

Another example of France's commitment to nuclear non-proliferation in the post-Cold War era has been its strong engagement, as early as 2003 and alongside its European partners, in the negotiations with Iran which led to the Joint Comprehensive Plan of Action (JCPOA), signed in July 2015 between Iran, the United States, China, Russia, France, the United Kingdom, Germany, and the European Union (Fabius, 2016). The agreement was designed to curb Iran's nuclear activities through a mix of sanction-lifting and monitoring. The dossier became a diplomatic priority for France due to its implications for the security of France and its allies – including its partners in the Middle East – for the future of non-proliferation, and for Europe's strategic credibility (Tertrais, 2017, pp. 143–144). When coming to power in 2017, the Trump administration denounced the Iran deal as "flawed" and announced a strategy of "maximum pressure" on Iran, aimed at financially draining the regime of Teheran and making it stop its activities in other domains, including its ballistic missile program and terrorism financing (Pompeo, 2018). After the Trump announcement, the European parties to the agreement did maintain their commitment to the agreement and endeavoured to circumvent the United States' unilateral reestablishment of sanctions against Iran. France led a mediation attempt in summer 2019 amid rising tensions between the United States and Iran, and attempted to make both parties fall back into line and respect their engagement.

70 *Nuclear deterrence*

Arms control and disarmament

As we have explained, France maintains a policy of strict sufficiency when it comes to its nuclear weapons. It is thus committed to not pursuing an arms race. Now, alongside non-proliferation activities, since joining the NPT as a nuclear weapon state, France is legally bound to a disarmament obligation, according to article 6 of the treaty. Yet, while France has been a very "good student" in the past decades when it comes to non-proliferation, it has been more conservative when it comes to its own disarmament. France is not alone in that: nuclear weapon states collectively refuse interference in their affairs and often speak with one voice, including at various NPT review conferences (Haupais, 2019, p. 38). It can be said that there is tension between France's efforts towards non-proliferation and the belief, among the French political establishment, in the stabilising effects of nuclear weapons. Illustratively, in its submission to the International Court of Justice 1996 to provide an opinion on the lawfulness of nuclear weapons, the French government argued:

> The Court cannot ignore in its decision on the desirability of an answer that it is impossible to examine the problem of nuclear weapons regardless of their real purpose, which is to avoid war. It cannot ignore the fact that, for decades, deterrence has helped to avert the risk of a new global conflict. (cited by Ibid., p. 29.)

In 2014, Defence Minister Jean-Yves Le Drian expressed a similar risk that French nuclear disarmament would pose, suggesting that "we must avoid that the generous call for 'a world without nuclear weapons' prepares the ground for a world where only dictators would possess such weapons", pointing to the fact that some countries – including India, China, Russia, Pakistan, or Israel – do not have the slightest intentions to disarm (Le Drian, 2014). More forcefully, former Foreign Minister Hubert Védrine exclaimed that he did "not believe in the exemplarity of suicide", referring to the possibility of unilateral disarmament (Jurgensen, 2019, p. 141).

This assessment, together with France's principle of "strict sufficiency", and the worsening of the international security climate since the late 1990s – starting with the Indian and Pakistani nuclear tests in 1998 – encouraged French authorities to double down on non-proliferation efforts while taking limited disarmament measures. French authorities did commit to cease the production of plutonium and enriched uranium; they have also engaged in recycling fissile material at its most protected nuclear facilities in Valduc, Burgundy. France is committed to concluding a treaty banning the production of fissile material for weapons, the Nuclear Fissile Material Cut-off Treaty (Tranchez, 2019, p. 7). In 2015, France tabled a draft "cut-off" treaty at the UN Disarmament Conference and actively participated in the high-level preparatory group on the subject. Today, French authorities consider that their deterrence capabilities are defined without excess and at a level strictly measured to guarantee its security, and therefore do not envisage new unilateral disarmament measures (Gautier, 2009, p. 185). As Hollande declared:

> France has been exemplary in terms of the volume of its weapons stockpile: 300. Why maintain 300? Because of our assessment of the strategic context. If the level of the other arsenals, particularly those of Russia and the United States, were to fall one day to a few hundred weapons, France would respond accordingly, as it always has. But today, that scenario is still a long way off. (Hollande, 2015)

In this understanding, so long as general and complete disarmament is not a reality, nuclear weapons will remain a necessity for France (Gautier, 2009, p. 185).

France's approach to arms control is "comprehensive", as described by Céline Jurgensen: it must go hand in hand with confidence-building measures, agreements to limit conventional forces, and a generally favourable international environment. Jurgensen notes that said international environment has been rather unfavourable to arms control in the 21st century. Even the United States contributed to shifting the gear away from disarmament efforts. Notably, after 9/11, the United States under the George W. Bush (2001–2009) administration adopted a critical attitude towards traditional institutions of non-proliferation and deterrence, preferring the doctrine of counter-proliferation, and focusing on weapon miniaturisation as well as missile defence (Aloupi, 2019, p. 103). Besides, the 2000s and 2010s have been, in contrast, characterised by the resumption of proliferation in the Middle East and Asia. New nuclear threats emerged, in particular nuclear proliferation, following the successful tests of India and Pakistan in 1998, followed by a conflict between India and Pakistan in 2001–2002 that risked leading to a nuclear escalation; the proliferation of ballistic systems, in particular from Iran and North Korea; the threat of state-sponsored nuclear terrorism; a greater emphasis on nuclear weapons in Russia's military strategy; the Ukraine crisis from 2014 onwards; the decision by President Trump in May 2018 to withdraw from the JCPOA; and, in 2019, the end of the 1987 US–Russia Treaty on Intermediate Nuclear Forces (INF).

François Hollande's speech was pronounced in February 2015, a few months after the beginning of the Ukraine crisis. The speech illustrates this changed context, with its particular emphasis on renewed international tensions with a nuclear dimension, and the threat of nuclear proliferation:

> what has been happening in Eastern Europe for the last year shows that peace can never be taken for granted [;] the arms race has resumed in many world regions, with a considerable, even rapid increase in defence spending and in arsenals, in a context of rising tensions [;] countries that had, up to now, possessed nuclear weapons and talked of the urgency of disarming, have even increased their capabilities by developing new nuclear components or continuing to produce fissile material for weapons... tactical nuclear arsenals are growing, giving rise to fears of a reduction in the threshold for using nuclear

72 *Nuclear deterrence*

weapons [;] France has therefore decided to tackle one of the most serious threats to global stability: the proliferation of weapons of mass destruction (WMD). (Hollande, 2015)

The French 2017 Strategic Review, drafted under Macron's presidency, similarly noted the "rapid and lasting deterioration of the strategic environment" overall and from many directions (Ministère des Armées, 2017, p. 16). In his February 2020 speech on defence and deterrence strategy, Macron further noted that while the fight against terrorism had been a priority at the beginning of his presidency, it should not overshadow the "global uninhibited strategic competition" that was unfolding, characterised by nuclear multipolarity, the proliferation of advanced missile technologies, and breaches of norms on chemical, biological, radiological and nuclear (CRBN) weapons (Macron, 2020). Multilateralism and international norms were at the heart of Macron's foreign policy strategy, with arms control and disarmament viewed as key to European security, after the demise of the INF treaty. The president thus suggested that Europe – and France – should be involved in international negotiations which otherwise would likely include only the United States, Russia, and China. That being said, given France's position whereby nuclear disarmament is part of a whole and linked to general and complete disarmament, there are little chances that France would join any agreement that would imply any reduction of its arsenal.

Modernising or questioning French deterrence?

Current debates about deterrence in France as in other nuclear-armed democracies focus, on the one hand, on the financial cost of deterrence, especially in the context of the modernisation of arsenals, and, on the other, on the ethical and humanitarian implications of nuclear deterrence, especially in the context of the ICAN. First is the question of cost. The resources allocated to deterrence went down, as we mentioned earlier, with the end of the Cold War. In 1965, nuclear deterrence mobilised 450,000 personnel, and the development, maintenance, and operationalisation of nuclear forces used up 50% of France's defence budget, which was 4.5% of France's GDP (Briefing by a former chef d'état-major particulier, November 2015). This had consequences for conventional forces, their conditions, equipment, etc. After the end of the Cold War, partial nuclear disarmament lowered the cost of France's nuclear deterrent and the human resources involved. The cost of maintaining the nuclear deterrent still represented more than 22% in 2015–2019 (*Journal Officiel de la République Française*, 2013, §5.2) of the French defence budget, which as of 2019 represents 1.84% of France's GDP (NATO, 2019, p. 8).

That being said, towards the end of the 2010s, the cost of deterrence has been going up again, with the plan to modernise the French nuclear arsenal. As provided for in the 2019–2025 military programming law, France is currently completing the modernisation of all SSBNs, the commissioning of the M51.3 missile, the development of the future version of the M51 missile, and the design work for the third-generation nuclear-powered ballistic missile submarine (SNLE 3G) (*Journal Officiel de la République Française*, 2018, §3.2.2). As for the airborne component, the late 2010s/early 2020s will see the transition to a single Rafale, the mid-life refurbishment of the air-to-surface missile ASMPA, and development studies for the successor missile (the ASN 4G). The renewal of French nuclear capabilities is aimed at ensuring the undetectability of French SSBNs, the ability of future versions of the M51 submarine launched ballistic missile (SLBMs) to reach its targets, and the protection of the airborne component from surface-to-air threats (Brustlein, 2017, p. vii). These are responses to progress in hostile anti-submarine warfare capabilities and missile defence systems, both of which increasingly challenge Western military superiority (Ibid.). Reflecting these needed investments, the budget of deterrence is planned to increase significantly between the mid-2010s and the mid-2020s. Illustratively, the share of defence equipment spending allocated to deterrence for the period 2014–2019 was €23.3 billion, that is to say, €3.88 billion per year (*Journal Officiel de la République Française*, 2013, §5.2). For the period 2019–2023, it is planned to be approximately €25 billion, that is to say, around €5 billion per year (*Journal Officiel de la République Française*, 2018, §4.1.2). This represents an increase of approximately 22.5% compared to the previous period. The cost of French nuclear deterrence thus remains significant and is even increasing. General Desportes, former director of the *École Militaire*, denounced the effects of the cost of nuclear deterrence on the resources allocated to conventional forces (Desportes, 2013), while a former CEMP described French atomic weapons as "a costly pride" (Briefing by a former chef d'état-major particulier, November 2015).

The "old" nuclear powers, which developed their nuclear weapons in the 1950s (the five permanent members of the UN Security Council (UNSC) are all undergoing a phase of modernisation. For the three democracies that are the United States, the United Kingdom, and France, this raises, once again, the question of the justification of the maintenance of these capabilities. In the United Kingdom, there were significant debates in 2006, 2010, and 2016 on the replacement of the fleet of Vanguard-class SSBNs and extension of the service life of the US-manufactured Trident II D5 missile (Berger and Lasconjarias, 2019). In France, decisions to maintain or renew nuclear deterrence lead to few public debates or mobilisations.

While there has historically been political polarisation in Western European countries about deterrence, with the socialist and social-democratic parties adopting anti-nuclear policies, France has been an exception: the socialist party has supported nuclear deterrence since the 1970s (Yost, 1990, p. 392). Socialist President Mitterrand, himself, despite being initially sceptical, became very active on nuclear issues during the two terms of his presidency (Guisnel and Tertrais, 2016). More to the left, the French Communist Party (PCF) even supported it, too, during the Cold War (Dobry, 1986, p. 49). As recently as 2017, the PCF – despite now being officially in favour of "a world without nuclear weapons" (PCF, 2018) – supported the presidential candidacy of Mélenchon, of the radical left party, *France Insoumise*, who does not oppose nuclear deterrence. What opposing parties, such as the radical left and the greens indeed do is to try and limit, on the

74   *Nuclear deterrence*

margin, the budgetary expenses dedicated to deterrence, for instance by opposing modernisation programs (Assemblée Nationale, 2018). Only a few public figures who once had roles in government have expressed stronger opposition to nuclear deterrence altogether, including Michel Rocard, a former prime minister who in 2009 signed an op-ed, following Obama's Prague speech, in favour of global nuclear disarmament,[3] and Paul Quilès, defence minister 1985–1986, who since 2016 is the head of the French NGO *Initiatives pour le Désarmement Nucléaire* (IDN, "Initiatives for nuclear disarmament") (Juppé et al., 2009).

When it comes to public opinion, the extent of public support has gone down since the Cold War decades but remains high and increased over the decade of the 2010s. Illustratively, in the 1980s, public support for national nuclear forces ranged between 67% and 72% of the French population (Dobry, 1986, p. 62). In the late 1980s and 1990s, in the context of the Chernobyl incident and France's newly accepted membership to the NPT, the attention of anti-nuclear movements in France had shifted to an opposition to nuclear tests on the one hand, and the risks associated with civilian nuclear power on the other (Collin, 2019, pp. 155–156). In January 2010, a law was passed relating to the recognition and compensation of the victims of the French nuclear tests, following work that had started since 1990. As of 2017, a poll indicated that 69% of the French were "in agreement" with the statement according to which, "to ensure its defence, France needs the nuclear deterrent force and conventional forces" (Ministère de la Défense, 2017). This figure shows a significant and regular increase from 53% in 2012. The idea of modernising the deterrent was, for its part, supported by 60% of the respondents. More than in other countries, there was and remains in France an exception when it comes to public acceptance of nuclear weapons (Yost, 1990; Lafont Rapnouil, Varma and Whitney, 2018).

France thus is not confronted with a public opinion problem when it comes to nuclear deterrence, but political elites are prudent. Today, the problem for French authorities is perceived to come mostly from the fact that France and the United Kingdom are isolated in Europe: international talks – including speeches by US President Barack Obama – in favour of global disarmament in the 2000s ("global zero"), and the International Campaign for the Abolition of Nuclear Weapons have mobilised public opinion in all other European countries since 2007. The socialist government of François Hollande, which came to power in 2012, included two ministers from the green party (*Europe Ecologie – Les Verts*, EELV), who decided to open a dialogue with the ICAN campaign. In 2014, the French ICAN campaign was heard by the defence committee: it was the first time that members of an NGO for disarmament were consulted as experts on the subject of deterrence (Collin, 2019, p. 161).

Despite engaging with civil society, however, the French government did not switch its position on the treaty, and opposed and denounced the ICAN campaign. The arguments put forward by France, together with the United States and the United Kingdom, against the ICAN treaty have been the following (see for instance Maitre, 2017). First, the treaty does not account for the reality of contemporary strategic realities and international tensions, or the intentions of non-NPT nuclear-armed countries. It is thus naive and will be ineffective. Secondly, it strikes a fatal blow to step-by-step international disarmament processes, which produces partial but effective successes, and could evolve to include the prohibition of fissile material production and the universalisation of the test ban. It is thus counter-productive. Thirdly, it creates particular difficulties for democracies (nuclear weapon states, host states, or democratic members of nuclear alliances), as these are the countries where public opinion can indeed be mobilised through campaigns to challenge the status quo defended by traditional political parties. It is thus, in the view of the French nuclear community, unfair. To signal their opposition to the treaty, French authorities did not attend the session when the treaty was voted at the UN in July 2017 or participate in the signing ceremony organised on 20 September 2017. France, the United Kingdom, and the United States also worked to convince EU member states and NATO allies to not sign it. Eventually, 122 countries adopted the text of the ICAN treaty in July 2017, including two European countries (Ireland and Austria). On 24 October 2020, Honduras was the 50th country to ratify the treaty, meaning that it would come into force 90 days later, in January 2020. The French government vehemently opposed ICAN and qualified the campaign and its signatories as "irresponsible" (Le Drian, 2017).[4]

Conclusion

Successive French governments have remained steadily committed to maintaining an independent nuclear deterrent. This independence has been pursued, and achieved, by having a national capacity for designing, producing, maintaining, and using nuclear weapons to defend national interests defined autonomously by the French government. While France got rid of its land-based systems (both tactical and strategic) in the decade following the Cold War, it has since maintained a dyad of airborne and submarine-based nuclear weapons. As a corollary to the ambition of independence, France is the only NATO member that does not participate in the Atlantic Alliance's NPG. Nonetheless, France has maintained close cooperation with the other two nuclear-armed members of the Alliance, the United Kingdom and the United States. With them, it has also sought to advance international arms control and disarmament agendas. French governments have done so with a rather conservative stance, as the maintenance of a national nuclear deterrence at "strictly sufficient" levels, as is the case today, is not called into question. Public opinion supports nuclear deterrence in France, and the modernisation of the arsenal is underway. Since the United Kingdom's departure from the European Union in January 2020, France has become the only nuclear power of the Union. Emmanuel Macron, like other presidents before him, has sought to involve European partners in a discussion about the role of the French deterrent. Macron also wants Europeans to be involved in the future of arms control in Europe. This dual endeavour is proving a little harder for governments as public opinions around Europe are either uninterested in or wary of getting involved too directly in nuclear strategy matters.

76 *Nuclear deterrence*

Notes

1 *"Les armes nucléaires ont été et doivent rester conçues en termes de menace d'emploi et de dissuasion"*.
2 That is to say x-ray radiography used in the simulation of nuclear blast effects for the design of nuclear weapons.
3 Alain Juppé, also a former prime minister, had also signed that op-ed. However, only three years later, Juppé qualified Rocard's call for a unilateral French disarmament as "irresponsible". Juppé had, in the meantime, held the post of Minister of Foreign affairs (Libération, 2012).
4 *"Une telle démarche ne peut qu'affaiblir le Traité de non-prolifération nucléaire [....] Sur ce sujet, la politique de l'incantation confine à l'irresponsabilité"*.

References

Aloupi, N. (2019), "La Position des Etats Nucléarisés Face à la Prolifération", in N. Haupais (ed.), *La France et l'arme nucléaire au 21ème siècle*. Paris: CNRS Editions, 101–116.
Arms Control Association (2019), *Nuclear Testing and Comprehensive Test Ban Treaty (CTBT) Timeline*. June. Available at: https://www.armscontrol.org/factsheets/N uclear-Testing-and-Comprehensive-Test-Ban-Treaty-CTBT-Timeline (last access, 16 December 2019).
Assemblée Nationale (2018), "PLF pour 2019 - (No.1255), Amendement No.II-634", 29 October.
Assemblée Nationale (2019), "Audition du Général Bruno Maigret, Commandant des Forces Aériennes Stratégiques", *Commission de la Défense Nationale et des Forces Armées, Compte Rendu No.43*, 12 June.
Axe, D. (2019), "Russia's Deadly Iskander-M Ballistic Missile is Headed to Kaliningrad Exclave", *National Interest*, 2 January. Available at: https://nationalinterest.org/blog /buzz/russias-deadly-iskander-m-ballistic-missile-headed-kaliningrad-exclave-40397 (last access, 16 December 2019).
Baille, L.-M. (2019), "L'épisode nucléaire tactique: 1957–1996", in Haupais, N. (ed.), *La France et l'arme nucléaire au 21ème siècle*. Paris: CNRS Editions, 61–79.
Barbit, C. and Maître, E. (2020), "Discours de l'École de guerre: Quelles réactions internationales?", FRS, Observatoire de la Dissuasion: Bulletin No.73, February 2020.
Berger, C. and Lasconjarias, G. (2019), "La modernisation des arsenaux nucléaires dans le monde", in Haupais, N. (ed.), *La France et l'arme nucléaire au 21ème siècle*. Paris: CNRS Editions, 205–224.
Berghofer, J. (2020), "Breaking the Taboo: Why It Is so Hard to Lead a Strategic Nuclear Dialogue with Germany", *FRS*, Note 29/20, 27 April.
Brustlein, C. (2017), "France's Nuclear Arsenal: What Sort of Renewal?", *Politique Etrangère*, 2017/3, 113–124.
Butcher, M., Nassauer, O. and Young, S. (1998), "Nuclear Futures: Western European Options for Nuclear Risk Reduction", BASIC-BITS, Research Reports 98.5.
Cameron, D. and Hollande, F. (2014), "UK-France Summit: Declaration on Security and Defence", *RAF Brize Norton*, 31 January.
Chirac, J. (1996), *Discours du Président de la République à l'École Militaire*. Paris, 2 February.
Chirac, J. (2006), "Discours à l'Ile Longue sur la Politique de Défense de la France, Notamment la Dissuasion Nucléaire", 5 Brest, 19 January.

Chirac, J. and Major, J. (1995), *British-French Joint Statement on Nuclear Co-operation*. London, 29–30 October.

Collin, J.-M. (2019), "La marche en avant du désarmement nucléaire", in Haupais, N. (ed.), *La France et l'arme nucléaire au 21ᵉᵐᵉ siècle*. Paris: CNRS Editions, 153–173.

CTBTO (2017), "CTBTO Completes Hydroacoustic Part of the International Monitoring System", *Press Release*, 20 June. Available at: https://www.ctbto.org/press-centre/press-releases/2017/ctbto-completes-hydroacoustic-part-of-the-international-monitoring-system/ (last access, 16 December 2019).

Desportes, V. (2013), "Sanctuariser le nucléaire, c'est condamner la dissuasion", *Libération*, 6 June. Available at: https://www.liberation.fr/societe/2013/01/06/sanctuariser-le-nucleaire-c-est-condamner-la-dissuasion_871986 (last access, 7 January 2020).

Dobry, M. (1986), "Le jeu du consensus", *Pouvoirs*, 38, 47–66.

Dumoulin, A. and Wasinski, C. (2010), "Justifier l'arme nucléaire: Le cas français pendant les années 1990", *Etudes internationales*, 41/1, 79–96.

Duval, M. (1989), "The Prospects for Military Cooperation Outside Europe: A French View", in Boyer, Y., Lellouche, P. and Roper, J. (eds.), *Franco-British Defence Cooperation: A New Entente Cordiale?* London: Routledge, 67–83.

Euractiv (2020), "AKK lehnt atomare Kooperation mit Frankreich ab", 4 February. Available at: https://www.euractiv.de/section/europakompakt/news/akk-lehnt-atomare-kooperation-mit-frankreich-ab/ (last access: 12 June 2020).

Fabius, L (2016), "Inside the Iran Deal: A French Perspective", *The Washington Quarterly*, 39/3, 7–38.

Gautier, L. (2009), *La Défense de la France après la Guerre Froide*. Paris: Presses Universitaires de France.

Gerogelin, J.-L. (2010), "Pertinence et permanence de la dissuasion", *Revue Internationale et Stratégique*, 79/3, 113–118.

Guisnel, J. and Tertrais, B. (2016), *Le Président et la Bombe: Jupiter à l'Elysée*. Paris: Odile Jacob.

Haupais, N. (2019), "Introduction: La Dissuasion Française Entre Force et Droit", in Haupais, N. (ed.), *La France et l'arme nucléaire au 21ᵉᵐᵉ siècle*. Paris: CNRS Editions, 13–48.

Hollande, F. (2015), "Speech by the President of the French Republic on the Nuclear Deterrent", *Speech, Official Translation*, 19 February. Available at: https://cd-geneve.delegfrance.org/Nuclear-weapons-statement-of-Mr-Francois-Hollande-in-Istres-on-the-19th-of (last access, 16 December 2019).

Howorth, J. (1997), "France", in Howorth, J. and Menon, A. (eds.), *The European Union and National Defence Policy*. London: Routledge, 23–48.

Irondelle, B. (2005), "Stratégie Nucléaire et Normes Internationales: La France Face au Tabou Nucléaire", Presented at the Congress of the Association Française de Science Politique, Lyon, 14–16 September.

Journal Officiel de la République Française (2009), "Décret No.2009-1118 Relatif au Contrôle Gouvernemental de la Dissuasion Nucléaire", 18 September.

Journal Officiel de la République Française (2013), "Loi No.2013-1168 Relative à la Programmation Militaire pour les Années 2014 à 2019 et Portant Diverses Dispositions Concernant la Défense et la Sécurité Nationale", 18 December.

Journal Officiel de la République Française (2018), "Loi No.2018-607 Relative à la Programmation Militaire pour les Années 2019 à 2025 et Portant Diverses Dispositions Intéressant la Défense", No.0161, 14 July.

78 Nuclear deterrence

Juppé, A., et. al. (2009), "Pour un Désarmement Nucléaire Mondial, Seule Réponse à La Prolifération Anarchique, MM. Juppé, Norlain, Richard et Rocard", *Le Monde*, 14 October.

Jurgensen, C. (2019), "La France, la Maitrise des Armements et le Désarmement", in Haupais, N. (ed.), *La France et l'Arme Nucléaire au 21ème siècle*. Paris: CNRS Editions, 117–150.

Lafont-Rapnouil, M., Varma, T. and Witney, N. (2018), "Eyes Tight Shut: European Attitudes Towards Nuclear Deterrence", ECFR, "Flash Scorecard" Report, December.

Laval, P.-F. (2019), "La France et la non-prolifération", in Haupais, N. (ed.), *La France et l'Arme Nucléaire au 21ème Siècle*. Paris: CNRS Editions, 83–100.

Le Drian, J.-Y. (2014), *Déclaration sur la Dissuasion Nucléaire*. Paris, 20 November.

Le Drian, J.-Y. (2017), *Conférence de Presse à l'Assemblée Générale des Nations Unies*. New York, 18 September.

Lewis, J.G. and Tertrais, B. (2019), "The Finger on the Button: The Authority to Use Nuclear Weapons in Nuclear-Armed States", James Martin Center for Nonproliferation Studies, Occasional Paper No.45, February.

Libération (2012), "Tollé Contre Rocard, Qui Proposait de Supprimer la Dissuasion Nucléaire", 20 June.

Macron, E. (2020), *Speech on the Defense and Deterrence Strategy*. Paris, 7 February 2020, official translation. Available at : https://www.elysee.fr/en/emmanuel-macron/2020/02/07/speech-of-the-president-of-the-republic-on-the-defense-and-deterrence-strategy (last access, 12 June 2020).

Maitre, E. (2017), "A Treaty Banning Nuclear Weapons: Diversion or Breakthrough?", Fondation pour la Recherche Stratégique, Note de la FRS 08/2017, 16 March.

Macron, E. and May, T. (2018), *United Kingdom-France Summit communiqué, Annex on Security and Defence*. Royal Military Academy Sandhurst, 18 January.

Mélandri, P. (1994), "Aux origines de la coopération nucléaire franco-américaine", in Vaïsse, Maurice (ed.), *La France et l'atome*, Bruxelles: Bruylant.

Ministère de la Défense (1972), *Livre Blanc sur la Défense Nationale, Tome 1*. Paris: Centre de Documentation de l'Armement.

Ministère de la Défense (2017), "Baromètre Externe: 'Les Français et la Défense'", DICOD/IFOP May. Available at: https://docplayer.fr/73919947-Barometre-externe-les-francais-et-la-defense-resultats-mai-2017.html (last access, 16 December 2019).

Ministère des Armées (2017), *Defence and National Security Strategic Review*.

Mitterrand, F. (1991), "Interview accordée au journal 'NRC Handelsblad', notamment sur la Communauté européenne, le rôle du Conseil de sécurité dans le règlement du conflit du Golfe et dans l'instauration d'un 'Nouvel ordre mondial' et les relations franco-allemandes", 2 March. Available at: https://www.vie-publique.fr/discours/136296-interview-de-m-francois-mitterrand-president-de-la-republique-accorde (last access, 16 December 2019).

Mohr, C. (1989), "U.S. Secretly Helped France Develop Nuclear Weapons, an Expert Writes", *New York Times*, 27 May.

Mongin, D. (2018a), *Résistance et Dissuasion: Des origines du programme nucléaire français à nos jours*. Paris: Odile Jacob.

Mongin, D. (2018b), "La Dissuasion Nucléaire a-t-elle Encore un Avenir?", *Revue Esprit*, July/August.

Mongin, D. (2019), "Perspectives Historiques", in Haupais, N. (ed.), *La France et l'Arme Nucléaire au 21ème Siècle*. Paris: CNRS Editions, 49–60.

NATO (1974), *Declaration on Atlantic Relations Issued by the North Atlantic Council*. Ottawa, 19 June.

Nuclear deterrence 79

NATO (2010), "Active Engagement, Modern Defence: Strategic Concept for the Defence and Security of the Members of the North Atlantic Treaty Organisation", Adopted by Heads of State and Government at the NATO Summit in Lisbon, 19–20 November.

NATO (2016), "Summit Communiqué", *Warsaw*, 9 July.

NATO (2019), "Defence Expenditure of NATO Countries (2012–2019)", *Press Communiqué PR/CP(2019)069*, 25 June.

Nuclear Threat Initiative (2019), *North Korea: Overview*. August. Available at: https://ww w.nti.org/learn/countries/north-korea/ (last access, 16 December 2019).

PCF (2018), "Discours de Fabien Roussel −38ème Congrès du PCF", *Ivry-sur-Seine*, 25 November. Available at: http://www.pcf.fr/article_fr_25novembre (last access, 16 December 2019).

Pompeo, M.R. (2018), "After the Deal: A New Iran Strategy", *Remarks US Secretary of State*. Washington, DC: Heritage Foundation, 21 May. Available at: https://www.state .gov/after-the-deal-a-new-iran-strategy/ (last access, 16 December 2019).

Pouponneau, F. (2015), *La Politique Française De Non-Prolifération Nucléaire. De La Division Du Travail Diplomatique*. Brussels: P. I.E. Peter Lang.

Premier Ministre (2008), *The French White Paper on Defence and National Security*. Paris: Odile Jacob.

Présidence de la République (1992), "Communiqué de la Présidence de la République, en Date du 9 Juin 1992, sur la Réduction du Niveau D'alerte des Forces Nucléaires en Temps de Paix", 9 June. Available at at: https://www.vie-publique.fr/discours/130 825-communique-de-la-presidence-de-la-republique-en-date-du-9-juin-1992-su (last access, 16 December 2019).

Présidence de la République (2013), *White Paper on Defence and National Security*.

Roche, N. (2017), *Pourquoi la Dissuasion?* Paris: Presses Universitaires de France.

RND (2020), "Atomare Abschreckung: AKK offen für Dialog mit Macron", 20 February. Available at: https://www.rnd.de/politik/atomare-abschreckung-akk-offen-fur-dialog-mit -macron-NARTHFHYZM2J5DD65HBZX6CO7Q.html (last access: 12 June 2020).

Sarkozy, N. (2008), *Déclaration sur le Livre Blanc sur la Défense et la Sécurité Nationale, la Dissuasion Nucléaire et sur la Non Prolifération des Armes Nucléaires*. Cherbourg, 21 March.

Soutou, G.-H. (2011), "La France et la Non-Prolifération Nucléaire: Une Histoire Complexe", *Revue Historique Des Armées*, No.262.

Tertrais, B. (2012), "Entente Nucléaire: Options for UK-French Nuclear Cooperation", BASIC Trident Commission Discussion Paper No.3, June.

Tertrais, B. (2017), *La France et la Dissuasion Nucléaire*. Paris: La Documentation Française.

Tranchez, O. (2019), "La Simulation des Essais Nucléaires, une Rupture Stratégique Française?", in Meszaros, T. (ed.), *Repenser Les Stratégies Nucléaires*. Brussels: Peter Lang, 2019, 281–293.

Yost, D.S. (1990), "La Dissuasion Nucléaire en Question?", *Politique Etrangère*, 55/2, 389–407.

Yost, D.S. (1996), "France's Nuclear Dilemmas", *Foreign Affairs*, 75/1.

4 Defence industry and procurement

Scholars usually distinguish three main tendencies in the evolution of the French defence industry since the end of the Cold War (Bellais, 2011) that reflect broader trends in the global defence economy. The first trend has been an overall decrease in defence budgets in the West following the end of the Cold War. In France, defence spending went down by one-third in the 1990s, while the international defence market shrunk by almost 50% (Fleurant and Quéau, 2014, p. 10). While the downward tendency ceased in the 2000s, we have seen an upward trend since 2015. However, meanwhile, Europeans have also been gradually losing ground in defence spending at the global level due to decreasing defence budgets in the region that has coincided with significant increases in other regions – overall world spending increased by 40% between 1995 and 2011 (in constant 2001 US dollars). Despite these trends, Europe remains one of the world's biggest defence spenders and makes up much of the defence industry. Most of that is inherited from the Cold War, which had led to massive investments in defence, and so did the many military interventions that took place in the 2000s and 2010s. Thus, in absolute numbers, the United States and Western Europe today are the countries that spend the most on defence – in 2013 they represented 54% of world defence spending. However, the balance continues to shift: in 2017 China became the second-largest defence spender.

In this context of ever-growing international competition and shrinking domestic demand, the second tendency has been a restructuring of defence industries worldwide, especially in the 1990s (Dunne and Smith, 2016, p. 14). This trend has been led by the United States and the emergence of major American groups (Boeing, Lockheed Martin, Northrop Grumman, Raytheon) (Masson, 2003). In turn, facing transatlantic competition became a challenge for smaller European companies. Changing dynamics in the world defence economy led them to adapt, either through rationalisations, merger, or diversification.

Thirdly, another major development since the end of the Cold War has been technological progress, which has made the cost of single equipment increase dramatically (Droff, 2013; Hartley and Solomon, 2016). Since the second half of the 20th century, the defence needs of Western states have become more sophisticated, giving rise to an inexorable increase in the cost of equipment (of the order of 5% to 10% per unit per year) (Kirkpatrick, 2004, pp. 262–263). This race in

Defence industry and procurement 81

technological progress has been especially led by the United States. Given the tight links between the United States and Europe, US investment in defence and the revolution in military affairs has impacted European countries who have had to try and keep up with US technology, including information and communication systems. This has been necessary both in order to remain militarily interoperable and able to compete in the export market.

In this chapter, we examine how France has adapted to – and shaped – these international evolutions over the past three decades. We start by analysing the evolution of the French defence budget and equipment spending, before moving on to presenting the institutions and processes of French defence procurement. We then examine France's procurement practices, explaining the country's preference for national systems and its accommodation of necessary cooperation with European partners. Finally, we analyse the growing importance of arms exports for the preservation of the French defence industry and the constraints that accompany this dependency.

The economic importance of the French defence industry and the evolution of defence equipment spending

The notion of a defence technological and industrial base – DTIB – emerged in the 1990s to help decision-makers circumscribe those companies that are deemed essential in the preservation of defence industrial competences (Serfati, 2014, p. 34). In France, the underlying understanding of the importance of the DTIB, however, dates back to the 1950s, as the provision of arms has since been considered as one of the components of the founding principles of national independence. Since the beginning of the Fifth Republic, the defence industry has indeed been approached as a cornerstone of national strategic autonomy, together with nuclear deterrence (Fontanela and Hébert, 1997; Malizard, 2019). As Fleurant and Quéau argue, despite the geopolitical and geo-economic shifts of the 1990s and 2000s and their consequences for defence policies (e.g., professionalisation of the armed forces, restructuring and reform of the Ministry of Defence, consolidation and Europeanisation of the industrial base, etc.), the basis of the approach designed during the Cold War still guides France's defence policy today (Fleurant and Quéau, 2014, p. 4). These factors continue to justify a willingness to dedicate significant resources to the maintenance of high-end industrial activities through structuring programs that favour advanced technologies, as illustrated in the 2013 defence white paper:

> The defence industry is a key component of France's strategic autonomy. It also contributes to a coherent political, diplomatic and economic ambition. It alone can guarantee the secure supplying of equipment supporting our sovereignty and of critical weapons systems and ensure that it matches operational needs as defined by the Ministry of Defence. (Présidence de la République, 2013, p. 117)

France made financial and organisational efforts during the Cold War to build a performant defence industry, which allows it to remain today a member of the

82 *Defence industry and procurement*

restricted club of countries that are able to provide for themselves the full spectrum of military capabilities, such few other countries include the United States, Russia, and China.

In turn, the industrial sector is of significant importance to France's economy. Illustratively, the defence industry provided 165,000 direct and indirect jobs in France in 2012, and up to 200,000 in 2018 (Fleurant and Quéau, 2014, p. 8; Malizard et al., 2019, p. 145). In 2013, among the 50 biggest factories in France, 15 belonged to groups that had some military activity, just behind the car manufacturing industry, which possesses 17 of the largest factories (Serfati, 2014, p. 16). Besides, the defence industry provides jobs in parts of France that are otherwise under-industrialised: it represents 10% to 20% of industrial jobs in the south-west, in particular, due to aerospace activities; 20% in Finistère (Brittany) and Var (south of France) where the naval shipyards are located; and 25% in Cher, in the centre of France, where land equipment is produced (Dussauge and Cornu, 1998, p. 24). In 2010, the DTIB received €11.1 billion worth of payments from the Ministry of Defence, to which one can add exports. In 2012, the overall revenue of the defence industry was estimated at €15.1 billion (Fleurant and Quéau, 2014, p. 8), a figure that climbed to €49.6 billion in 2017 (Wyckaert, 2019).

These economic activities are heavily supported by the state: about three-quarters of France's public investments are made by the Ministry of Defence (Serfati, 2014, p. 22). Despite a tense financial situation, defence has remained the third most important published budget in the post-Cold-War era, as well as the first source of investment spending (Fleurant and Quéau, 2014, p. 7). During the Cold War, defence innovation was thought to benefit civilian research and technology, and thus has even greater economic benefits: it was especially the case in France, with the development of space technologies and micro-processors (Vaisse, 2002). Today, defence is still fuelling research and development (R&D) and supports technology-intensive sectors in both military and civilian advanced sectors. As such, defence industries are central to the "national innovation system" (Belin et al., 2019), especially when they invest in fundamental research resulting in dual technologies (Acosta et al., 2018). However, others have argued that while arms production does mobilise considerable expenditure on R&D and attracts highly trained engineers, it does not have any noticeable effect on the general industrial dynamic (Moura, 2018). Either way, the ambition of strategic autonomy and the belief in technology makes it more acceptable in France, relative to other developed countries, to dedicate a significant share of its defence budget to defence equipment spending that benefits national industries. According to data provided by the Ministry of Defence in the Statistical Yearbook of Defence, on average, since 1980, the equipment budget (Titles 5 and 6 of the *Loi de Programmation Militaire*) accounts for half of the defence budget. This characteristic is shared only by the United Kingdom and the United States, which also benefit from a broad industrial defence base (Malizard, 2013, p. 1).

In spite of the economic importance of the sector and the willingness to maintain it for strategic purposes, France has had to adapt its defence equipment spending to macroeconomic evolutions. While it has continuously devoted significant resources to defence equipment, the sharp increase in spending from the 1970s to the 1990s was followed by a steady decrease that stabilised in the early 2000s and to today, with a drop around the 2008 financial crisis, as is illustrated in Figure 4.1. More precisely, from the beginning of the 1970s to the beginning of the 1990s, the resources devoted to equipping the armed forces increased dramatically, from 15 billion French francs (FRF) in 1973 to FRF103 billion in 1993, before falling back to FRF81 billion in 1998 (Dussauge and Cornu, 1998, p. 57). This trend reflected a more general tendency in the defence budget, which increased continuously between the 1970s and 1993. As a share of GDP, the budget went from 3.5% to 4% in the 1980s down to 3% in 1998 (Ibid., p. 61).

The decline in the budget in the 1990s had consequences mainly for equipment expenditure, and therefore for the industry. Indeed, the simultaneous decrease in national orders and of exports led the French defence industry revenue to drop from FRF125 billion in 1990 to FRF87 billion in 1995, that is to say, a 30% decrease in five years (Ibid., p. 9). This is because operating expenditures ("day-to-day expenditures" in Figure 4.1) are of a more incompressible nature in that they are largely made up of staff salaries. Indeed, the evolution of the disaggregated budget shows that operating expenses are relatively constant over time, with equipment expenditure being the main victim of budgetary adjustments (Malizard, 2013, pp. 75–80).

The austerity measures following the 2008 financial crisis led to a decrease in defence budgets, and in particular a decrease in equipment expenditure, although the defence ministry was not the most badly hit. However, 23,500 civilian and military jobs were cut (Fleurant and Quéau, 2014, p. 7). The effects of the financial crisis were felt on the budgets two years later: annual spending on equipment rose to almost €18 billion in 2009 and went down to €15.6 billion, approximately, yearly, from 2010 onwards (Foucault, 2012, p. 25). The 2014–2019 Military Programming Law froze defence spending and protected the €17

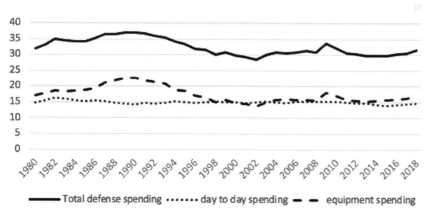

Figure 4.1 Change in total spending, day-to-day spending, and equipment spending. (Source: Belin, Malizard and Masson, 2019, p. 147.)

84 *Defence industry and procurement*

billion/year dedicated to equipment and the €730 million/year for defence R&D (*Journal Officiel de la République Française*, 2013). As Figure 4.1 illustrates, equipment expenditures still represented 53% of French defence spending in 2017 (Oudot, 2017, p. 1). A point has to be made, however, about planned versus effective equipment spending. The French military spending bill – the *Loi de Programmation Militaire*, LPM – is passed by the French parliament and "sets out the military budget and major capability investment projects over six-year periods" (Dyson, 2010, p. 158). This, together with the important role played by the Directorate General of Armaments (DGA) to control and streamline procurement has prevented the "overheating" of the French equipment program as severe as it was in the United Kingdom, for instance (Ibid.). Nonetheless, the LPMs are not always the best indicator of how much France actually invests in defence procurement as they tend to be contradicted by yearly budget laws. Indeed, as Foucault reports, since 1994 and until recently, no spending bill had been respected due to a combination of credit deferrals, program cancellations, and public financing crises (Foucault, 2012, p. 23). Therefore, there remained a cumulative shortfall for equipment credit that was estimated in 2012 at €46 billion – that is to say the equivalent of more than three budget years of equipment credits (Foucault, 2012, p. 28). The evolution of the security environment and the engagement of France in military theatres that proved demanding for equipment, together with increased revenues from arms exports led to a correction of that trend in the second half of the decade, and the 2014–2019 LPM was effectively implemented as planned (André and Pueyo, 2018). Overall, if we exclude the equipment related to nuclear deterrence, as well as maintenance cost, France, in the late 2010s, effectively spent on average €7–8 billion per year on procurement (Cour des Comptes, 2018, p. 5; Sénat, 2018, p. 85).

As an alternative to cutting equipment spending when in financial difficulty, French governments have opted, since the 1990s, for reducing the number of orders and extending delivery schedules. Illustratively, the number of A400M transport aircraft ordered by France went from 18 down to 8 (Foucault, 2012, p. 27). However, reducing series numbers questions the viability of certain production lines (Foucault, 2012, p. 25). Besides, regarding the postponement of delivery schedules, the Cour des Comptes – the French audit office – warned that postponing spending commitments could eventually lead to "structural disarmament where the armed forces would be supplied with equipment that is out of date before entering service and in quantities incompatible with operational requirement" (Cour des Comptes, 1997, p. 182). Another method to mitigate the effects of limited resources was to abandon the rule of annual payments: since 1997, France has passed multi-year orders in exchange for lower costs on the part of the industrialists (Dussauge and Cornu, 1998, p. 75). Finally, a means to gather exceptional income was found in 2010 with the sale of the Ministry of Defence's real estate, including several historical buildings in the centre of Paris, as well as its Hertzian frequency bands, both of which were estimated at approximately €3.5 billion – the amount that the financial crisis was estimated to have cost the French ministry of defence (Trucy et al., 2008, pp. 10 and 20).

The evolution of the structure of the industry and main producers

More than in other advanced economies, the structure of the French defence industry continues to reflect the political commitment to maintaining an autonomous supply of equipment to the armed forces. Adjustments have been necessary over the past three decades to compensate for the financial difficulties mentioned above, namely via a dual process of privatisation and concentration, nationally and at the European level.

Most of the potential of the French industry was destroyed during the Second World War, contrary to what happened in the United Kingdom or the United States. The bases of the contemporary French defence industry therefore were developed in the 1950s through to the 1970s. The industry expanded over that period due to the combined effects of the Indochina War, De Gaulle's great ambitions for national independence, and the exponential growth of exports. This period of growth has since been followed by a durable downward tendency that paralleled that experienced by government equipment spending, which we have discussed. In the 1980s, national economic growth slowed down, at the same time the international arms market became increasingly unstable towards the end of the decade, and the drop in both national orders and exports worsened in the 1990s. From the 1980s onwards, the industry has had to restructure and downsize: 100,000 jobs were lost in a decade (Dussauge and Cornu, 1998, p. 16).

Since the 1980s, both right-wing and left-wing governments have implemented a process of industrial privatisation and progressively withdrawn from the capital of the main defence companies in order to promote transnational rapprochements. Matra was privatised in 1988, Thomson-CSF in 1998, Aérospatiale in 1999, and Safran (ex-Sagem) and DCNS, partially, in the 2000s. In France, this process of privatisation has not been as complete as it has been across Europe. With the exception of Italy and Spain, France is one of the few European governments that has not gone as far as total privatisation of the sector, and it is in France that the level of public participation in the capital of the defence industries remains the highest (Masson, 2007, p. 1). Indeed, the capitalist links that connect the major defence groups reveal that the presence of the French state is either direct and total (e.g., Nexter and Naval Group – ex-DCNS), either it possesses large but minority shares (Safran, Thales), or is involved indirectly, through corporations created for this purpose in which the state itself is a shareholder (e.g., Dassault) (Serfati, 2014, p. 36; Fawaz et al., 2019). In 2014, the state acquired one share of the Dassault industrial group and signed an important convention "enabling the State to defend its essential interests in the event of changes in control of this strategic company, in particular, due to its contribution to the airborne component of nuclear deterrence" (Cabirol, 2014). Table 4.1 indicates in more detail the extent of the French government's participation in the main defence groups.

Despite links that are clearly stronger than in other countries, the French state's influence on defence companies has limits. For one, its shareholding overall has been in decline since the 2000s. Besides, the audit office (Cour des Comptes)

86 *Defence industry and procurement*

Table 4.1 Main French defence companies

Firm	Defence Activities	Shareholders	World Ranking and Value of Sales
Aerospace and Cross-Domain			
Airbus Group	Activities in aerospace, missiles, electronics	France: 11.08%; Germany 11.07%; Spain: 4.17%; Others: 73.68%	7th US$11,290 million
Thales	Electronics for the aeronautics and naval sectors	France: 25.7%; Dassault Aviation: 24.3%; Public float: 49.6%	8th US$9,000 million
Safran	Electronics for the land sector and infantry; aeronautical equipment	France: 13.16%; Others (incl. public float & employees): 86.84%	33rd US$2,910 million
Dassault Aviation	Combat aircraft and drones	Dassault Group: 62.17%; Airbus: 9.93%; Others: 27.90%	50th US$2,120 million
Land			
Nexter	Armoured vehicles; artillery; powder and propulsion; ammunition	France: 100%	83rd US$960 million[1]
Arquus[2]	Tactical armoured vehicles	Parent Company: Volvo	Sales <US$700 million
Naval			
Naval Group	Conventional- and nuclear-powered surface ships and submarines	France: 62.49%; Thales: 35%; Other: 2.51%	19th US$4,130 million
Missiles			
MBDA	Missiles for air, land, and naval platforms	Airbus: 37.5%; BAE Systems: 37.5%; Leonardo: 25%	26th US$3,380 million

Sources: Fleurant and Quéau, 2014, p. 8; SIPRI, 2018; Cabirol, 2018; Fleurant et al., 2018; Malizard et al., 2019.

regularly points to the government's mismanagement of its shareholding, for instance when the shareholding agency APE (Agence des Participations de l'État) and the DGA failed to coordinate their positions in a 2012 vote at Nexter's board (Cabirol, 2013a). But the acquisition of a share in Dassault indicates that the French government is still ready to control the shareholding of industries it deems strategic, when it can. Aside from large defence groups, in late 2017, the French government launched "DefInvest", a €50-million program whereby the French

Defence industry and procurement 87

state, via BPI France, became a shareholder in SMEs that are considered strategic for the Ministry for the Armed Forces – in particular those SMEs that play a critical role in the supply chain of armament programs and/or companies leading in disruptive innovations. The government identifies 400 such "strategic" SMEs (BPI France, 2017).

As a response to the triple dynamics of increased global competition, the rising cost of equipment, and the lowering defence budgets, France also had to undertake industrial concentration. Indeed, the fragmentation of the European DTIB started to become a problem in the 1990s, when the American DTIB was reinforcing itself around Boeing, Lockheed Martin, and Raytheon. At the end of the 1990s, French defence industrial activity was already centred around a small number of actors (Dussauge and Cornu, 1998, p. 15). The Commissariat à l'énergie atomique (CEA) managed nuclear activities, and the *Société Nationale des Poudres et Explosifs* (SNPE) produced powders and explosives, which was strategic both for nuclear weapons and Ariane-type space rockets. The SNPE was later taken over by Sagem and GIAT (Serfati, 2014, p. 61). In the aeronautical sector, three groups represented 70% of revenue: Aérospatiale, SNECMA, and Dassault Aviation. In the domain of electronics, five companies hired 60% of the workforce: Thomson-CSF, Matra, Sagem, Dassault Electronics, and Alcatel-Alstom. The shipbuilding industry was dominated by DCN, while 70% of the sales in land armament were generated by Aerospatiale, GIAT Industries, and Thomson-CSF.

Concentration has occurred not only nationally but also at the European level, through the creation of joint ventures. One example is the Airbus Group, the leading European company that came about from the reorganisation of the European aeronautic defence and space group (EADS). EADS was created in 2000, following a series of industrial consolidations that integrated several European companies, including the French Aérospatiale and Matra. France and Germany today possess 11.08% and 11.07% of the shares of the group, respectively, and are thus the biggest stakeholders. Defence and security represent 20% of the group's activities, which are dominated by civilian aircraft commercial activities. Another example is MBDA in the missile sector. The missile sector is a sector that produces few dual-use technologies, and it is thus highly dependent on state procurement. It is also a sector where European countries have cooperated regularly from the 1960s. The MBDA group was set up in December 2001. MBDA resulted from the fusion of Matra-BAe Dynamics (MBD; Franco-British), EADS-Aérospatiale Matra Missiles (French), and Alenia Marconi Systems (Italian-British). MBDA stakeholders are EADS (now Airbus) and BAE, with 37.5% of shares each, and Finmeccanica (now Leonardo), with 25%. The group then took over the German company LFK in June 2005.

Just like in the case of privatisation, however, France did not go all the way in terms of industrial concentration: in various sectors, competing companies have persisted. Indeed, where, on the international scene, the constitution of large defence groups has led to a diversification of activities, sectoral specialisations persist in France because of the strong links created between companies, the DGA, and the armed forces (Serfati, 2014, p. 48). These same links between

88 *Defence industry and procurement*

the state and the industry have also limited the number of transnational mergers (James, 2004, p. 108).

Today, the French industry remains concentrated around most of the same actors, despite some name changes, and thus there are national monopolies or duopolies in the different sectors, as illustrated in Table 4.1. Naval Group (which has replaced DCN, and later DCNS, in 2017), Thales (which replaced Thomson-CSF in 2000), Safran (which replaced Sagem in 2005), and Dassault together benefited from 66% of orders for weapons and 52% of Research and Technology (R&T) funds from the Ministry of Defence (if we exclude nuclear activities) in 2013 (Serfati, 2014, pp. 18–19). That year, the government's €10.83 billion worth of contracts were awarded to Airbus Group (€1.9 billion), Naval Group (€1.8 billion), and Thales (€1.4 billion) (Guillermard, 2014). As Table 4.1 indicates, according to 2017 rankings, Thales is the only French group that makes it to the top ten of world defence contractors, right behind Airbus Group (Macias, 2019; SIPRI, 2018). They are both well behind the British BAE Systems, Europe's largest defence company with US$22,940 million in arms sales in 2017, ranking as the fourth-largest company in the world. Italy follows, with Leonardo ranked ninth in the world.

The organisation of French defence procurement: the role of the DGA

The *Délégation Ministérielle pour l'Armement* (DMA, Ministerial Delegation for Armaments) was created under De Gaulle, in 1961, as part of his plans for national technological independence, and for a French nuclear deterrent. The DMA was later renamed *Direction Générale de l'Armement* (DGA, Directorate General for Armaments) in 1977. The DGA is under the direct authority of the minister of defence, and it supervises all the conception, studies, and production of armament programs. The creation of the DGA was a solution to the problem that "too many public agencies, along with the military services, were influencing the design and development of weapons systems" (Kapstein, 2009, p. 2). Except for some organisational reforms, the objectives and activities of the DGA have remained the same. Its main mandate is to provide the material necessary for the conduct of a defence policy free from any external dependence, and its associated goal is to help reconstitute and sustain the French defence industrial and technological base. What is more, the DGA manages international cooperation with partners for joint procurement projects, imports, as well as arms exports.

From the onset, the DGA has thus had a mission that combines equipping French armed forces in an efficient fashion and within budget, ensuring France's sovereignty in areas of critical technologies and supporting the French industry for the maintenance of national competencies. There has always been tension between these missions, and since the 1980s, several reforms of the organisation have attempted to shift the balance towards one mission or another. While in 1986 a first reform aimed to focus the DGA's activity on the mission of equipping the armed forces with relevant material, another reform in 1994 gave prominence instead to "industrial affairs", at a time when the French armaments industry

Defence industry and procurement   89

entered a period of very strong turbulence provoked by the fall in exports and the reduction of national orders (Dussauge and Cornu, 1998, pp. 32–35). Yet another reform in 1996 aimed at reducing the cost of programs by ensuring better control mechanisms with the integration of the principles of New Public Management (Hoeffler, 2008, p. 143). The compartmentalised, hierarchical organisation that prevailed during the Cold War was replaced in the 1990s by a so-called matrix organisation: the DGA was reorganised across directorates. These are the Strategy Directorate, which identifies operational needs, R&T prioritises and ensures the preservation of the DITB; the Operations Directorate, which executes research and studies, and manages ongoing armament programs; the Technical Directorate, which oversees the technical implementation of programs, conducts tests and ensures the DGA's continued technical expertise; and the Directorate for International Development, which ensures the promotion and control of arms exports (Ministère de la Défense, 2010). The full conduct of a program is thus the result of horizontal collaboration between different staff, under the responsibility of a program director who is the sole guarantor for the costs of and delays to the program (Hoeffler, 2008, p. 147).

Given the state's concern with the preservation of a national defence industry and the desire to therefore avoid resorting to external procurement, there is a strong mutual dependence between the DGA and French industrialists. The DGA compensates for its dependence on a limited number of suppliers by resorting to contractual practices that put a greater burden on the industry. In France, contracts are signed with a performance obligation (*obligation de résultat*) for the industry, whether in terms of deadline or technical performance; technological risks are estimated at the outset and are included in the initial prices; and the contracts involve full insurance for the client (the state). Besides, the client can modify its requirement during the process and controls the industry's activities as development and production progress, and contracts can be renegotiated. Fixed-price contracts, which are particularly attractive when the technology is mature, provide the DGA with a great deal of protection against ex-post contingencies (Oudot and Bellais, 2008, p. 90).

Arguably, the capacity to control the development of industrial programs is reinforced by the fact that the DGA is composed of armament engineers who possess technical expertise. Indeed, the peculiarities of the DGA and the *corps des ingénieurs de l'armement* – corps of armament engineers – distinguishes the French system from that of other countries. The DGA comprises 10,000 employees, of which half are engineers: technical experts hired on a permanent basis to run France's armament programs (Guillermard, 2014; Dyson, 2010, p. 158). Jean Joana calls it a "technico-scientific and administrative agency" (Joana, 2008, p. 45). It is noticeable that these engineers are characterised by their specialisation and their technological competence as well as their *"esprit de corps"* – if not their homogeneity: 80% of them studied at the Grande École Polytechnique (Cohen, 1994, p. 217). The DGA thus combines "technological expertise and management expertise, which gives it unparalleled authority […]. It is in a privileged position, which allows it, in most cases, to impose its choices" (Chesnais and Serfati, 1992, pp. 66–67).

90 *Defence industry and procurement*

Dyson argues that the DGA provides France with a stronger level of civilian control than in the United Kingdom and Germany (Dyson, 2010, p. 158). Now, the distinction between military and civilian control is not so clear, considering that armament engineers do have a military status, with corresponding ranks, even though their professional *ethos* is arguably more technical than military (Hoeffler, 2008, pp. 138–139). At the same time, there is also a blurred boundary between the defence ministry and the defence industry (Joana, 2008, p. 45). This is partly due to the integrated nature of the procurement process, where there is one client (the DGA) and a limited number of suppliers. Besides, this is explained by the persistence of a strong involvement of the French state in defence companies' shareholding, as we explained in the previous section. Finally, it is also to do with the professional and social links between the DGA and the industry. A recent study by Faure et al. (2019) finds, through case studies of the directors of Safran and Thales, the strong presence of actors both trained by the state and who have done a part of their career in the service of the state. These individuals have also been to the same schools, in particular, Polytechnique.

The organisation of acquisitions in France and the particular nature of the DGA affects the procurement choices that are made. From the onset, the system has been perceived as creating a power imbalance whereby industrial and/or technological logic are favoured over the needs of the services. This is true in particular when preference is given to French materiel or when colossal efforts are made for the development of technologies in which the armies do not have an interest (Joana, 2008, pp. 46–47). Indeed, some scholars wonder if the needs expressed by the services are not quite simply subordinated to the options that the DGA proposes, which themselves are primarily concerned with export prospects (Dussauge and Cornu, 1998, pp. 40–41). Indeed, the growing industrial constraint has resulted in a significant loss of influence from the services in the definition of their needs. First, historically, the development of the nuclear deterrent, and then the decrease in troop numbers at the end of the Cold War meant that the French defence industry could no longer be guaranteed a decent workload (Cohen, 1994, p. 213). The situation worsened over time, as national orders became insufficient to ensure an efficient industrial base, and exports gained even more strategic importance. As a result, the armed forces have no longer been able to oppose the acquisition of certain materiel aimed for export as this would compromise their sale to foreign customers and thus harm industrial interests. Overall, a side-effect of the French procurement system has been a preference for domestically produced equipment, and precedence given to industrial logic and technological development over the operational needs expressed by the armed forces.

French procurement: *grands programmes* and technological innovation

Because of the logic of national independence and the industrial mission attributed to the DGA, France has tended to opt-out of acquiring off-the-shelf equipment (i.e., importing arms), even when these could meet the services' needs

Defence industry and procurement 91

faster and at a lower cost (Joana, 2008, p. 49). Illustratively, between 1976 and 1996, France has only imported between 2% and 14% of equipment each year (Dussauge and Cornu, 1998, p. 68). According to the SIPRI database, imports to France come primarily from the United States, followed by Europe (between 1996 and 2019, the United Kingdom is France's third supplier on average, behind the United States and Spain). Notable recent off-the-shelf purchases include Reaper drones from the United States (*cf. infra*) and HK416 assault rifles from Germany.

The combination of France's foreign and domestic policy objectives and the professional profile of DGA staff has historically given rise to a specific weapons procurement system: the policy of major programs, or "high-tech Colbertism", is reflected in the idea that priority must be given to the technological excellence of French armament (Genieys and Michel, 2004; Hoeffler, 2008). Finally, and logically, France produces – and exports – mostly large platforms and weapon systems, and has weaker production in small material such as individual arms (Dussauge and Cornu, 1998, p. 8).

The Leclerc main battle tank (MBT) is a good example of historical French procurement practices and their adaptation to the post-Cold-War period. The policy of major programs combined with preparations for a direct confrontation between NATO and the Warsaw Pact had led to the establishment of "technological cathedrals" (Bellais and Droff, 2017, p. 779): a model of innovation in military capabilities based on a massive investment in R&D, clearly identified technological trajectories, and the "generational" development of equipment (Moura, 2018, p. 2). As soon as a platform came into service, it was necessary to start the development of its replacement to maintain the lead in the technological race. The Leclerc main battle tank was such a program. When the AMX30 came into service in 1966, the first considerations were given to its successor program (Genieys and Michel, 2004, p. 87). Designed from 1983 onward, the Leclerc was built by GIAT (which became Nexter and is now part of the Franco-German group KNDS) and entered service in 1993, that is to say in the new, post-Cold-War context. Initially conceived to be able to "stop on the ground the hordes from the East, while France would implement its nuclear strike force", it was then redefined around the notion of versatility (Ibid., pp. 90 and 98). More recently, in 2006, Nexter unveiled a new version of the tank optimised for urban operations (Army Technology, no date). The tank was designed with the most advanced technologies at the time, including its own computer system, as the goal was indeed to build "the best tank in the world" (Genieys and Michel, 2004, p. 99). The Leclerc was first engaged in Kosovo in 1999, and then in Lebanon in 2006. The Leclerc was then not deployed for almost a decade as it was considered inappropriate for operations in Afghanistan and in the Sahel (Maldera, 2016). Interestingly, the Leclerc was not even a success in exports, as it was only exported to the UAE. It nonetheless regained legitimacy with the Ukraine crisis and NATO's Operation Enhanced Forward Presence: France deployed four Leclerc twice, in 2017 and 2019, in Estonia as part of its participation in a UK-led multinational battlegroup (Lagneau, 2019).

92 *Defence industry and procurement*

The Char Leclerc is also an interesting example when it comes to technological adaptation and the integration of innovation in France's weapons acquisitions. In order to keep up with the changing character of war, technological progress, and in particular the durable move towards network-enabled operations, it was decided to further renovate the Char Leclerc and to embed it in a key transforming program for the French army: Scorpion. A €5 billion contract awarded in 2014 to Nexter, Renault Trucks Defence (now Arquus), and Thales, Scorpion aims to improve the fighting capabilities of the army through the acquisition of new intermediate combat vehicles, a digitalisation effort to improve battlefield awareness and fire coordination, and a new program of operational readiness. The first phase of the transformation program runs to 2025, and it brings together the Leclerc, armoured vehicles (the Griffon multirole armoured vehicle, the Jaguar armoured reconnaissance and combat vehicle), and a light multirole vehicle all organised in a network thanks to a single communication and information system (Armée de Terre, 2018; Sénat, 2018, p. 49). Scorpion is designed to evolve, with the addition of new equipment and capabilities such as tactical drones, combat support vehicles, protection against cyber and electronic warfare capabilities, land robots, and the successor to the FELIN (*Fantassin à Equipements et Liaisons Intégrés*; a digitalised, integrated equipment and communication system for infantrymen) (Maldera, 2016). The concept is supposed to facilitate the army's transition towards an era of new sensors and AI-enabled military capabilities by incrementally preparing the forces for the introduction of such capabilities.

As the adaptation of the Leclerc indicates, French procurement priorities have to adapt to the changing character of war and technological evolution. In the 1990s, most defence research funds were directed towards electronics and computing, airspace and missiles, and nuclear deterrence (Dussauge and Cornu, 1998, p. 47). Today, military innovation has become an even more important factor in the context of the resurgence of great power competition, which comes in addition to the asymmetric conflicts that characterised Western experiences of warfare in the 1990s and 2000s. Therefore, it fuels all aspects of defence R&D and procurement. Illustratively, in 2016, the French army published its own vision for the future operational environment. Overall, the army envisions a hardened battlefield, in which mass and command performance will be of critical importance in achieving military superiority, and human factors will, as always, determine the final victory. Actors that can integrate new technologies to facilitate command, cooperation, understanding, and influence will have the edge in this operational environment. The Scorpion is a response to those identified needs. The Armée de l'Air, for its part, envisions the end of the hitherto undisputed Western air supremacy through a combination of two factors: first, the development and diffusion of fourth- and fifth-generation fighters able to compete with Western planes; and second, the development of air defences, particularly new radar and new surface-to-air missiles (Brustlein et al., 2014; Steininger, 2017). In this context, maintaining military supremacy could require a "system of systems" of manned and unmanned vehicles linked together in a strike package (Anger, 2017; Pappalardo, 2018). The Marine Nationale envisions a future in which undersurface (from submarines and mines) and anti-ship (from naval missiles) threats are quickly proliferating, and in which electronic warfare is a key capability in achieving operational superiority (Marine Nationale, 2018). A way to tackle these challenges is gradual automatisation, including the use of drones: by 2030, all French ships are supposed to have an on-board drone capacity. The move towards autonomous systems is an important focus of modernisation and capacity innovation, provided that one or more human agents remain in control. Thus, aerial drone programs (such as the European medium altitude long endurance (MALE) drone or the SDAM naval drone), the future mine warfare system (SLAMF), or the terrestrial robots eventually integrated into the Scorpion information and communication systems will provide entirely new concepts based on collaboration between platforms and remotely piloted aircraft systems (RPAS) (Sénat, 2018, p. 48).

The 2000s have also seen the rapid development of cyberattacks and corresponding defence capabilities. In France, the theme of cybersecurity appears for the first time as a strategic issue in the 2008 defence white paper. The security of information systems is then identified as part of sovereign domains (Premier Ministre, 2008, p. 306), alongside the nuclear domain (nuclear deterrence, ballistic missiles, and SSNs) (Desforges, 2015, p. 69). In 2013, the Hollande government announced that the DGA's R&D budget dedicated to cybersecurity would be multiplied by three, going from €10 million to €30 million (Ibid.). Today, French official documents therefore emphasise the development of autonomous capabilities in cyberspace (SGDSN, 2018), including through the conduct of offensive cyber operations (Ministère des Armées, 2019a). Finally, to grapple with these fast-paced technological and strategic changes, ranging from cybersecurity to unmanned systems and increased competition, the French Ministry of Armed Forces announced in September 2018 the creation of an agency for defence innovation to "bring together all the actors of the ministry and all the programs that contribute to defence innovation", including civilian research (DGA, 2018). Headed by a civil servant specialised in artificial intelligence and military simulation, it aims to "guarantee France's strategic autonomy and the military superiority of armed force" (Marzolf, 2018).

Europeanising the French defence industry and procurement: achievements and frustrations

Despite the persistence of programs such as the Leclerc – we could also evoke the Rafale aircraft – and its ability to follow the pace of innovation in certain domains, France has had to increasingly internationalise – and especially Europeanise – its R&D and procurement for a long time. The necessity of bringing down costs led to an acceptance that, from the 1990s onward, it was no longer possible for France to maintain a strictly autonomous procurement policy. With the goal that economic rationality should be at the heart of future programs, it was acknowledged that weapon acquisitions may be done through off-the-shelf purchases or international cooperation. The 1994 defence white paper admits that while the

94 *Defence industry and procurement*

French defence industry was present in all the sectors from 1960 to 1985, the evolution of technology and of the domestic and international markets made it so that "such a situation [was] no longer possible [in 1994] and [would] be even less possible in the future", so that it was "no longer possible, or even desirable that France possesses and maintains, by itself, the whole of these competencies" (Premier Ministre, 1994, pp. 116–117). With national markets being too narrow, conducting programs in cooperation appeared and continued to be considered as one option to enhance competitiveness by reducing intra-European competition and reaching a greater number of markets. Cooperation is also supposed to take unit prices down through economies of scale. Finally, cooperation also offers access to technology not available to France.

Since the 1990s, French political decision-makers have thus been torn between different contradictory priorities: to ensure national independence with a limited defence budget; to preserve employment in a little-productive industrial sector; and to cooperate internationally without hurting the French industrial base, all the while providing the best possible equipment for the armed forces (Cohen, 1994, p. 251). The 1994 white paper did specify three possible levels of interdependence deemed acceptable for France, according to the strategic importance of different sectors of equipment. First, France must remain fully competent for all things nuclear and its environment, which includes strategic missiles equipped with nuclear warheads, launch systems, information and communication systems, and SSBNs. Secondly, for other strategic sectors, France could engage in cooperation but must retain the skills and ability to develop and manufacture alone if necessary. This included intelligence, information analysis, stealth, and electronic warfare. Thirdly, apart from the sectors mentioned above, there is no area that could not ultimately be shared with other European countries in the context of common objectives and procedures to be defined. The 2017 strategic review provides a more detailed picture of the desired degree of independence in each sector and for each type of systems: for example, "sovereignty" is envisaged for "core" communication systems and networks; while cooperation with "mutual dependence" is acceptable for land vehicles and some missile systems (Ministère des Armées, 2017, p. 67). Interestingly, cooperation is now considered the default option for producing air vehicles, except for stealth, sensors, command and control, and missile systems, where sovereignty is pursued.

Having collaborated with select European partners since the 1960s – in particular with the United Kingdom and Germany for the development of joint programs – France was a key player in the setting up of European institutions and mechanisms to oversee multinational procurement. France contributed to setting up the armaments branch of the Western European Union (the Independent European Program Group, which later became the Western European Armaments Group, WEAG). The WEAG was a forum for defence ministers and national armaments directors that closed in 2005 after the European Defence Agency was created. France, with the United Kingdom, Italy, and Germany, then created the *Organisation Conjointe de Coopération en Matière d'Armement* (OCCAr) in 1996. The OCCAr's role is to oversee the through-life management of cooperative

Defence industry and procurement 95

defence equipment programs. The organisation now also includes Belgium, Spain, and non-members that participate in certain projects. France, with Germany and the United Kingdom, was also key in promoting the idea of the European Defence Agency (EDA), on which the European Council agreed in 2003. Since 2004, the EDA has been promoting defence market integration, encouraging collective solutions to capability gaps, and fostering collaborative projects.

The EU has also played a role in altering the rules of defence procurement, with a view to fostering a Europeanised defence and technological industrial base. Directive 2009/81/EC of the European Parliament and of the Council of 13 July 2009 (*Official Journal of the European Union*, 2009), opened member states' defence procurement to competition across the single market. The rationale was that liberalising the defence market would bring prices down, avoid the coexistence of multiple similar programs and eventually create a rationalised European DTIB that would be competitive at the global level. With the directive, exemptions to the free-market approach in weapons acquisitions went from the default rule to case-by-case exceptions that need to be justified. There are indeed circumstances in which EU member states can legally get around the directive, including arguments on essential national security interests.

Cooperation among European countries through joint procurement has been limited in practice. Indeed, if the advantages of cooperation in defence procurement are well known, so are its difficulties, which range from differing operational requirements and calendars to disputes over workload distribution. This is the case even when transnational firms – such as Airbus – exist. According to Cornu, as long as they have branches in their national territories, governments will consider them like national companies (Cornu, 2001, p. 72). The creation of the OCCAr in 1996 and the EDA in 2004, and then the 2009 EU directive on intra-community transfer did not create a groundswell of joint European procurement. According to the European Defence Agency, across Europe, the percentage of European spending dedicated to collaborative defence projects rose from 5% to 15% between 1965 and 1990, and to just under 20% today. As Figure 4.2 illustrates, France in the 2000s–2010s procured an average of 23% of its equipment through European collaboration. This places France above the EU average (at 19.45%) and the other two largest spenders in Europe – Germany and the United Kingdom, which respectively procure on average 20% and 21% of their equipment through European collaborations – but well below other EU member states such as Belgium, Italy, or Spain which on average do so for 44%–49% of their expenditure (Figure 4.2).[3]

France collaborates specifically in the aeronautical domains, on satellites, and on missile programs. Illustratively, over the past three decades, France has cooperated on the Tiger, a Franco-German attack helicopter launched in the late 1980s, manufactured by Eurocopter (now Airbus Helicopter), which entered service in 2003. The Tiger is considered a technological success; however, it turned out to be significantly more expensive than planned (Cour des Comptes, 2018, p. 14). France also participated in the NH90, a multirole helicopter developed in cooperation between France, Germany, Italy, and the Netherlands in the 1990s, which

96 Defence industry and procurement

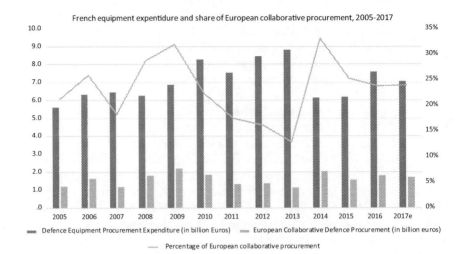

Figure 4.2 French equipment expenditure and share of European collaborative procurement, 2005–2017.

entered into service in 2007. For the French audit office, the lack of standardisation of needs has given rise to multiple versions of the helicopter, and its realisation shared between two competing industrialists (the main companies involved were Airbus and AgustaWestland, now Leonardo) is an example not to follow (Cour des Comptes, 2018, p. 14). Besides, France participated in the Airbus A400M transport aircraft. Launched in the 1990s, the A400M is a transport aircraft of intermediate size and range that has no equivalent. It was also the first program operating in European institutions (OCCAr and to a lesser extent EDA) and 'European' firms with a common European aim (Mawdsley, 2013, p. 16). Aside from the aeronautical domain, France has collaborated on many missile programs, with the firm MBDA, mostly with the United Kingdom and Italy.

The single most important failure in France's experience of collaborative procurement has probably been the plan for Franco-British aircraft carriers. Since the 1980s, French governments had envisaged the construction of a second aircraft carrier but had cancelled the project repeatedly for budgetary reasons (Cour des Comptes, 2014, pp. 128–137). In 1998, the British government took the decision to equip its forces with three aircraft carriers (the Carrier Vessel Future program, CVF), and the French saw an opportunity to cooperate. Cooperation was announced in 2002. When, in 2005, the British government announced that it planned to organise the construction of the carriers in British shipyards in order to boost local employment, the French government in 2006 chose to invest in Britain's program. Thus, the intent to cooperate was restated, but with a more limited extent as France would simply buy British industrial designs off the shelf. Eventually, the prospect of Britain not sharing industrial production led Nicolas

Defence industry and procurement 97

Sarkozy to suspend the construction of a second French aircraft carrier. France withdrew from the program in 2008, having spent €214 million and while gaining nothing from it.

A 2013 European Parliament report evaluated the "cost of non-Europe" in the defence realm – that is to say, the financial deficiency stemming from a lack of harmonisation and integration in defence – ranging between €26 billion and €130 billion (Ballester, 2013, pp. 77–78). From 2017 onwards, European governments enacted a change of approach in the incentive system created by the EU to encourage and facilitate cross-border procurement and joint programs. Launched in June 2017, the European Defence Fund includes a research component, which allows for the EU to finance research for defence technologies and to co-finance European armaments programs carried out in cooperation between several companies, themselves located in the territory of several member states.

Defence companies' and EU member states' interests are at stake in this EU project to fund defence R&D and co-fund cross-border armament programs. This is evidenced in the definition of the eligibility criteria for the European Defence Industrial Development Programme (EDIDP) and the European Defence Fund (EDF): the objective is that only EU companies should be able to receive funds. Thus, while derogations could be made for foreign companies located in EU territory, these would be awarded only against certain guarantees and if they do not put at risk the interests of the EU, in terms of technology, jobs, and intellectual property. France was one of the strongest proponents of strict eligibility criteria that would allow non-EU companies to participate on a case-by-case basis, but not to receive funds. A restrictive definition of the European Defence and Technological Industrial Base is indeed seen as a way to protect national defence industries from American competition and protectionist practices. But aside from the defence industries, the emergence of new technologies (5G, AI) and the growth of China's international role prompted new debates about the potential risks stemming from foreign investments into EU critical infrastructures. Finally, the COVID-19 pandemic was seen in Brussels as further highlighting the importance of having EU-based manufacturing capacity in a wider array of strategic sectors, as the digital domain, data, health, intellectual property, and critical infrastructure made their way into yet a broader understanding of security. As such, the pandemic accelerated the consolidation of the pursuit of a "European technological sovereignty" that France has pushed for since the early 2000s (Darnis, 2020).

Looking at the defence industry, strictly speaking, the ultimate objective for an effective European Common Security and Defence Policy is that the annual defence review serves as a basis for the identification of multinational capability projects that would fill real gaps that would be financed by the European Defence Fund and conducted under the governance of Permanent Structured Cooperation (PESCO), an EU mechanism also launched in 2017. In this new European context, a report from the French Sénat announced a 36% increase in the number of programs conducted in cooperation with European partners envisaged for the period 2019–2025 compared to the 2014–2019 period (Sénat, 2018, p. 33). Indeed, as

98   *Defence industry and procurement*

of 2019, France was already participating in projects under this umbrella (it is the second state participating in the greatest number of PESCO projects, behind Spain; Fiott, 2019) such as the development of a modular unmanned ground system, future MALE drones, a cyber-threat intelligence-sharing platform and "rapid response" teams, and the improvement of the Tiger attack helicopter (European Council, 2018).

Aside from domestic procurement and cross-border cooperation, there are off-the-shelf purchases. France buys material off the shelf when national production cannot be envisaged, for example, if the number of units needed is insufficient, e.g., C-130 transport aircraft (Dussauge and Cornu, 1998, p. 70), when faced with urgent operational requirements, which multiplied during the war in Afghanistan, or when European cooperation fails. This was the case with MALE drones when France eventually decided in 2013 to acquire US Reapers off the shelf as an interim solution. In parallel, as we mentioned earlier, France has launched new cooperation programs with the United Kingdom, and then with Germany, on a future combat air system, including unmanned air vehicles. On other occasions, France does rent equipment from foreign countries. The large Antonov aircraft used for heavy transport, for example, belong to a Ukrainian company, but 98% of their parts come from Russia.

French arms exports: opportunity or constraint?

French arms exports grew from 2.3 billion francs in 1970 to 23.4 billion francs in 1980, and from 20% to 40% of the sector's turnover (Dussauge and Cornu, 1998, p. 9). During that period, France was the world's third arms exporter, representing 10% of the global market, far behind the United States and the USSR, but well ahead of Germany and the United Kingdom (Ibid., p. 79). France was in fact the first exporter if one considers the amount of arms sales against the GNP or the number of inhabitants. Since the mid-1980s, France's position has weakened: its global market share went from 12% in 1986 down to 6% by 1995 (Béraud-Sudreau, 2017, p. 19). During the Cold War, France benefited from the opposition between the two blocks led by the United States and the USSR, by positioning itself as an alternative provider. Thus, France exported mainly to Arab countries in the Middle East and North Africa that sought to decrease their dependency on the two main suppliers. This approach – that supposedly did not assign political ties to arms sales – was put forward in political discourses. The Minister for Commerce, Michel Jobert, stated in 1981: "when France sells arms to a country, it does not deprive it from its freedom" (Le Monde, 1981). This approach however meant that France's market share in developed countries was comparatively lower: in 1988–1992, France represented around 5% of arms sales to those countries, against 50% for the United States and 18% for the USSR/Russia (Dussauge and Cornu, 1998, p. 95).

As we explained above, with the end of the Cold War, the strategies of both client states and producers changed. The decrease in defence budgets among Western countries led to the shrinking of domestic defence markets. As a result,

Defence industry and procurement 99

the United States became more aggressive in the export markets (Dussauge and Cornu, 1998, p. 108). Russia, for its part, engaged in an offensive strategy of commercialisation at low prices of some advanced equipment it had until then refrained from exporting. The 2000s were more favourable to defence companies, due to the conflicts in Afghanistan and Iraq, and the modernisation of arsenals both in Western countries and in emerging economies. While the 2008 financial crisis led to a new decrease in the defence budgets of the United States and Europe, this was not the case in the rest of the world (Béraud-Sudreau, 2017, p. 17). Illustratively, China now is the third-largest arms exporter in the world, before France, the United Kingdom, and Germany (Ibid., p. 18).

That France should sustain a strong arms export policy has been and remains a matter of cross-party consensus. Before its coming to power in 1981, the socialist party had the intention to reduce arms sales and to redeploy certain industrial activities from defence into civilian activities. However, soon after, the government announced that arms exports were in fact indispensable for maintaining France's industrial potential due to their contribution to the balance of trade. Indeed, at the end of the 1990s, Thomson-CSF (now Thales) was 65% military activity, of which 35% depended on foreign sales, and Eurocopter was 60% military activities, of which half was exported (Dussauge and Cornu, 1998, p. 112). Importantly, unlike other economic sectors, the defence industry displays a persistent positive balance (Serfati, 2014, p. 16). Today, while the companies composing the French DTIB represent about 1% of the exporting companies located in France, they realise a quarter of the total of France's exports (if we combine their civilian and military activities) (Moura and Oudot, 2014, p. 1). Because of this particular performance of the defence sector, comparative to others, economic considerations – rather than political or diplomatic goals – appear to have become increasingly important in France's approach to arms exports (Dussauge and Cornu, 1998, p. 85).

Rather than limiting the importance of arms sales, successive French governments in fact have increasingly been supporting arms exports. When it comes to the laws and institutions surrounding French arms exports, as we have explained, the DGA plays a role in favour of exports via its Directorate for International Development (DGA/DI). The DGA assists industrialists by conducting market analysis, by participating in negotiations, by meeting with potential clients, and by representing and promoting the French industry in international arms fairs (Béraud-Sudreau, 2017, p. 14). Since the Sarkozy presidency, the French defence staff and the defence attachés have also been involved in export support activities ("*soutex*") which were previously only devolved to the DGA and armaments attachés (Béraud-Sudreau, 2017, p. 22). In parallel, the control mechanisms for arms sales were also simplified (Ibid.).

As a result of these efforts to support French exports, the 2010s saw a sharp increase in arms sale, especially from 2015 onwards. That year, the number of sales (as per contracts signed) doubled compared to the previous year, amounting to €16.9 billion (Béraud-Sudreau, 2017; Fouquet and Bauer, 2019). This sharp increase was possible thanks to the signing of several large contracts ("*grands*

100 *Defence industry and procurement*

contrats"), including Rafale sales to India, Egypt, and Qatar. Sales went slightly down to €13.9 billion in 2016, and since have remained higher than the then average of €7 billion/year, still amounting to €9 billion in 2018 (Fouquet and Bauer, 2019). That year, Europe, for the first time, represented a significant level in French contracts: more than a quarter of the total amount, compared with an average of 10% recorded over the past decade. Indeed in 2018, the first two clients were Belgium, to which France sold 382 Griffon armoured vehicles, and Spain, which acquired two dozen NH90 helicopters (Ministère des Armées, 2019b, p. 35). The year 2019 marked a new record, with the Naval Group signing an €8 billion contract with Australia for the sale of 12 conventional attack submarines. This represented the largest arms sale contract ever signed by France (Guillermard, 2019). Aside from these exceptional sales, France's main clients for the period 2009–2018 were India, Saudi Arabia, Qatar, Egypt, Brazil, the UAE, the United States, Singapore, Malaysia, and Kuwait (Ministère des Armées, 2019b, p. 112).

France's increasing dependence on arms exports since the end of the Cold War creates a number of constraints. A first constraint that we have already mentioned concerns its effects on national procurement: orders by the French armed forces for some material that is also offered for export is a key selling point. Conversely, if equipment is developed in France but not used by the French forces, it has no chance of being exported. This explains why the French Air Force had to acquire Mirage aircraft in the 1990s, while the aircraft had been developed by the industry on its own accord, and French forces were to be equipped with the Rafale: the acquisition of the Mirage by the Air Force was key in securing the sale of 60 aircraft to Taiwan (Dussauge and Cornu, 1998, p. 89).

A second constraint is the growing power of client states over suppliers. With increased international competition, shrinking demand in the domestic market of weapon-producing countries, and economic growth outside the West, the past three decades have shifted the balance of power in the global arms market: client states have gained increasing leverage and have been exercising increasing pressure on arms exporters. Commercial or industrial compensation (offsets) are now included in a growing share of contracts: in exchange for an arms sale, providers commit to import, in return, locally produced goods, or to procure locally some components involved in the production of the exported material (Dussauge and Cornu, 1998, p. 111). Since the 1990s, clients' demands have been increasingly significant and in certain cases, such as India or Brazil, some of France's main clients, these demands are clearly aimed at facilitating the development of their own defence industrial base (Fleurant and Quéau, 2014, p. 13). Most recently, the contract signed between the Naval Group and the Australian navy will ensure that the submarines will be designed and conceived in France, which will secure 200–250 jobs, but more jobs will be created in Australia, where the submarines will be built, creating 3,000–4,200 jobs locally (Guillermard, 2019).

Finally, arms sales pose ethical and/or legal constraints. Illustratively, voices were raised internationally against arms sales to Saudi Arabia – France's second most important client in 2018 – in the context of the war in Yemen against Houthis, and after the assassination of journalist Jamal Khashoggi in October

2018. In France, the issue gained publicity after a new media outlet, *Disclose*, conducted an investigation based on a leaked document from the French military intelligence agency, which revealed that the French government was aware that arms sold by France to Saudi Arabia and the United Arab Emirates were used by those countries in offensive operations in Yemen that led to civilian casualties (*Disclose* NGO, 2019). In particular, the systems involved were CAESAR canons sold to Saudi Arabia, a Damocles targeting pod on Saudi aircraft, and Leclerc MBT, Mirage 2000 aircraft, as well as frigates sold to the UAE. The Macron government denied France's awareness that the French systems were used in attacks against civilians, and continued arms trade with those countries, despite having signed the international treaty on arms trade that prohibits arms sales in cases of attacks against civilians and risks of war crimes (Blandin, 2019). In 2015, President Hollande had cancelled the sale of Mistral-class amphibious assault ships to Russia, following Putin's annexation of Crimea and destabilisation of eastern Ukraine (the sale had been agreed by President Sarkozy in 2011, only three years after Russia's war against Georgia). In 2019, Macron's Minister for the Armed Forces Florence Parly said about Middle Eastern clients that their armaments first and foremost serve these countries' "legitimate security needs", and that maintaining economic relations with these countries allows France to "keep a hold over these regions that are key for our [France's] security, for our energy provisions" (Blandin, 2019).

Conclusion

Like many other aspects of France's defence policy, the understanding of the strategic importance of the DTIB and the institutional features of weapon procurement date back to the 1950s. The provision of arms has since been considered as one of the components of the founding principle of national independence. The strong preference for nationally produced equipment has required significant and steady spending on R&T, R&D, and procurement. Additionally, consolidations in the post-Cold-War era have led to the emergence of powerful national monopolies or duopolies – that is to say, reduced competition nationally. As a result, the French defence industry has a significant influence on procurement. In turn, the French state also maintains shares in some defence companies to a larger extent than other European governments or the United States do and seeks as much as possible to control the shareholding in these companies. State–industry relations are indeed close throughout the procurement process, under the supervision of the DGA, and the government is also strongly involved in supporting French arms exports. While this whole state of affairs has persisted over the past three decades, a rise in the cost of individual equipment, a decrease in defence budgets, greater international competition, and a need to access new technologies have led successive French governments to resort to transnational mergers or joint ventures to conduct about a quarter of equipment programs in cooperation (mostly with European partners), or to buy foreign equipment off the shelf. In the second half of the 2010s, the EU has more than ever been seen as a necessary vehicle for preserving the defence and technological industrial base.

Notes

1 Nexter merged with the German Krauss-Maffei (KMW) in 2015. KMW ranked 56 in 2017 with sales worth US$1,750 million.
2 Named Renault Trucks Defence until 2018.
3 Note that EDA data is not always complete for all member states.

References

Acosta, M. et al. (2018), "Patents and Dual-Use Technology: An Empirical Study of the World's Largest Defence Companies", *Defence and Peace Economics*, 29/7, 821–839.

André, F. and Pueyo, J. (2018), *Rapport d'information sur l'exécution de la loi de programmation militaire 2014–2019, Assemblée Nationale*, Report No.718, 22 February.

Anger, T. (2017), "Penser l'armée de l'air de demain: le système de combat aérien futur (SCAF)", *Revue Défense Nationale*, 93–96.

Armée de Terre (2018), "Scorpion: Modernising the Medium Combat Capabilities of the Combined Arms Battlegroup", 19 September. Available at: https://www.defense.gouv.fr/terre/equipements/scorpion/scorpion/scorpion2/presentation2 (last access, 13 December 2019).

Army Technology (n.d.), "Leclerc Main Battle Tank", no date. Available at: https://www.army-technology.com/projects/leclerc/ (last access, 13 December 2019).

Ballester, B. (2013), "The Cost of Non-Europe in Common Security and Defence Policy", European Parliamentary Research Service, CoNE 4/2013.

Belin, J. et al. (2019), "Defence Firms Adapting to Major Changes in the French R&D Funding System", *Defence and Peace Economics*, 30/2, 142–158.

Belin, J., Malizard, J. and Masson, H. (2019), "The French Defence Industry", in Hartley, K. and Belin, J. (eds.), *The Economics of the Global Defence Industry*. London: Routledge, 145–160.

Bellais, R. (2011), "Restructuration et Coopérations, l'Avenir de l'Industrie de Défense Française?", *Géoéconomie*, 57.

Bellais, R. and Droff, J., (2017), "Innovation et technologie dans l'armement: un modèle en nécessaire Transformation", *Annuaire Français des Relations Internationales*, 18.

Beraud-Sudreau, L. (2017), "La politique française de soutien aux exportations d'armement: raisons et limites d'un succès", *Focus stratégique*, 73, June.

Blandin, B. (2019), "Les exportations d'armement de la France restent confidentielles", *La Croix*, 5 June.

BPI France (2017), "Fonds d'investissement Definvest: pour qui, pour quoi?", 20 November. Available at https://www.bpifrance.fr/A-la-une/Actualites/Fonds-d-investissement-Definvest-pour-qui-pour-quoi-37744

Brustlein, C., de Durand, E. and Tenenbaum, E. (2014), *La Suprématie aérienne en péril: menaces et contre-stratégies à l'horizon 2030*. Paris: La Documentation Française.

Cabirol, M. (2013a), "Armement : les cinq erreurs capitales de l'Etat actionnaire", *La Tribune*, 9 April.

Cabirol, M. (2014), "Comment l'Etat s'est invité à la succession de Serge Dassault", *La Tribune*, 1 December.

Cabirol, M. (2018), "Renault Trucks Defense: Le Rebond Plutôt que le Crash?", *La Tribune*, 24 May.

Chesnais, F. and Serfati, C. (1992), *L'Armement en France: Genèse, Ampleur et Coût d'une Industrie*. Paris: Nathan.

Cohen, E. (1992), *Le Colbertisme High-tech: Economie des Telecom et du Grand Projet*. Paris: Hachette.

Cohen, S. (1994), *La défaite des généraux: Le pouvoir politique et l'armée sous la Vème République*. Paris: Fayard.

Cornu, C. (2001), "La forteresse Europe: Réalité ou virtualité?", in Schmitt, B. (ed.), *Entre coopération et concurrence: Le marché transatlantique de la défense*. Paris: European Union Institute for Security Studies.

Cour des Comptes (1997), *La Gestion Budgétaire et la Programmation au Ministere de la Défense*.

Cour des Comptes (2014), Rapport Public Annuel 2014, Tome 1, Vol. I-1.

Cour des Comptes (2018), "La coopération européenne en matière d'armement: Un renforcement nécessaire, soumis à des conditions exigeantes", *Rapport public Thématique – Synthèse*, April.

Darnis, J.P. (2020), "European Technological Sovereignty: A Response to the Covid-19 Crisis?", *Note de la FRS*, 45, 29 May.

Delerue F. (2018), "Stratégie juridique pour la cyberdéfense française", *Les Champs de Mars*, 30, 297–306.

Desforges, A. (2015), "Cybersecurité, Cyberdéfense: Une Nouvelle Demande pour une Nouvelle Menace", in Fleurant, A.-E (ed.), *Quelles Stratégies Face aux Mutations de L'économie de Défense Mondiale?*. Paris: IRSEM, 68–77.

DGA (2018), "Création de l'Agence de l'innovation de défense et nomination d'Emmanuel Chiva au poste de directeur", 5 September. Available at: https://www.defense.gouv.fr /dga/actualite/creation-de-l-agence-de-l-innovation-de-defense-et-nomination-d-emma nuel-chiva-au-poste-de-directeur (last access, 13 December 2019).

Disclose NGO (2019), "Made in France". Available at: https://made-in-france.disclose .ngo/fr/ (last access, 13 December 2019).

Droff, J. (2013), "Technological Change and Disruptive Trends in the Support of Defense Systems in France", *Journal of Innovation Economics & Management*, 12, 79–102.

Dunne, J. and Smith, J.P (2016), "The Evolution of Concentration in the Arms Market", *The Economics of Peace and Security Journal*, 11/1, 12–17.

Dussauge, P. and Cornu, C. (1998), *L'Industrie française de l'armement: Coopérations, restructurations et intégration européenne*. Paris: Economia.

Dyson, T. (2010), *Neoclassical Realism and Defence Reform in Post-Cold War Europe*. Basingstoke: Palgrave MacMillan.

European Council (2018), "Permanent Structured Cooperation (PESCO) Updated List of PESCO Projects—Overview", 19 November. Available at: https://www.consilium.eur opa.eu/media/37028/table-pesco-projects.pdf (last access, 13 december 2019).

European Defence Agency (2018), "EDA Collective and National Defence Data 2005– 2017e", *Defence Data Portal*. Available at: https://www.eda.europa.eu/info-hub/defen ce-data-portal.

Faure, S., Joltreau, T. and Smith, A. (2019), "Qui gouverne les grandes entreprises de la défense? Contribution sociologique à l'étude des capitalismes en France et au Royaume-Uni", *Revue Internationale de Politique Comparée*, online first.

Fawaz, M. et al. (2019), "Shareholder Nationality among the Major European and American Defense Contractors: An Exploratory Data Analysis", *Finance Bulletin*, 1/2, 36–49.

104 *Defence industry and procurement*

Fiott, D. (2019), *Yearbook of European Security*. Paris: European Union Institute for Security Studies.

Fleurant, A. et al. (2018), "The Sipri Top 100 Arms Producing and Military Services Companies, 2017", *SIPRI Fact Sheet*, December. Available at: https://www.sipri.org /sites/default/files/2018-12/fs_arms_industry_2017_0.pdf (last access, 13 December 2019).

Fleurant, A.-E. and Quéau, Y. (2014), "L'Industrie de Défense Française: Une Autonomie Stratégique sous Contrainte", *GRIP, Note d'Analyse*, 1 September.

Fontanela, J. and Hébert, J.-P. (1997), "The End of the 'French Grandeur Policy'", *Defence and Peace Economics*, 8/1, 37–55.

Foucault, M. (2012), "The Defence Budget in France: Between Denial and Decline", *Focus stratégique*, 36 bis, December.

Fouquet, C. and A. Bauer (2019), "Bond de 30 % des exportations françaises d"armement en 2018", *Les Echos*, 18 April.

Genieys, W. and Michel, L. (2004), "Le Leclerc ou l'invention du 'meilleur char du monde'", in Genieys, W. (ed.), *Le choix des armes: Théories, acteurs et politiques*. Paris: CNRS éditions, 83–113.

Guillermard, V. (2014), "La Direction générale de l'armement se réforme", *Le Figaro*, 18 February.

Guillermard, V. (2019), "Sous-marins: Naval Group et l'Australie signent un partenariat stratégique", *Le Figaro*, 13 February.

Hartley, K. and Solomon, B. (2016), "Special Issue: Defence Inflation", *Defence and Peace Economics*, 27/2, 172–175.

Hoeffler, C. (2008), "Les réformes des systèmes d'acquisition d'armement en France et en Allemagne: un retour paradoxal des militaires?" *Revue internationale de Politique Comparée*, 15/1, 133–150.

James, A.D. (2004), "L'évolution de la Coopération Franco-britannique en Matière d'Armements: du Jaguar au Futur Porte-avions", in Hébert, J.-P. and Hamiot, J. (eds.), *Histoire de la coopération européenne dans l'armement*. Paris: CNRS éditions, 99–121.

Joana, J. (2008), "Armée et industrie de défense: cousinage nécessaire et liaisons incestueuses", *Pouvoirs*, 2/125, 43–54.

Journal officiel de la République française (2013), *LOI n° 2013-1168 du 18 décembre 2013 relative à la programmation militaire pour les années 2014 à 2019 et portant diverses dispositions concernant la défense et la sécurité nationale*, 19 December.

Kapstein, E. (2009), "Smart Defense Acquisition: Learning from French Procurement Reform", Policy Brief, Center for a New American Security.

Kirkpatrick, D. (2004), "Trends in the Costs of Weapon Systems and the Consequences", *Defence and Peace Economics*, 15/3, 259–276.

Lagneau, L. (2019), "Otan: L'armée de Terre sera bientôt de retour en Estonie, avec 4 chars Leclerc et 13 VBCI", *Opex 360*, 12 April. Available at: http://www.opex360.com/2019 /04/12/otan-larmee-de-terre-sera-bientot-de-retour-en-estonie-avec-4-chars-leclerc-et -13-vbci/ (last access, 13 December 2019).

Le Monde (1981), "M. Jobert: lorsque la France vend des armes à un pays, elle ne le prive pas de sa liberté", 12 October.

Macias, A. (2019), "American Firms Rule the $398 Billion Global Arms Industry: Here's a Roundup of the World's Top 10 Defense Contractors, by Sales", *CNBC*, 10 December. Available at: https://www.cnbc.com/2019/01/10/top-10-defense-contractors-in-the-worl d.html (last access, 13 December 2019).

Maldera, N. (2016), "La Mutation Technologique de l'Armée de Terre, le Cas du Programme Scorpion", *Fondation IFRAP*, 20 June. Available at: https://www.ifrap.org/etat-et-colle ctivites/la-mutation-technologique-de-larmee-de-terre-le-cas-du-programme-scorpion

Malizard, J. (2013), "Dépenses de défense et activité économique: quelles influences?", *Revue Défense Nationale*, 75–80.

Malizard, J. (2019), "Introduction", *Defence and Peace Economics*, 30/2, 133–141.

Marine Nationale (2018), *Plan Mercator*.

Marzolf, E. (2018), "Comment va fonctionner la nouvelle Agence de l'innovation de défense", *Acteurs Publics*, 15 November. Available at: https://www.acteurspublics .com/2018/11/15/comment-va-fonctionner-la-nouvelle-agence-de-l-innovation-de-de fense (last access, 13 December 2019).

Masson, H. (2003), "Les industries de défense en Europe", *Géoéconomie*, 26, 41–65.

Masson, H. (2007), "L'industrie de défense française à la croisée des chemins. Partie 1: Industries de défense et actionnariat public: une singularité française", in Fondation pour la Recherche Stratégique (ed.), Annuaire Stratégique et militaire 2006–2007, Fondation pour la Recherche Stratégique. Paris: Odile Jacob.

Mawdsley, J. (2013), "The A400M Project: From Flagship Project to Warning for European Defence Cooperation", *Defence Studies*, 13/1, 14–32.

Ministère de la Défense, (2010), "La DGA prend une nouvelle direction", *Direction Générale de l'Armement*, October. Available at: https://www.defense.gouv.fr/content /download/17136/149046/plaquette_organisation_dga_vf_201010.pdf

Ministère des Armées (2017), *Defence and National Security Strategic Review*.

Ministère des Armées (2019a), *Eléments Publics de Doctrine Militaire de Lutte Informatique Offensive*.

Ministère des Armées (2019b), *Rapport au Parlement sur les exportations d'armement de la France*.

Moura, S. (2018), "La R&D militaire: Le lien industrie-état", Ecodef No.117, Ministère des Armées. Available at: https://www.defense.gouv.fr/content/download/549341/936 4770/EcoDef%20117.pdf (last access, 14 January 2020).

Moura, S. and Oudot, J.-M. (2014), "Le rôle clé de la BITD dans les exportations civiles et militaires de la France", Ecodef No.68, Ministère des Armées. Available at: https:/ /www.defense.gouv.fr/content/download/440815/6885702/Ecodef68.pdf (last access, 13 December 2019).

Oudot, J.-M. (2017), "Efforts d'Equipement de Défense: Un Coût Net Modéré pour l'Etat", Ministère de la Défense, Bulletin de l'Observatoire Economique de la Défense, No.91.

Oudot, J.-M. and Bellais, R. (2008), "Choix contractuels et innovation: le cas de l'approvisionnement de Défense", *Innovations*, 28, 85–103.

Pappalardo, D. (2018), "The Future of the French Air Force: A Future Combat Air System as a Strategy to Counter Access Denial", *Over the Horizon*, 5 February.

Premier Ministre (1994), *Livre Blanc sur la Defence*. Paris: La Documentation Francaise.

Premier Ministre (2008), *The French White Paper on Defence and National Security*. Paris: Odile Jacob.

Présidence de la République (2013), *White Paper on Defence and National Security*.

Secrétariat Général à la Défense et la Sécurité Nationale (2018), *Revue Stratégique de Cyberdéfense*.

Sénat (2018), *Rapport Annexé à la loi n° 2018-607 relative à la programmation militaire pour les années 2019 à 2025 et portant diverses dispositions intéressant la défense*.

Serfati, C. (2014), *L'Industrie française de l'armement*. Paris: La Documentation française.

106 *Defence industry and procurement*

SIPRI (2018), "Global Arms Industry: US Companies Dominate the Top 100; Russian Arms Industry Moves to Second Place", 10 December. Available at: https://www.sipri.org/media/press-release/2018/global-arms-industry-us-companies-dominate-top-100-russian-arms-industry-moves-second-place (last access, 13 December 2019).

Steininger, P. (2017), "Vers un durcissement des conditions d'engagement des forces aérospatiales", *Revue Défense Nationale*, 77–81.

Trucy, F., Masseret, J.-P. and Guené, C. (2008), *Avis présenté au nom de la commission des finances sur le projet de loi relatif à la programmation militaire pour les années 2009 à 2014 et portant diverses dispositions concernant la défense, Sénat, Session extraordinaire de 2008–2009.*

Vaïsse, M. (ed.) (2002), *Armement et Vème République*. Paris: CNRS Editions.

Wyckaert, M. (2019), "Près de 30 Milliards de Chiffre d'Affaires Militaire pour les Entreprises Industrielles de la BITD en 2017 2019", Ecodef No.133, Ministère des Armées. Available at: https://www.jpgilon.insee.fr/jspui/bitstream/1/105565/1/EcoDef_Stat_%20133.pdf (last access, 13 December 2019).

5 At war: French military operations since 1991

For the RAND senior political scientist Michael Shurkin,

> There is a French way of warfare that reflects the French military's lack of resources and its modest sense of what it can achieve. They specialise in carefully apportioned and usually small but lethal operations, often behind the scenes; they can go bigger if they have help from the U.S. and other allies—which they will probably have in any case and know how to put to good use.
> (Shurkin, 2015; See also Chivvis, 2016)

For Shurkin, the French military's sense of its relative lack of resources compared with Paris' high international ambitions has several consequences:

> One is an insistence on modest objectives, on limiting strictly the aims of a military invention in line with a modest assessment of what the military can accomplish. The French thus aim low and strive to achieve the minimal required. (…) Another feature of the French way of war is scale. Whereas the U.S. military tends toward a 'go big or go home' approach to war—American planners arguably take for granted their ability to marshal vast resources and firepower—the French military embraces "going" small. (…) This requires knowing how much is enough, not to mention accepting risk that Americans would prefer not to run and largely do not have to.
> (Shurkin, 2015)

Shurkin may be slightly optimistic. The French are no stranger to mission creep (Le Flem and Oliva, 2018) and the relative lack of resources may have some benefits but is also an important challenge. Yet, it is undeniable that recent military interventions, particularly in Mali and the Sahel, have demonstrated that French forces are capable of planning and conducting effective military operations. As Olivier Zajec has documented, French military interventionism has taken several forms since the 1960s: post-colonial warfare in Africa in support of regimes with which France had defence agreements, followed by participation in peacekeeping operations in the 1990s, and the subsequent participation in coalition warfare through NATO operations in Kosovo and Afghanistan (Zajec, 2018). In a

108   *French military operations since 1991*

sense, the Serval and Barkhane operations in the Sahel are a culmination of several trends in French warfare, since they involve robust use of force in Africa, a degree of cooperation with the UN in a peacekeeping operation, foreign military assistance, and coalition warfare.

This chapter traces the evolution of French military operations in the post-Cold-War era and discusses their role in the achievement of the French grand strategic objectives.

The Gulf War: the "mother of all battles"

As discussed in chapters 1 and 2, the Gulf War triggered a number of major transformations of the French defence system, including the move towards jointness and the eventual implementation of an all-volunteer force model. The Gulf War was politically challenging for France, which aimed to maintain a degree of independence while still appearing as a responsible stakeholder in the international system. French policy-makers faced the difficulty of having to reconcile several diverging incentives. First, Iraq was a long-time trade partner for France and the Iraqi army was partly equipped with French material. However, the invasion was clearly recognised as a breach of international law, was condemned in a day, and Iraqi financial assets were immediately frozen. More important to French diplomacy was the need to maintain good relations with other Arab countries. In that perspective, the best outcome for French diplomacy would have been an Arab solution to the crisis. However, when it became clear that a US-led and Arab-backed intervention was inevitable, and that French attempts at independent diplomacy were not producing the desired effect, François Mitterrand decided to engage more firmly on the coalition's side.

Reconciling politicians' desire to appear autonomous, while also contributing to Saudi Arabia's defence proved difficult to military professionals. When the French were informed of the coalition's plans for the war in November 1990, they had to decide how they would be integrated. Defence Minister Chevènement favoured an assault with the Arab forces, which would signal the French ties with the Arab world while being independent of the United States. Admiral Lanxade, chief of Mitterrand's private military staff, favoured a central assault with the US VII Corps, while the Chief of Staff General Schmitt (concerned about the lightly armoured French vehicles) advocated protecting the flank of the main offensive, alongside the US XVIII Airborne Corps. As Head of the Armed Forces, Mitterrand had to make the decision of which option to pursue and finally decided to cooperate with the XVIII Airborne Corps. According to DeVore:

> While sensitive to military advice, Mitterrand's choice was shaped by political calculations. By operating on the coalitions' westernmost edge, French forces would possess greater autonomy and only encounter second-line Iraqi units. France could keep its casualties to a minimum and have the cache of

operating deep inside Iraq. The downside of this choice was that the mission was peripheral, rather than essential, to the coalition's effort.

(DeVore, 2012, p. 72)

The force generation process was cumbersome. Mitterrand promised on 9 January 1991 (a week before the end of the UN ultimatum) that he would not send conscripts to the conflict, an important decision that contributed to the establishment of an all-volunteer army five years later (Irondelle, 2011). But this decision posed important operational problems. For example, the French navy ships routinely had between 20% and 30% of their crew made of conscripts and had to stop their operations for a week before new volunteers could arrive. About half of the conscripts signed a three-year contract with the navy and stayed onboard their ships (Bonnot, 2001).

The same problems appeared for the army, and the French division (codename Daguet) was made of several already professionalised battalions drawn from various regiments. This "patchwork" ended up working relatively well in practice during the military action, but the logistical and organisational constraints raised by Mitterrand's decision were intense. The political decision ultimately limited the size of the French contribution: due to her other commitments for example in Africa, France could not generate more than 15,000 professional soldiers to make up the Daguet division. The other members of the coalition, in particular the Americans, recognised the tactical and operational skills of the French forces. Cordesman and Wagner write that: "French forces fought well during *Desert Storm* and played a major role in securing the coalition's western flank and the Advance of the XVIII Corp" (Cordesman and Wagner, 1996, p. 170), while Houlahan calls the commander of the Daguet division, General Janvier, a: "very competent office" (Houlahan, 1999, p. 238). Nevertheless, the limited French contribution meant that the Daguet division was assigned a peripheral role in the campaign. Overall, "The integration and quality levels of the French forces were lower than those of the British, and that strongly reduced the utility of the French participation" (Schmitt, 2018, p. 68).

The Gulf War illustrated a number of lacking capabilities in the French armed forces and many lessons had to be learned from it. First, contrary to the previous French doctrine, a major engagement of the French forces could happen outside of the European territory, and France had to be ready for such a contingency. Second, a high-intensity crisis could not be managed by a single European power alone: major interventions would have to be conducted in a multinational/coalition framework. Third, the political decision to not mobilise the conscripts created logistical difficulties but also eroded the social basis and justification for the draft: what good are conscripts if they are not to be sent to war on behalf of their country? Finally, the Gulf War illustrated the growing need to modernise key systems in the armed forces. As such, the lessons learned from the Gulf War largely shaped the transformation of the French post-Cold-War defence apparatus.

110   *French military operations since 1991*

Peacekeeping in practice: the Balkans, Somalia, and Lebanon

The Balkans

While the French forces were still learning the lessons from the Gulf War, they were quickly engaged in a peacekeeping operation in the Balkans. Created in 1992, the UNPROFOR (United Nations Protection Force) was tasked with creating the peace and security conditions required for solving the unfolding conflict in ex-Yugoslavia, applying the peace plan drafted by Cyrus Vance, and envisioning a combination of a ceasefire between the different belligerents, the establishment of a "safe area", and a demilitarisation of the population. As part of the UNPROFOR (which comprised a total of 30,000 soldiers from 17 different nationalities), France deployed 2,200 soldiers in April 1992. However, the security situation kept getting worse, and the UNPROFOR did not have the relevant rules of engagement at its disposal in order to effectively enforce the ceasefires and safety zones. Following the declaration of independence of Bosnia-Herzegovina in 1992, which triggered an intervention of both Croatian and Serbian forces backing armed groups along ethnic lines, the conflict expanded to the rest of the country. As early as 4 May 1992, the Bosnian leadership asked for an extension of the UNPROFOR to the country, but it was only after François Mitterrand staged a dramatic visit to Sarajevo on 28 June that the Security Council agreed to such an extension. In 1993, the security and political situation kept worsening, and the commander of the UNPROFOR, the French General Morillon, obtained the authorisation to deploy heavier weapons (such as mortars and artillery) and a relative relaxation of the rules of engagement, specifically in cases of self-defence. General Morillon also visited Srebrenica in order to raise awareness of the Serbian siege of the city, which led to the city being added to the list of "safe area" allegedly protected by the UNPROFOR. This concept of safe areas was particularly supported by France, which saw it as an alternative to the more coercive approach that was favoured in Washington. However, this solution was not sustainable in the long term in the absence of a political will to grant the UNPROFOR more coercive means to enforce the agreements. The UNPROFOR's relative weakness was illustrated by the attack on the Markale marketplace in Sarajevo on 5 February 1994, which led to the killing of 68 civilians, wounding 144. This attack shocked international public opinion, leading to NATO's involvement in the crisis.

In 1995, the UNPROFOR was reorganised. While its mandate was limited to Bosnia-Herzegovina, two other missions were created: the United Nations Preventive Deployment Force (UNPREDEP) in Macedonia and the United Nations Confidence Restoration Operation in Croatia (UNCRO). At this stage, the UNPROFOR comprised 38,000 soldiers, of which 7,100 were French. On 26 and 27 May 1995, following aerial bombardment by NATO airplanes, the Serbian forces captured 200 blue helmets from the UNPROFOR in order to hold them as hostages. French soldiers were captured by the Serbian forces near the Vrbanja bridge. This event outraged the newly elected President Jacques Chirac, who gave the order to take back the position on the bridge by force. On 27 May 1995, a section from the first section of the third *Régiment d'Infanterie de Marine*

French military operations since 1991   111

led the assault on the bridge, killing four Serbian soldiers and capturing four others (two French soldiers were killed in the engagement). This combat action became famous in the French armed forces in the post-Cold-War era for two reasons. First, after what was perceived as four years of humiliation imposed by the Serbian armed forces because of the extremely restricting UN rules of engagement (that prevented French troops from conducting offensive operations), the assault symbolically marked the new policy of refusing further abuses from the belligerents. Second, the assault is, to date, the last combat action in which French troops had to engage in such close-quarter battles that they had to make use of their bayonets against enemy forces: in an era in which the "combat" dimension of soldiers' identity was blurred through the constant messaging of being "soldiers for peace" (see chapter 1), the brutality of the action resonated with a heroic imaginary (Sandahl, 2019). The officer commanding the assault on the ground, Captain Lecointre, would end up having a stellar career in the armed forces, being appointed as chief of the general staff in 2017.

Following the Serbian attempt to coerce the UN forces, France pushed for the establishment of a Rapid Reaction Force (RRF), adopted by a UNSC resolution on 15 June 1995. This RFF was made up of 4,200 British, Dutch, and French soldiers (2,000 were French). While officially part of the UNPROFOR, it was under the operational command of the UN military authorities (not the civilian ones) and could rely on air support from the NATO operation Deliberate Force. Because the RRF had more operational flexibility, France insisted that the troops composing it operated under a national uniform, without the blue helmet and the white vehicles. The Serbian-committed massacre of Srebrenica (from 11 July onwards) led to an intensification of the NATO airstrikes, which accelerated the political solution to the crisis: the Dayton agreements were signed in December 1995, and the UNPROFOR was replaced by the Implementation Force – IFOR – under NATO command (60,000 soldiers, of which 7,500 were French). The IFOR was subsequently replaced by the Stabilisation Force (SFOR) in December 1996 (32,000 soldiers, of which 5,500 were French). The peacekeeping experience in the Balkans has been marked by what André Thiéblemont (2002) called "the tactical breakdown". Thiéblemont argues that the operational concept underpinning the peacekeeping operations between 1992 and 1995 was a form of "pacifist-deterring ideology" that was a side effect of the French strategic preference for nuclear deterrence. In short, the logic of deterrence at the strategic level had gradually been diffused to the operational and tactical levels, leading to concepts of force employment (imposing peace through the *presence* and not the *actions* of foreign troops) that were disconnected from the actual dynamics of the conflict. As such, the fundamentals of military planning were overlooked in the Balkans, contributing to the general ineffectiveness of the UN troops in establishing peace: bases were established in the middle of disputed areas (under Serbian or Bosnian fire) or in the middle of Serbian forces (thus becoming willing hostages). This planning without strategic intent logically diminished the freedom of action of the French troops, which sometimes had to negotiate safe passage (or renounce when challenged) and had difficulties mounting basic manoeuvres in which units

112 *French military operations since 1991*

would be mutually supportive, and thus effective support for coercive action. This operational approach (or rather, the lack thereof), created numerous frustrations among the units deployed on the ground, until the end of the UNPROFOR. Once the IFOR/SFOR was established (and later the Kosovo Force – KFOR – following the 1999 war to stop the mass massacres ongoing in Kosovo), military and civilian leaders acknowledged that the "pacifist-deterring ideology" had led to an abysmal operational failure, which triggered an adjustment of the rules of engagement and operational concepts towards more controlled aggressiveness. For example, French troops were authorised to be more coercive, and thus more efficient, during their KFOR mandate: they were deployed in the northern part of Kosovo (near Serbia), which included the disputed city of Mitrovica; on several occasions (most notably in 2000 and 2008), French troops had to use force to enforce the peacekeeping mandate, and the mission led to the doctrinal development of more robust forms of peacekeeping in the French armed forces. French troops would remain in the Balkans until 2014 when the last remaining 320 French soldiers still deployed in Kosovo as part of the KFOR were repatriated.

Somalia

While French troops were being deployed in the Balkans, they were simultaneously being sent to Somalia, as part of the United Nations Operations in Somalia I and II (UNSOM I and II). On 3 December 1992, UN Resolution 794 authorised the deployment of a military force tasked with establishing a safe environment for humanitarian operations. The second-largest contingent of this United Task Force (UNITAF) was the French contingent (2,000 troops): President François Mitterrand had deemed it important to show the French diplomatic commitment to the peace process, and also had an eye on potential post-conflict reconstruction contracts. During the first phase of the deployment, French troops intervened in the Bakool, a border region with Ethiopia of strategic interest as it was used as an entry point by foreign fighters and was hosting 20,000 refugees. The tasks assigned to the French troops were both counter-guerrilla warfare and the protection of humanitarian aid. After the UNSOM 2 was established in April 1993, the French troops were redeployed to the Baidoa region. The first phase of the deployment was clearly coercive, as French troops had to establish control of the major cities and axes of communication. After about a month, the main effort shifted to political-administrative building.

However, the brutal degradation of the security situation in Mogadishu had an impact on the overall French contribution. On 5 June 1993, 24 Pakistani soldiers were killed in an ambush, which led to a counter-operation by members of an American quick reaction force and other UN troops already present (including a French company of 200 soldiers). The intense urban fighting that occurred between 16 and 18 June was considered a tactical success but generated a number of frustrations for France. First, during the operation itself, the general staff in Paris was left in the dark, without regular updates, while the French officers inserted within the UNSOM II headquarters were relegated to secondary roles.

French military operations since 1991 113

This frustration led to the decision to withdraw the French forces earlier than was originally planned, and the bulk of the French contingent withdrew from Somalia between December 1993 and January 1994. Interestingly, the intervention in Somalia, albeit generally overlooked, was announcing a number of battlefield conditions that the French troops would encounter in the 21st century: the return of high-intensity urban warfare, the challenge of coordinating contingents from different countries (the first example of coalition warfare that France would experience again in Afghanistan, Libya, and the Sahel), and the blending of combat and humanitarian activities.

Lebanon

Finally, another major peacekeeping operation for the French forces in the post-Cold-War era has been the participation in the United Nations Interim Force in Lebanon I and II (UNIFIL I and II). After the Litani operation – the Israeli intervention in Lebanon in 1978 – the UN Security Council adopted Resolution 425 calling for the respect of the Lebanese sovereignty and created the UNIFIL to monitor the withdrawal of the Israeli force. The UNIFIL was composed of 4,000 blue helmets, of which 730 were French. However, the UNIFIL troops were quickly embroiled in the local dynamics of the emerging civil war and were being targeted by the belligerents. The French contingent gradually increased in order to adjust to this degraded environment, and reached 1,400 soldiers in 1984, in particular following the Beirut attacks of 23 October 1983, in which 241 US Marines and 58 French soldiers were killed. However, due to a lack of resources and a limiting operational mandate, the UNIFIL had to witness three Israeli interventions in Lebanon (1982, 1986, 1996) without being able to enforce its mandate. In 2005, the main contingents manning the UNIFIL were coming from China, Ghana, and India, with the French contribution limited to 200 soldiers.

The 2006 war between Israel and Hezbollah led to a reinforcement of the French presence. The UNIFIL II was created by UN Resolution 1701 (August 2006), with a more coercive mandate than UNIFIL I. Initially 1,600 French soldiers were deployed, with heavy armaments such as the Leclerc main battle tanks and artillery units, and 900 French soldiers are still in operation at the time of writing. The peacekeeping experience of the French forces in Lebanon was starkly different from the one in the Balkans between 1992 and 1995. Emboldened by a mandate asking for the demilitarisation of the area, French troops usually engaged in tactics revelatory of a culture of "controlled assertiveness" (Ruffa, 2019). French troops conducted frequent patrols in order to prevent weapons smuggling, used the Leclerc MBTs as a show of force and granted little attention to civil–military cooperation (CIMIC) activities:

> from a French unit perspective, in an area where Hezbollah was very strong, it was pivotal to show their presence and deter hostile activities with frequent night patrols with heavy vehicles. The drawback of this approach was that the local population perceived it as aggressive, as the heavy tanks destroyed

114 *French military operations since 1991*

roads. (...) However, by dedicating less attention to humanitarian activities, the French unit was better able to accomplish the mandate's aim of creating an area free from weapons smuggling and preventing hostile activities at the border.

(Ruffa, 2019, p. 56)

The French participation in UNIFIL II is a good illustration of how peacekeeping practices have evolved within the French armed forces since the initial deployment in the Balkans: the body of doctrine has been reinforced and the experience acquired in more demanding operations, such as in Afghanistan, coupled with the overall evolution of peacekeeping mandates towards more robust forms of engagement contributed to overcome the "tactical breakdown" observed just after the end of the Cold War.

Learning coalition warfare: Kosovo, Afghanistan, Libya, and Syria/Iraq

An important trend for French military operations in the post-Cold-War era has been the discovery of coalition warfare, first during the Gulf War, but mostly through the interventions in Kosovo, Afghanistan, Libya, and Syria/Iraq. While France was officially not part of NATO's integrated military structure during the Cold War (and until 2008), military arrangements existed between the French armed forces and NATO for joint planning in case of conflict. But this cooperation was orders of magnitude more limited than the integration with other military forces that French forces had to implement after the Cold War. Such integration was first experienced, with difficulty, during the 1999 NATO intervention in Kosovo.

Kosovo

France played an active, albeit sometimes confusing role during the 1999 Kosovo crisis. In particular, the French government was divided on the issue, and the rampant rivalry between the left-wing government and the right-wing President Chirac (a political situation known as "cohabitation") complicated the matter further. Overall, France was uncomfortable letting NATO operate without the political blessing of the United Nations, which also resonated with some of the country's concerns for the future of the European security architecture. Nevertheless, the good personal relations between Bill Clinton and Jacques Chirac eased the tensions between the two countries (de la Sablière, 2013).

When the tensions in Kosovo restarted at the beginning of January 1999, France proposed hosting a conference in Rambouillet Castle on the model of the 1995 conference hosted by the United States in Dayton. French Foreign Minister Hubert Védrine co-presided the debates with his British counterpart Robin Cook. The conference lasted from 6 to 23 February 1999. In the meantime, Jacques Chirac was on an official trip to Washington, DC, during which he insisted on his

French military operations since 1991   115

"unrestricted" support for Bill Clinton and encouraged Milosevic to choose the "path of wisdom, and not the path of war" (Nouzille, 2012, p. 511). After the failure of the Rambouillet negotiations, France supported the airstrikes that started on 24 March 1999. France was committed to the intervention for two main reasons. First, French political leaders stressed on numerous occasions that the crisis in Kosovo could endanger the stability of the entire Balkan region and create security and migration problems for the European Union. The fear of a long-standing regional instability that would have followed almost a decade of complicated missions in the Balkans was a powerful motivation for French policy-makers. France had an ambition of proving that, after the Cold War, Europe was able and ready to take care of its own security and that NATO's role and structures had to be adjusted to a new strategic context (see chapter 6; see also Schmitt, 2017a). In that sense, France had to participate in the strikes, as it could not afford to appear inconsistent on issues pertaining to European security.

However, France was deeply uncomfortable with the decision to launch military action without the approval of the United Nations Security Council. As a permanent member of the UNSC, France traditionally sees the legitimacy and the standing conferred by this position as a force multiplier and a possibility to punch above its weight on the international stage. Thus, the bypassing of the United Nations could potentially backfire and possibly undermine France's diplomatic standing in the medium term. Throughout the crisis, France took great pains to insist on the fact that the intervention was an exception and that any settlement should be obtained through a UN resolution. This willingness to put the UN at the centre of a peace agreement clashed with the preferences of many in the United States who preferred bypassing the UN entirely. However, this issue was of crucial importance to the French, who insisted on discussing it during the NATO summit and did not hesitate to publicly express their differences with the United States (Davidson, 2011).

France put a particular emphasis on the relationship with Russia. With NATO just expanding to former members of the Warsaw Pact in 1999, tensions with Russia were on the rise. The air campaign against a country obviously supported by Moscow did nothing to improve the climate. In this context, France emphasised the necessary inclusion of Russia in any post-war settlement. This was consistent with the French willingness to obtain a UNSC resolution after the conflict that would serve as a peace agreement, which required Russian cooperation. French diplomacy maintained permanent contact with Russia during the crisis, both bilaterally and in multinational settings, in order to prepare the ground for the discussions at the UNSC. The main locus of this diplomatic activity was the G8, which had the advantage of reuniting four of the five permanent members of the Security Council. In fact, the resolution adopted by the G8 on 6 May 1999 served as the basis for the UNSC resolution adopted in June.

On the issue of deploying ground forces, there seems to have been diverging opinions amongst French policy-makers. One week before the offensive, Prime Minister Jospin refused to exclude the possibility of using ground forces, although Foreign Minister Védrine had claimed the contrary the day before, an option that

116 *French military operations since 1991*

Jospin himself deemed "completely premature" one week later. Health Minister Kouchner declared several times that he would favour the use of ground troops, while Védrine consistently opposed the idea. At a meeting in Bonn at the end of May, the British, French, German, Italian, and American defence ministers seriously considered a ground invasion, which would have taken place in late June or early July. Yet, the French publicly declined that they seriously considered this option, probably for internal political reasons. With the communists in the government opposed to the war, and a large part of the traditional right-wing electorate also denouncing a US-led intervention, the government had to walk a fine line to strike the right balance between the preservation of French strategic interests and the management of the internal political context (MacLeod, 2000). As a result, France sent mixed signals on the issue of the ground troops, secretly considering the option and discussing it with partners, while in the meantime publicly denying this possibility.

To summarise, France played its traditional role as a reliable NATO ally in a time of crisis while also trying to bridge the gap between the West and Russia on the Kosovo issue. In a sense, the crisis is typical of the French diplomatic preferences: siding with the allies while trying to maximise its degree of autonomy.

In military terms, France was the primary European contributor to the campaign, both in terms of aircraft deployed and in the number of sorties flown. The French military contribution was meaningful because of the specific capabilities deployed. French planes could conduct all-weather reconnaissance and strike missions, engage high-value targets with precision-guided munitions (PGMs), and operate relatively smoothly with allied planes, a significant improvement from the Gulf War. Moreover, France deployed the aircraft carrier *Foch* in the Adriatic Sea, which allowed the Super Étendard aircraft to operate from a location close to the area of operations (Schmitt, 2018).

As it turned out, France was very much aware of the diplomatic advantage associated with a high level of integration in the campaign. As McLeod (2000) argues, the expected diplomatic gain in the medium term was a rearrangement of the European security architecture that would leave more responsibilities to the Europeans (see Chapter 6). But France also vetoed a number of targets within Serbia in order to avoid civilian casualties. The French officials opposed targeting television towers, bridges, oil refineries, or the Yugoslavian power grid. Chirac also opposed the targeting of the socialist party headquarters in Belgrade because intelligence estimated that the worst-case scenario would be a loss of 350 people, including 250 in the apartments nearby (Cordesman, 2001). This led to some frustration in the United States, the focus of which was the French refusal for some time to bomb two television towers and a number of key bridges in Belgrade. The differences in the approaches were clear: to the USAF planners, hitting such targets would inflict suffering on the Milosevic regime and would facilitate its compliance. On the contrary, the French argued that punishing and antagonising the Serbian population would be disastrous for the post-conflict political climate. This issue became the most central point of friction between the United States and France and the lens through which French participation became interpreted

French military operations since 1991   117

in American circles. For the French armed forces, the operation demonstrated the possibility of integrating with a coalition framework, despite a number of frustrations related to the US domination of the campaign.

Afghanistan

Shortly after the end of the Kosovo operation, the United States was attacked by Islamist terrorists affiliated with Al-Qaeda on 9/11. The United States and a coalition of willing allies decided to overthrow the Taliban regime in Afghanistan in retaliation for having sheltered Al-Qaeda. The objective was to deny Al-Qaeda the safe haven the organisation had enjoyed with the cooperation of the Taliban regime in order to diminish the threat of future attacks. The quick defeat of the Taliban regime led to the establishment of several international mechanisms at the Bonn conference of December 2001 to build, or re-build, the country; one such mechanism being the creation of the International Security Assistance Force (ISAF). Although initially restrained from supporting the American initiatives (which was useful per se but limited), France gained momentum in 2008 by forcing NATO to think strategically about Afghanistan at the Bucharest summit, and has been a proactive country since then, as demonstrated at the Lisbon and Chicago summits. In military terms, the French contribution was extremely limited until 2008. The French then moved to the Kapisa and Surobi districts until 2012, where they managed to improve the security conditions while on the ground, but these successes were short-lived because, despite its tactical excellence during the last two years of the French campaign, the lack of available troops prevented France from achieving lasting success in these two districts.

While France did not participate in the military campaign that toppled the Taliban, Paris sent troops to Afghanistan as early as December 2001. Yet, the French strategy was still unclear and did not go beyond a display of solidarity for the United States. The initial objective was then limited to ensure the security of the new Afghan administration. Prime Minister Lionel Jospin explained to the National Assembly on 12 December that the mission would be short, "no more than a few months", and that France could participate by providing security to the buildings and personnel of the newly established Afghan administration, and eventually participate in the training of the Afghan security forces. Thus, France initially tried to properly balance its support for the United States with an apparent lack of strategic interests in Afghanistan. Between 2001 and 2004, there was a lack of interest in Paris for the Afghan mission, which translated into a fairly limited military commitment but did not contradict the official political support for the mission, expressed on several occasions.

In fact, French political support was fluctuating and certainly not linearly (Barat-Ginies, 2011). In 2003–2004, France agreed to let NATO take responsibility for the ISAF mission, in large part because it would help heal the wounds of the transatlantic crisis over Iraq. France even increased its commitment and took command of ISAF through the Eurocorps between August 2004 and February 2005, and deployed (in agreement with Germany) elements of the Franco-German

118   *French military operations since 1991*

Brigade to Kabul to provide security to the city. This increased commitment was supposed to be proof of France's commitment to the mission and transatlantic relations, while at the same time giving a European blueprint for the mission through the participation of the Eurocorps and the Franco-German Brigade. Yet, France had its own separate agenda that antagonised its partners. First, France was keen on keeping NATO limited to purely military tasks, a key aspect of France's security policy at the time. Thus, it refused to contribute to the establishment of Provincial Reconstruction Teams (PRTs) that mixed military and civilian resources, which were extremely important to the Germans. Moreover, France tried to erect a firewall between Operation Enduring Freedom and the ISAF mission, with the explicit goal of not conflating the ISAF mission with counter-terrorism. When ISAF expanded to the whole of Afghanistan in 2006, the allies contributed by sending more troops on the ground. Yet, President Chirac, still very sceptical about the soundness of the strategic approach and the utility of conducting the campaign, refused to increase the French commitment at NATO's Riga summit in 2006.

This attitude changed with the election of President Nicolas Sarkozy in 2007. One of the most visible signs of France's new diplomatic posture was the president's willingness to reintegrate France within NATO integrated military command. France's return to the military structure contributed to changing NATO's Afghan policy. The return became official during NATO's 50th summit jointly organised by France and Germany in 2009, but negotiations began as soon as Sarkozy arrived in power in 2007. One of the defining moments was the Bucharest summit in April 2008, during which Nicolas Sarkozy laid out the necessity of a strategy for Afghanistan. This move was in fact successful as NATO adopted the Comprehensive Strategic Political-Military Plan (CSPMP), which became the blueprint for the action of the alliance in Afghanistan. France also supported the Intequal strategy adopted at Lisbon in 2010 and was one of the key countries during the 2012 NATO summit in Chicago, where the exit strategy was officially adopted (Schmitt, 2017b).

Yet, France's commitment changed after François Hollande was elected in May 2012. One of his campaign pledges was to withdraw French "combat troops" from Afghanistan by the end of 2012, which he did, thus substantially reducing the French presence in the country.

In military terms, the first French forces to arrive in Afghanistan were ISR planes of the French Air Force (Transall Gabriel and Mirage IVP), based in the United Arab Emirates, which began gathering intelligence as early as October 2001 (Tanguy, 2011). Although France did not participate in the airstrikes, it conducted post-strike assessment missions of which the results were shared with the United States through the French exchange officer that joined the United States Central Command (CENTCOM) in September 2001. The frigate *Courbet*, which arrived in the Indian Ocean on 17 October, was the first naval asset to participate in Operation Enduring Freedom in the area and was subsequently joined by the aircraft carrier *Charles de Gaulle*. In December 2001, the French ground troops (500) arrived in Kabul as a component of the Kabul Multinational Brigade,

French military operations since 1991   119

which comprised 3,500 soldiers from various countries. As of February 2002, the French Air Force had established two bases in Dushanbe (Tajikistan) and Manas (Kyrgyzstan). Six Mirage-2000D and two C-160 transport aircraft were based in Dushanbe, while one C-135 aircraft (designed for air-to-air refuelling) was based in Manas. Yet, despite this capability, Paris was reluctant to allow French planes to be used in strike missions and favoured shows of force over the use of violence. Overall, during the 2001–2004 period, French engagement was limited and in line with the strategic objectives laid out in Paris: showing solidarity at the minimum cost. Afghanistan was clearly not a priority for the French armed forces at this time.

This logic of minimal engagement remained the same between 2004 and 2007, despite marginal organisational changes in the French contribution. Between 2001 and 2007, the most useful asset France deployed was its Special Forces (SF). Back in 2001, the French SF units were still relatively young, as they had only been organised in a separate command (*Commandement des Opérations Spéciales* – COS) in 1992, following the lessons learned in the Gulf War (see chapter 2). Most importantly, the French general staff was doubtful about the SF's capability of deploying and sustaining a number of units so far from the traditional French logistical lines. Yet, the COS surprised the higher ranks by fielding the units and conducting high-visibility operations such as the reopening of the Mazar-e-Sharif airport, secured by the navy commandos.

The French campaign plans fundamentally evolved with the election of Nicolas Sarkozy, who decided to increase the French contribution, with a clear strategic objective: improving France's relationship with the United States. France agreed to take responsibility for the Kapisa and Surobi regions, two small and mountainous areas north of Kabul and of critical strategic importance because of their proximity to both Kabul and the Salang highway. The provinces geographically command access to the northern part of Afghanistan from Kabul, but also to Pakistan through Laghman province. Because of its strategic importance, the area was already viciously fought over by the Mujahedeen and the Soviets during the Soviet invasion of Afghanistan. The French decided to deploy a brigade to the region and thus were put under the command of Regional Command East (RCE). However, because France had earlier refused to participate in the PRT system, the division of labour between Europeans and Americans was turned on its head in Kapisa. While most European countries run their own PRT with American troops providing the main battlefield force, the opposite happened: an American PRT conducted civilian actions with French military forces conducting combat (Lasconjarias, 2011).

In retrospect, the difficulties of the Afghan terrain seem to have been underestimated. The transformative moment was the ambush in the Uzbin Valley on 19 August 2008, during which 10 soldiers were killed and 21 were wounded (Schmitt, 2017c). This loss, the most important for French forces since the attack of the Drakkar building in Lebanon in 1983, was a shock for both the French population and the armed forces. First, the Ministry of Defence drastically improved the quality of the equipment. But mostly, the potential violence of the fights was

120 *French military operations since 1991*

acknowledged. In the autumn of 2009, the French forces underwent a deep restructuring with the creation of the La Fayette task force (TF). A brigade-size unit, TF La Fayette united under a single command the French forces in Surobi and Kapisa. The units deployed in these two areas were renamed (from "task force" to "battlegroup"), and their structure changed. Each battalion-sized unit was expanded and included four companies instead of three previously. Moreover, artillery capability was deployed as well as light tanks, in order to raise the firepower of the French troops. In total, the TF La Fayette amounted to about 2,800 troops. The mix of kinetic and population-centric actions that had characterised the action of the task force "Korrigan" were carried out by other battlegroups. For example, the legionnaires of the battlegroup Altor, deployed in the Surobi district between December 2009 and May 2010, conducted major operations in order to keep the insurgents at bay (operations Septentrion and Dragon) and aimed to secure the Tagab valley, while in the meantime they politically engaged with the population through the dissemination of combat outposts, the use of political officers, and the mentoring of the Afghan National Army (ANA).

Yet, two main factors limited the effectiveness of the French campaign. First, at the end of 2010, an "operational pause" was imposed on the French troops by their political authorities following the capture of two French journalists by the Taliban in December 2009. It appears that the French intelligence services made serious contact with their captors at the end of 2010 and requested an operational pause in order to facilitate their liberation, which was finalised in June 2011. In the meantime, French forces were instructed to avoid large-scale operations and almost stop the patrols and the engagement with the local population. Second, divergences of strategic priority emerged between the TF La Fayette and the RCE. While the French troops wanted to secure the gains obtained in the Tagab and Alasay Valleys, the American command of the RCE wanted them to focus on the securing of the main supply road (MSR) Vermont, an important logistical axis. French troops simply did not have enough resources to conduct both actions simultaneously. They eventually succeeded in securing MSR Vermont as requested, but this was at the expense of the security in the Kapisa and Surobi districts, where Taliban fighters could re-infiltrate. Yet, the situation had improved, as Kapisa and Surobi were transferred to the Afghan forces in 2012, before the withdrawal of the French combat troops decided by President Hollande was completed. Nevertheless, these two districts are still violent, even by Afghan standards, and the French ultimately failed to secure Kapisa and Surobi (Lafaye, 2016).

Libya

While the French operations in Afghanistan peaked in 2010–2011, protests related to what would later be called the Arab Spring started to erupt in the Maghreb and the Middle East. From February 2011 onwards, protests reach Libya, particularly the city of Benghazi. The first French military operations started on 22 February (evacuation of French citizens) and 25 February (closing of the embassy). Naval

French military operations since 1991 121

assets were also deployed in the Mediterranean in order to monitor the situation on the ground. The diplomatic turning point was the adoption of Franco-British UNSC Resolution 1973 that authorised the use of force in protection of the endangered populations on 17 March (Pannier, 2020). On 19 March, a meeting in Paris defined the coalition that would enforce the resolution. On the same day, the French Air Force conducted the first strikes on Libyan territory, destroying four artillery pieces and marking the beginning of what would be called Operation Odyssey Dawn (and Operation Harmattan in France). Between 19 and 20 March, US forces (supported by British forces) proceeded to destroy the enemy air defences (112 cruise missiles were launched from US ships), thus granting air superiority to the coalition forces. The establishment of the institutional mechanism for the operation was complicated by the necessity to coordinate different layers of cooperation (Rynning, 2013): a coalition operating within the framework of an alliance and in coordination with a broader political club. Between 19 and 31 March, the operations were coordinated by the US Africa Command (AFRICOM), which delegated command to a joint task force based on the *USS Mount Whitney* and commanded by Admiral Samuel L. Locklear. However, very early on the United States announced that they would rather "lead from behind", which led to a gradual transfer of the command and control of the operation to NATO. This dynamic frustrated French policy-makers, who hoped that some Franco-British cooperation could be established, which would materialise in the Lancaster House Agreement, which had been signed the year before. However, French policy-makers were alone in their desire not to involve NATO, which led to the transfer of the operation to the alliance's command and control structure (Notin, 2012). However, the French military kept operational control of high-value assets, such as the aircraft carrier *Charles de Gaulle* and the attack submarines, which were then deployed as "associated support" to Operation Unified Protector.

The operation had three main phases: halting the Libyan forces (19–31 March), attrition of the adversary forces and support to the rebel troops culminating with the fall of Tripoli (27 August), and destruction of the last areas of loyalist resistance leading to the death of Muammar Qadhafi on 20 October. During the first phase, the French armed forces deployed an aircraft carrier group and two dozen fighter jets (and their support) operating from Air Base 126 in Solenzara, Corsica. The operation demonstrated the improvement of France's long-range strike capabilities, as the French forces used the Scalp-EG cruise missile in combined air force/navy raids for the first time. During the second phase, the coalition delivered on average 120 strikes per day, of which about 30 were conducted by the French forces. However, while the airstrikes were unable to end the conflict, operational and tactical adjustments were required. For the French navy, it involved rediscovering naval gunfire support, and for the army, the deployment of a helicopter group operating mostly at night and conducting operations in closer contact with the enemy. The French airmobile forces embarked on the Tonnerre landing helicopter dock on 16 May for a mission that lasted about two weeks. The helicopters served to conduct precision strike missions against pro-Gaddafi military installations, vehicles, and command posts to help the rebels "unlock" Brega, a town

122   *French military operations since 1991*

on the road to Tripoli (Pannier, 2020). Special Forces were also deployed on the ground as support to the insurgents.

The operation highlighted a number of challenges for the French forces in terms of operating within a NATO framework (Schmitt, 2015): the reintegration within the command structure was too recent, and French officers were not all equally proficient at going through the NATO channels. Yet, while the nuts and bolts of coalition warfare were still challenging, the campaign illustrated a clear improvement in French military capabilities: France conducted about 30% of the strikes and deployed an aircraft carrier group including submarines and Special Forces. During the Gulf War, France had conducted 1.9% of the strikes, and 5% during the intervention in Kosovo. Of course, the proportional increase in the number of French strikes is related to the US decision to "lead from behind" and the logistical comfort to operate not too far from French bases. But the improvement in technologies (illustrated by the use of cruise missiles) and operational concepts (demonstrated jointness through army/navy and army/air force cooperation) was clear. The intervention in Libya was thus a good demonstration of the results of the transformation of the French armed forces: increasing the level of professionalism but decreasing the ability to sustain long-term engagements because of the lack of redundancy and slack in an organisation under constant transformation.

Iraq and Syria

Following the degradation of the security situation in Iraq/Syria and the rise of Islamic State, the UNSC adopted in 2014 Resolution 2170, which provided the legal basis for the US-led operation Inherent Resolve (Saideman, 2016). The French mission was called operation Chammal, and consisted of both an air campaign, ground troops (in particular, artillery troops), supported by naval forces. Unlike the previous operations we have mentioned so far, Chammal was more directly a response to a terrorist threat to France. France engaged in missions against Islamic State in Iraq in June 2014, and in September 2015, President Hollande decided to authorise French strikes on ISIS in Syria, evoking the necessity of "self-defence", based on intelligence suggesting the preparation of terrorist attacks against France (Pannier and Schmitt, 2019, p. 903). For the French forces, Chammal was the culmination of several trends in modern warfare they had experienced for more than a decade. First, it was a US-led intervention in which the French forces were a "junior partner", which is consistent with the gradual mastery of coalition warfare: the operational and technological integration with US and allied forces, improved during the Afghanistan and Libya interventions, is reportedly extremely high. Clearly, the practice of multinational military intervention has been largely improved since 1999. Second, operation Inherent Resolve does not have a large ground component, since Western forces provide mentoring and support (through indirect fire) to local forces. This is also the culmination of a trend towards proxy warfare (albeit in a different way than during the Cold War) (Groh, 2019), which was experienced in Afghanistan (through the training and monitoring of Afghan troops) and in Libya. Third, Western forces have to operate in a contested environment and do not necessarily have air supremacy since the Russian intervention in 2015: the fact that air forces are not able to freely operate is a development (compared with the entirely permissive Afghan environment and the destruction of the Libyan anti-air capabilities in the first days of the campaign), which announces future military challenges for Western forces. The is already implementing the lessons it learned from operation Chammal in the design of its new aircraft. There is then a stark contrast between the challenges of coalition warfare observed during the Kosovo intervention and the current conduct of multinational military operations by Western forces, and the French armed forces contributed to interactions becoming more fluid.

Defending the *"pré carré"*: French interventions in Africa

While the interventions in Kosovo, Afghanistan, Libya, and Syria/Iraq illustrate the gradual French involvement in multinational military operations, Paris was also active in Sub-Saharan Africa. In fact, France is the only European country that still regularly deploys its military forces on combat missions in the area, following a Cold War practice of projecting power and influencing events as a key element of France's international status as a major power. Since the end of the Cold War, Paris has conducted a number of interventions on the continent (Table 5.1).

Going through all the details of those interventions would be outside the scope of this chapter,[1] but it is still possible to make some general observations. The independence of France's colonies in the 1960s was not a disappearance of colonial relations, but "a restructuring of the imperial relationship" (Chafer, 2001, p. 167). Bilateral defence agreements were established (containing secret clauses for intervention as well as technical and cultural cooperation) between France and its former colonies, often relying on the strong and personalised relations between the French and African political and business elites (see chapter 6). Therefore, for more than three decades after the *de jure* independences, "France exercised a 'virtual empire' in Sub-Saharan Africa, premised on cultural, economic, linguistic and personal ties forged during the colonial period" (Gregory, 2000, pp. 435–436). Of course, this domination was only possible because the African elites had a vested interest in the relationship (Bayart, 2000), a relationship summarised by the label *"Françafrique"*. Since the end of the Cold War and the transformations of the global system that have accompanied it, French policy towards Africa has evolved, displaying both elements of continuity and elements of change. Whether this change amounts to some sort of decline in Franco-African relations is open to question (Bovcon, 2013). For example, Bruno Charbonneau (2008) argues that the past three decades demonstrate more a restructuring than a decline in the hierarchical relationship between France and African countries, and he laments the persistence of "outdated values, practices and structures of a particular kind of knowledge, that of French security policy in Africa" (Charbonneau, 2009, p. 558).

124 *French military operations since 1991*

Table 5.1 List of major French military interventions in Africa since the end of the Cold War

Target country	Operation code name	IO endorsement	Launch date
Comoros	Oside	None	December 1989
Gabon	Requin	None	May 1990
Rwanda	Noroît	None	October 1990
Togo	Verdier	None	November 1991
Djibouti	Iskoutir	None	February 1992
Rwanda	Turquoise	UNSC	June 1994
Comoros	Azalée	None	September 1995
Cameroon	Aramis	None	February 1996
Central African Republic	Almandin	None	April 1996
Ivory Coast	Licorne	ECOWAS/UNSC	September 2002
Democratic Republic of the Congo	Artemis	UNSC/EU	June 2003
Chad	EUFOR Chad-CAR Epervier	UNSC/EU	January 2008
Libya	Harmattan	UNSC/Arab League	March 2011
Ivory Coast	Licorne II	UNSC/ECOWAS	April 2011
Mali	Serval	UNSC/ECOWAS	January 2013
Central African Republic	Sangaris	UNSC/African Union	December 2013
Burkina Faso, Chad, Mali, Mauritania, Niger	Barkhane	UNSC/G5 Sahel	July 2014

Other authors note a decline in French interests and the French capability to shape political outcomes (Châtaigner, 2006).

In military terms, some continuities are worth observing. First, while some interventions are based on humanitarian grounds (evacuation of citizens or multi-national peacekeeping), major operations are generally launched in order to maintain or restore political order in targeted states. This observation is still true in the post-Cold-War era (currently being epitomised by the Barkhane operation), which reveals underlying and enduring patterns of perceptions of Africa within French decision-making circles, from the alleged "African experience" of the armed forces (in fact a specific type of knowledge based on limited interactions with African populations) to the definition of French interests by the political elites. Nathaniel Powell perfectly summarises this nexus and its self-defeating consequences:

> First, French policymakers have consistently construed threats to their sphere of interest in ideological terms that privilege grand narratives over local agency and issues. Second, the conflation of the security of France's African allies with French security has given those allies an outsized importance and

French military operations since 1991 125

influence in determining policy. The desire to maintain 'credibility' has reinforced this dynamic. Third, this strategic orientation has provided powerful disincentives for political reforms by African elites who have benefited from French backing. Ultimately, this has meant that past interventions often contributed to the very processes of political and social decomposition that French policymakers hoped to prevent.

(Powell, 2017, p. 49)

As such, the persistence of this specific type of knowledge and construction of French national interests helps explain the patterns of military intervention (Erforth, 2020).

However, there has also been a shift towards a multilateralisation of French military activities. Some locate the shift with the disastrous military intervention in Rwanda (1994), which led the French government to be questioned about its policy shortcomings (and potential contribution) to the genocide, while others argue that the Ivory Coast intervention (2002–2004) was a turning point as it revealed that the French presence could be mobilised by local politicians for local gains, and that Paris needed another source of legitimation. While the legitimation aspect is certainly important, in line with the trend towards multinationalisation discussed by Finnemore (2003), issues of burden-sharing also certainly matter. These attempts to multinationalise French military interventions have been supported by a training program of the African armed forces called RECAMP (*Renforcement des Capacités Africaines de Maintien de la Paix*), launched in 1994, which had very mixed results. Multinationalisation of the African policy has, in any case, been a contested issue among the French elites, some circles contending that the French commitment to bilateral security agreements was the key to the country's influence in Africa. In any case, there has been an observable (albeit limited) shift towards gaining international legitimacy through the blessing of an international institution (France being a member of the P5, it always looks for UN approval, ideally combined with the approval of a regional organisation) and the multinationalisation of military interventions. These attempts at multinationalising French policy have sometimes been resented by Paris' partners, for example when Germany declined to participate in the EUFOR-Chad mission in 2007 on the grounds that it was a French operation with an EU make-up (Schmitt, 2012). This trend explains why the French authorities have attempted to involve international troops in the Sahel in support of the Barkhane operation: local troops through the G5-Sahel and international troops through a UN and an EU mission. Moreover, the Barkhane operation (which is a follow-up to Serval), is itself a legacy of the Epervier operation in Chad, first launched in 1986 and maintained ever since, before being finally subsumed under Barkhane. The Serval operation also benefited from the infrastructure of the French military power in Africa, namely the prepositioned forces in Senegal.

Africa is historically seen in France as a potential source of power, and the current trends show no sign of overturning the primarily securitised prism through which French elites perceive their interactions with their African counterparts:

126 *French military operations since 1991*

French interventions are thus likely to keep happening in the foreseeable future. However, the relative French decline in the international system has led Paris, out of necessity, to gradually multinationalise its African interventions; there is here again a tension between the autonomous ambitions of a middle power and the need to rely on allies and partners.

Managing political and diplomatic contingencies

French decision-makers have repeatedly used the armed forces as a flexible tool to promote specific policies after the end of the Cold War. The most visible operation in that regard has been Operation Sentinelle deployed on French territory after the Charlie Hebdo attacks in January 2015. It is not unusual for the French armed forces to contribute to civilian tasks. For example, in the absence of a dedicated unit, the French Navy also provides coast guard functions. Similarly, the army has been routinely deployed in support of civil protection units in the wake of natural disasters, or as a light counter-terrorism protection force under the "Vigipirate" plan, according to which French troops have, since the mid-1990s, been deployed to protect sensitive sites and infrastructures, including train stations. However, Sentinelle's magnitude is unprecedented, since it has mobilised between 7,000 and 13,000 troops at any time on French territory since 2015 (Tenenbaum, 2016). In fact,

> given its scale and duration, *Sentinelle* has taken a considerable toll on French military resources, affecting the availability and readiness of the country's armed forces for other deployments. Consequently, it has also had a negative impact on the morale of the military.
>
> (Pannier and Schmitt, 2019, p. 906)

The format of the operation has been further adjusted, but it has become politically difficult for current (and future) French leaders to terminate the operation altogether, as it could easily be portrayed as "sacrificing the security of the French population" by the opposition: it is likely that Sentinelle will endure, and gradually fade away through continuous adaptation.

Finally, French troops have been deployed in the Baltics in the framework of the NATO Enhanced Forward Presence (eFP) military posture since 2017. French troops were deployed in Estonia in 2017 (with the United Kingdom as a "framework nation" for the battlegroup), in Lithuania in 2018 (with Germany as a "framework nation"), and again in Estonia in 2019. In any case, the eFP's role in case of a conventional conflict is very much a tripwire that could probably but not meaningfully contribute to halting invading Russian troops: estimates of the correlation of forces that it would take NATO 90 days to outnumber Russian conventional forces in the area (notably due to challenges of military mobility in Europe). In that context, the French engagement is modest, with about 300 troops, 4 Leclerc main battle tanks, and 13 APCs. This limited commitment is the result of both operational priorities in the Sahel, but also French reasoning that even a small tripwire

French military operations since 1991 127

provided by a nuclear-armed nation is enough to credibly boost the eFP's deterring effect: French commitment is then calibrated to signal commitment to the NATO alliance.

These two operations illustrate the way French governments tend to rely on the armed forces in order to provide flexible policy options, here in the areas of counter-terrorism and NATO politics, which is part of a broader pattern of making the military front and centre in the definition of French foreign and security policy (discussed in chapter 1).

The COVID-19 crisis had a limited impact on French military operations but was nevertheless felt. While multinational military exercises have been suspended, the operational tempo did not slow down, especially in the Sahel. This created a small controversy when it was found that more than 1,000 sailors on the *Charles de Gaulle* aircraft carrier (2/3 of the crew) were infected with COVID-19, but the onboard doctors had failed to estimate the severity of the virus spread, ultimately forcing Defence Minister Parly to abort the planned mission and order the ship back to its harbour in Toulon. The armed forces also established temporary field hospitals in order to help treat civilian patients in the heavily infected area around Mulhouse.

Conclusion

Military operations are a cornerstone of the French armed forces' identity. The military considers itself combat-proven and has integrated a professional ethos of delivering tactical results, regardless of the actual resources at its disposal. This "gritty" mentality is quite similar to the one observed in the British armed forces and is sometimes self-defeating since it incentivises military leaders to keep telling politicians that the armed forces will deliver what is required of them, which is then used as an argument to further diminish the format of the military. Beyond this civil–military dimension, the use of military force is often perceived by the French leadership as a way to bolster French positions and status in the international system, including at the UNSC.

Yet, when it comes to military operations, the gap between the proclaimed French ambitions worldwide and the limited military resources available leaves both military and political circles frustrated. In that regard, a redefinition of the French grand strategic objectives, taking stock of the changing international system and the concomitant decline of France's relative power, would necessarily lead to a prioritisation of French military commitments abroad.

Note

1 For an overview of French military operations in Africa, see French Ministry of Defence, '50 Ans d'Opex en Afrique, 1964-2014', *Cahier du RETEX*, Paris, 2014.

References

Barat-Ginies, O. (2011), *L'Engagement Militaire Français en Afghanistan, 2001–2011*. Paris: L'Harmattan.

128 *French military operations since 1991*

Bayart, J.F. (2000), "Africa in the World : A History of Extraversion", *African Affairs*, 99/395, 217–267.

Bonnot, P. (2001), "La Marine dans la Guerre du Golfe", in Maurice Vaïsse (ed.), *La Participation Militaire Française À La Guerre Du Golfe*. Paris: Cahiers du Centre d'Etudes Historiques de la Défense N°21, 59–77.

Bovcon, M. (2013),"Françafrique and the Regime Theory", *European Journal of International Relations*, 19/1, 5–26.

Chafer, T. (2001),"French African Policy in Historical Perspective", *Journal of Contemporary African Studies*, 19/2, 165–182.

Charbonneau, B. (2008), *France and the New Imperialism: Security Policy in Sub-Saharan Africa*. Aldershot: Ashgate.

Charbonneau, B. (2009), "What is so Special about the European Union? EU-UN Cooperation in Crisis Management in Africa", *International Peacekeeping*, 16/4, 546–561.

Châtaigner, J.M. (2006), "Principes et Réalités de la Politique Africaine de la France", *Afrique Contemporaine*, 220/4, 247–261.

Chivvis, C. (2016), *The French War on Al Qa'ida in Africa*. Cambridge: Cambridge University Press.

Cordesman, A.H. (2001), *The Lessons and Non-Lessons of the Air and Missile Campaign in Kosovo*. Westport: Praeger Publisher.

Cordesman, A.H. and Wagner, A.R. (1996), *The Lessons of Modern War, vol. IV. Gulf War*. Boulder: Westview Press.

Davidson, J.W. (2011), *America's Allies and War. Kosovo, Afghanistan, and Iraq*. Basingstoke: Palgrave McMillan.

de la Sablière, J.-M. (2013), Dans les Coulisses du Monde. *Du Rwanda à la Guerre d'Irak, un Grand Négociateur Révèle le Dessous des Cartes*. Paris: Robert Laffont.

DeVore, M. (2012)"Armed Forces, States and Threats: Institutions and the French and British Responses to the 1991 Gulf War", *Comparative Strategy*, 31/1, 56–83.

Erforth, B. (2020), *Contemporary French Security Policy in Africa. On Ideas and Wars*, Basingstoke: Palgrave.

Finnemore, M. (2003), *The Purpose of Intervention: Changing Rules about the Use of Force*. Ithaca: Cornell University Press.

Gregory, S. (2000), "The French Military in Africa: Past and Present", *African Affairs*, 396, 435–448.

Groh, T. (2019), *Proxy War. The Least Bad Option*. Palo Alto: Stanford University Press.

Houlahan, T. (1999), *Gulf War. The Complete History*. New London: Schrenker Military Publishing.

Irondelle, B. (2011), *La Réforme des Armées en France, Sociologie de la Décision*. Paris: Presses de Sciences Po.

Lafaye, C. (2016), *L'Armée Française en Afghanistan. Le Génie au Combat, 2001–2014*. Paris: CNRS Éditions.

Lasconjarias, G. (2011), "Kapisa, Kalachnikov et Korrigan", *Cahiers de l'Irsem n°9*. Paris: Irsem.

Le Flem, J.G. and Oliva, B. (2018), *Un Sentiment d'Inachevé. Réflexion sur l'Efficacité des Opérations*. Paris: Éditions de l'École de Guerre.

Macleod, A. (2000), "France: Kosovo and the Emergence of a New European Security", in Martin, Pierre and Brawley, Mark R. (eds.), *Alliance Politics, Kosovo, and NATO's War. Allied Force or Forced Allies?* Basingstoke: Palgrave, 113–130.

Notin, J.C. (2012), *La Vérité sur Notre Guerre en Libye*. Paris: Fayard.

Nouzille, V. (2012), *Les Dossiers de la CIA sur la France, 1981–2000. Dans le Secret des Présidents*. Paris: Fayard.

Pannier, A. (2020), *Rivals in Arms. The Rise of UK-France Defence Relations in the Twenty-First Century*. Montréal: McGill-Queen's University Press.

Pannier, A. and Schmitt, O. (2019), "To Fight Another Day: France between the Fight against Terrorism and Future Warfare", *International Affairs*, 95/4, 897–916.

Powell, N. (2017), "Battling Instability? The Recurring Logic of French Military Interventions in Africa", *African Security*, 10/1, 47–72.

Ruffa, C. (2019), *Military Cultures in Peace and Stability Operations*. Philadelphia: University of Pennsylvania Press.

Rynning, S. (2013), "Coalitions, Institutions and Big Tents: The New Strategic Reality of Armed Intervention", *International Affairs*, 89/1, 53–68.

Saideman, S. (2016), "The Ambivalent Coalition: Doing the Least One Can Do against the Islamic State", *Contemporary Security Policy*, 37/2, 289–305.

Sandahl, E. (2019), Vrbanja. *Le Mandat de la Rupture*. Paris: Lavauzelle.

Schmitt, O. (2012), "Strategic Users of Culture. German Decisions for Military Action", *Contemporary Security Policy*, 33/1, 59–81.

Schmitt, O. (2015), "A War Worth Fighting? The Libyan Intervention in Retrospect", *International Politics Reviews*, 3/1, 10–18.

Schmitt, O. (2017a), "The Reluctant Atlanticist. France's Security and Defence Policy in a Transatlantic Context", *Journal of Strategic Studies*, 40/4, 463–474.

Schmitt, O. (2017b), "International Organization at War. NATO Practices in the Afghan Campaign", *Cooperation and Conflict*, 52/4, 502–518.

Schmitt, O. (2017c), "French Military Adaptation in the Afghan War. Looking Inward or Outward?", *Journal of Strategic Studies*, 40/4, 577–599.

Schmitt, O. (2018), *Allies That Count. Junior Partners in Coalition Warfare*. Washington, DC: Georgetown University Press.

Shurkin, M. (2015), "The French Way of War", *Politico*, 17 November.

Tanguy, J-M (2011), "L'armée Française au Combat. Afghanistan, 10 Ans d'Opérations", RAIDS Hors-*Série*, 41, 6–11.

Tenenbaum, E. (2016), "La Sentinelle Égarée? L'Armée de Terre Face au Terrorisme", *Focus Stratégique*, 68.

Thiéblemont, A. (2002), "Unités de Combat en Bosnie (1992–1995): la Tactique Déstructurée, la Débrouille, le Ludique", *Les Champs de Mars*, 12, 85–122.

Zajec, O. (2018), "French Military Operations", in Meijer, Hugo and Wyss, Marco (eds.), *The Oxford Handbook of European Defence Policies and Armed Forces*. Oxford: Oxford University Press, 797–812.

6 France and its partners

French defence policy is not conceived in a vacuum: being a member of NATO and the EU, and having multiple allies and partners, is both an opportunity for France to shape those institutions and a constraint for reaching one's ends in a context of interdependence with partners who display different strategic cultures and diverging preferences. In this regard, the effect of the end of the Cold War on France's conception of its alliances and security partnerships cannot be overstated. As we highlighted in previous chapters, changes included the move from a bipolar world to one dominated by the United States, as well as a reduced centrality of nuclear weapons in international security. In parallel, the 1990s also saw a broadening of the definition of "defence", which became increasingly conceptualised as "security" and viewed as a collective endeavour (Howorth, 1997 p. 40). In this modified geostrategic context, France's voice in "the concert of European states" was reduced, while its security interests became increasingly interdependent with those of its allies and partners (Gautier, 2009, p. 67). Indeed, France found itself having to invent a new foreign policy for a new international order where attempting individually to balance between the United States and the USSR would no longer be sufficient as a way to have influence (Pannier and Schmitt, 2019, p. 899). In Europe more specifically, changes included the German reunification, the opening up of central and eastern European countries, and the removal of many US troops. Besides, the 1990s were marked by new forms of foreign military interventions and peacekeeping missions (in the Gulf, the former Yugoslavia, and Somalia) requiring an ability to insert French military forces into multinational coalitions (see chapter 5). Cooperation in defence and even the integration of military forces in Europe appeared to successive French governments as necessary and desirable for managing these multiple challenges. This, however, posed new problems for the maintenance of the principle of national independence as well as for balancing European and transatlantic defence arrangements.

This chapter analyses the evolution of French defence policy vis-à-vis the EU, NATO, and individual privileged partners from the end of the Cold War to today. Notably, the chapter reviews France's approach to the development of the EU's Common Security and Defence Policy (CSDP), as well as the process of French reintegration into NATO's integrated military structures and the role France has made for itself in the organisation since 2009. Then, the chapter moves

France and its partners 131

on to discuss France's bilateral relationships with its main partners: Germany, the United Kingdom, and other European partners, as well as the United States, but also France's relations with partners in Africa and Asia. Overall, this chapter shows that contextual changes led successive French presidents to partially adapt and push for more of the same vision when it comes to defence cooperation in a new context, rather than rethinking the fundamentals of France's orientations towards the roles of allies and partners. France has looked to combine national strategic autonomy with influence on and with allies, inside and outside international organisations, without ever specifying how these different goals could be reconciled.

France and the EU's security and defence policy

The development of the EU's Common Security and Defence Policy

Ever since the end of the Second World War, France has pursued a European defence cooperation mechanism. In so doing, the goals were both to reduce western Europe's reliance on the United States and to exert French influence via a power multiplication effect (Charillon and Ramel, 2010, p. 31). France's efforts failed during the Cold War when the French proposal for a European Defence Community (EDC) was called off in 1954. The EDC was ambitious: it was about creating another institutional arrangement for a European army within which token German units would be integrated. Because of the failure of the EDC, the project of having a European pillar in defence and security, alongside the transatlantic pillar, had to be rethought. What emerged was the Western European Union (WEU), which became an embryo of European defence and security policy, but much looser. The WEU remained a ten-member forum for restoring confidence and for coordinating their participation in multinational operations. It was dissolved in 2010, after having been dormant for lack of executive powers. Meanwhile, NATO remained dominant throughout the Cold War (see next section).

As the Cold War ended, unlike most of its European partners, France pushed for a deep rethinking of Europe's security architecture. There has always been a French hesitation, if not reluctance, to have the western European security system move eastward (Menon, 1995, p. 28). Thus, while most European partners went about reforming and adapting NATO to the new context, including by enlarging the Alliance's mandate and membership, France tried to push an alternative agenda (Menon, 1995). In 1990, Mitterrand emphasised the role of the Conference on Security and Cooperation in Europe (CSCE, which later became the OSCE), as a means for stabilising relations with Russia and as a forum for building partnerships with the former communist bloc, in complementarity to NATO (Saunier and Vial, 2015, p. 447). More importantly, the French vision saw the European Community at the core of a western European collective defence effort. Besides, France pushed for a radical "restructuring of NATO based on a reduced political role for the Alliance and concomitant military adjustments, [as well as] the emergence of an increasingly autonomous European security entity" (Howorth, 1997,

132 *France and its partners*

pp. 25–26. See next section on NATO). To summarise, after the Fall of the Wall, France tried and failed to block NATO's expansion and to reorganise Europe's security architecture around an EC/EU with a common defence policy, a small NATO limited to territorial defence, and a pan-European CSCE/OSCE managing disarmament and conflict prevention.

So, the creation and development of the European Security and Defence Policy (ESDP, which later became the Common Security and Defence Policy), has been for France primarily a politico-strategic goal, towards the completion of the European project. After the Fall of the Wall, French officials referred to European defence "in more far-reaching terms than ever before" (Menon, 1995, p. 23). The ambiguity of how this would relate to NATO was palpable early on. Mitterrand explained:

> It is not about creating a defence organisation [for western Europe] that would substitute NATO, it is simply about knowing the limits of the Atlantic alliance and of its military organisation, limiting its competences, limits in its geographical area, to know that Europe as such should lose no opportunity to restructure itself through a common policy and, thereby, its own defence.
> (François Mitterrand cited in Saunier and Vial, 2015, p. 508)

As Jolyon Howorth recalls, it was France who pushed for a clause in the 1992 Maastricht Treaty establishing a Common Foreign and Security Policy (CFSP) to deal with "all questions related to the security of the Union, including the eventual framing of a common defence policy which might in time lead to common defence" (Howorth, 1997, p. 23). Under the CFSP, the EU should be able to carry out the "Petersberg Tasks", including humanitarian and rescue tasks, peacekeeping, and crisis management, including peace-making. But France's ambitions always went further and included the necessity of European autonomous military capabilities. Published in 1994, the first French defence white paper of the post-Cold-War era read:

> [French] defence policy must [contribute] to build progressively a European common defence. [The WEU] must have as an objective the possibility of an autonomous military action by the Europeans. It is necessary to this end that the Europeans have their own military capabilities.
> (Premier Ministre, 1994, pp. 32–33)

The unfolding of the 1990s seemed to confirm Mitterrand's analysis that in the new international context, France could do little on its own, that EU member states no longer had the resources to get necessary capabilities individually, and that they needed to be able to intervene without the United States, which may be disinterested in European interests (Howorth, 1997, p. 34). Yet, as fears of a "duplication" between NATO and an EU defence policy arose, the idea of a common European defence had to be presented as reinforcing the European pillar

France and its partners   133

and the "European identity" in NATO. Illustratively, Hervé de Charette, France's foreign minister, said in 1996 at the WEU assembly:

> WEU is essential for turning Europe into a power that is capable of playing a full part within the new strategic context. WEU must genuinely become the European pillar of the Alliance and the defence component of the Union. This means that WEU occupies a pivotal position between the Alliance and the Union; it has to derive the full operational dimension from the former and its political legitimacy as the military branch of the European Union from the latter.
>
> (Assembly of the Western European Union, 1997, p. 172)

This European ambition could not come to fruition without the support of key allies. This support came, in particular, in the context of the Balkan wars, which were characterised by Europe's sloppy reaction and lack of capabilities. The German 1994 defence white paper, while presenting NATO as the foundation of Germany's security, defended the idea of Europe being able to act autonomously, and of the WEU becoming the defence component of the EU (Federal Republic of Germany, 1994). Aside from Germany, winning Britain's support was essential. For its part, the British 1998 Strategic Defence Review (SDR) referred to the Western European Union as having a role to play in "conflict prevention, and especially peacekeeping" (Ministry of Defence, 1998, p. 16). That is to say that from the beginning of the EU defence and security policy, the United Kingdom's position was that it should not be dealing with missions in the higher end of the military spectrum, which should be left to NATO. According to Clara O'Donnell, this proactivity resulted from pressure from Washington for Britain to push European partners to a bigger defence effort through NATO or, this failing, through the EU (O'Donnell, 2011, p. 422).

This uncomfortable compromise permitted Jacques Chirac to team up with Tony Blair to draft the famous Saint Malo declaration, which read:

> The European Union needs to be in a position to play its full role on the international stage. [It] must have the capacity for autonomous action, backed up by credible military forces, the means to decide to use them, and a readiness to do so, in order to respond to international crises.
>
> (Blair and Chirac, 1998)

To this end, with the support of both the United Kingdom and Germany, the EU under the new European Security and Defence Policy launched a number of initiatives, some operationally focused on the area of defence capabilities, including the "Helsinki Headline Goal" in 1999 (revised as the "Headline Goal 2010" in 2004), the 2001 "Capability Action Program", the creation of the European Defence Agency (EDA) in 2004, the drafting of the 2003 European Security Strategy, and the setting up of "EU Battlegroups".

134 *France and its partners*

As we explained in chapter 4, French governments supported European collaborative weapons programs for two main reasons: one political – considering the symbolic value of European cooperation (Irondelle, 2003, p. 217) – and the other economic, as a way of maintaining a robust industry in the face of lowering defence budgets. Thus, the portion allotted to armament programs in cooperation with European partners constantly increased: from 1996 to 2002 the share of the cooperation programs increased from 15% to 34% of the defence budget (cf. chapter 5). For Chirac, indeed, the priority was for the ESDP to produce outputs, and in particular to build European defence capabilities as well as operational command and control mechanisms (Mizlow, 2006).

Implementing European defence: from ambition to frustration to revival

The first EU operations under the ESDP took place in 2003, with a police mission in Bosnia and Herzegovina, a peacekeeping mission in the Former Republic of Macedonia, and a military operation in Congo. The following five years were characterised by a relatively intense pace of military ESDP missions. Added to the progress in institutional developments, including in the area of capabilities, the early 2000s was a period of optimism with regards to European defence, especially in France. Illustratively, several of the EU's missions were conducted in areas of French interest, and under French leadership. For Operation Artemis in the Congo, France provided the majority of the troops (Bagayoko-Penone, 2004), and for EUFOR Chad/RCA France contributed about 2,000 troops, and an operational headquarter, out of a total of 3,700 troops (EU Council Secretariat, 2009). Besides, NATO recognised in 2002 the notion of "European Security and Defence Identity" (ESDI) to designate a European pillar in NATO, or at a minimum, a partnership agreement between the EU's Security and Defence Policy and NATO. This came with an accord to coordinate tasks in crisis management and in particular the "Berlin Plus" agreement that provides the EU with access to NATO's planning capabilities when the Alliance does not wish to intervene.

Gradually, however, the absence of support from other EU member states and unresolvable political-institutional deadlocks created a general frustration in France about the Common Security and Defence Policy (the CSDP replaced the ESDP with the Lisbon Treaty in 2008). Despite an ambitious rhetoric, the ESDI had no practical consequences (Gautier, 2009, p. 83), and Berlin Plus "did not lead to a new phase in EU-NATO relations" as the two organisations "have to a large extent operated next to, and even in competition with, each other" (Duke and Vanhoonaker, 2016, p. 157). What is more, by that time it was clear that NATO successfully adapted to the post-Cold-War context and became the primary instrument not only for territorial defence but also for military operations outside of Europe (cf. next section). The space left for the EU to play a role in defence and security was thereby reduced at the same time as Europeans became engaged in the lengthy and resource-consuming war in Afghanistan and, for some, in Iraq. Effectively, since 2003, the majority of EU missions have taken in zones of strategic interest to France, notably in Africa, but they have been much more limited in scope and mandate than national, coalition, or NATO operations. What is more, as France endeavoured to "multilateralise" its Africa policy through the EU and the UN (Bagayoko-Penone, 2004), many have portrayed France as defending its own interests in Africa under the guise of EU missions (Charbonneau, 2008).

Besides, the debate on an EU "duplication" of NATO continued. In 2003, in the midst of a major transatlantic diplomatic crisis over the invasion of Iraq, France, Belgium, Germany, and Luxembourg held what came to be known as the "Chocolate Summit" where they pledged support for the EU to have an operational headquarters (known as OHQ) to conduct EU operations. The initiative met with British and the US opposition: "The chocolate summit reflected the worst fears of US hardliners about the dangers of ESDP going off in a NATO-incompatible direction", the then British ambassador to the United States was reported saying (Black, 2003). The debate in Europe about the OHQ – which came to crystallise debates about the compatibility of EU and NATO defence efforts – continued throughout the decade. In September 2011, France, Germany, Italy, Spain, and Poland signed a letter to Catherine Ashton instructing her to set up an OHQ without Britain's involvement, after the British government threatened to veto such a proposal (Waterfield, 2011). The letter suggested using the Permanent Structured Cooperation (PESCO) mechanism, in the 2008 Lisbon Treaty, which allows a group of member states to move ahead on a defence cooperation project without the need to have the whole of EU member states on board. In fact, it had become increasingly evident by the late 2000s that France's (and other "old" EU member states') ambitions for EU defence would not be supported by all. Aside from Britain's opposition, the new members who joined in 2004 also envisaged their defence policies in a transatlantic rather than a purely European context. Finally, the development of EU defence also took place at a period of lowering defence budgets, which worsened after the financial crisis of 2008, and which limited the bandwidth available for investing in EU initiatives.

So, to the detriment of France's vision, from the mid-2000s onwards, the momentum for European defence got lost, not least due to Britain's opposition. The EU increasingly focused on enhancing internal security cooperation, developing partnerships in the neighbourhood, and conducting limited, non-kinetic training and advisory missions further afield. As a reflection of this trend, the 2008 French defence white paper carefully underlined the "fragile" development of the CSDP in the previous years (Premier Ministre, 2008, p. 78). The document still called for the EU to have "a permanent and autonomous strategic planning capability" and to invest in its added value, identified as the complete range of instruments for crisis management (combining military, humanitarian, diplomatic, and financial tools. Ibid., p.84). It was at that point that France reinvested NATO as a forum for defence cooperation, as we explain in the next section.

While the EU's operational role proved by the end of the 2000s to be de facto quite limited, France supported other EU initiatives that concerned collaboration in defence procurement and industrial integration. As we explained in chapter 4, these initiatives such as Directive 2009/81/EC, or the European Union Defence and Security Procurement Directive, sought to open EU member states defence

136 *France and its partners*

procurement to competition across the Single Market. In practice, its effects on cross-border procurement proved to be limited. Hence, François Hollande, later followed by Emmanuel Macron, sought to double down on enhancing the EU's role in the areas of capability development and industrial integration. Hollande, in a speech made during the 2012 presidential campaign, insisted on two aspects in stating his objectives for the EU's role in defence:

> collective programming of future equipment, specialisation of tasks, strengthening of joint capacities [and] to work towards the consolidation of the European technological and industrial base, which supposes common support for aeronautics and defence research, but also joint ventures.
>
> (Hollande, 2012)

It took a few years for these priorities to make their way in Brussels. Importantly, the degradation of the security situation in Europe after the Russian annexation of Crimea and destabilisation of eastern Ukraine, the rise of ISIS and a wave of terrorist attacks in Europe, and the refugee crisis from 2015 onwards encouraged Europeans to reinvest in their defence budgets and opt for greater European cooperation, as evidenced by the publication of the 2016 EU Global Strategy, the first such document since 2003. A final factor that permitted progress was the United Kingdom's decision to leave the EU. On the day after the Brexit referendum in the United Kingdom, Paris and Berlin made statements reaffirming their commitment to the European Union and their desire for a major European plan for security and defence. EU defence was indeed a priority of the very pro-European candidate Emmanuel Macron. Once he became president, that was exemplified in his famously ambitious "Sorbonne speech" in September 2017 in which he called for Europe to develop strategic autonomy as well as its own "strategic culture" (Macron, 2017).

Helped by the support of Germany, the President of the EU Commission Jean-Claude Junker and the High Representative for Foreign Policy Federica Mogherini, the lifting of the British veto, the leadership of François Hollande and later Emmanuel Macron, amidst doubts about the United States' commitment to European security prompted by Donald Trump's election in November 2016, the EU decided on the following: an implementation plan for the EU global security strategy; the setting up of a military planning and conduct capability (a sort of small OHQ) for overseeing EU missions; a European Defence Fund (EDF) for co-funding cross-border defence R&D and procurement; a Coordinated Annual Review on Defence (CARD) for identifying capability gaps; and the launch of PESCO for committing member states to jointly defined capability, support, and training projects. Disagreements, however, existed between France and Germany, in particular on the goal and format of PESCO. While the EDF is clearly a pan-EU, long-term project for supporting the European Defence and Technological Industrial Base (EDTIB) and developing up-to-date military capabilities, Paris had hoped for a more ambitious, exclusive PESCO group that would gather the most willing and able Europeans around an operational focus, with the eventual

France and its partners 137

aim of addressing the most demanding missions, as specified in the Treaty on European Union (art. 42.6). Eventually, a compromise resulted in a looser version of PESCO, with 25 EU member states taking part in mostly capability-oriented projects on a case-by-case basis.

France and NATO

1966–2009: France outside of NATO's integrated military structures

While France consistently persisted in enhancing the EU's role in defence throughout the past 30 years, it is its relation to NATO that has changed the most, even though it remains somewhat uncomfortable. The sources of France's famously difficult relations with NATO date back to the 1950s. Even though France was a founding member of the Alliance, successive French presidents' desire to maintain an independent defence policy combined with distrust in US reliability has always shaped their ambiguous position vis-à-vis NATO. Distrust became especially prominent in the context of the Suez crisis of 1956, which revealed and accelerated the French "strategic malaise" (Lellouche, 2009, p. 39). De Gaulle had tried, but failed, to strengthen ties with the United Kingdom and the United States to set up a "tripartite world 'directorate'" (Duval, 1989, p. 78) and was unable to influence NATO's nuclear strategy on which it disagreed (cf. chapter 3). As a consequence of distrust and disagreement, France refused to subsume its military forces to American control and withdrew from NATO's integrated military structures in 1966. Throughout the Cold War, there was a "consensus" among French political representatives that France would remain a member of the Atlantic Alliance but not participate in the integrated command, thus having a "special status" (François Mitterrand, cited in Védrine, 1996, p. 75). France continued to participate in "the political and financial aspects of the Alliance": it had a seat at the North Atlantic Council – the main political decision-making body – and had a small number of military liaison officers within the headquarters (Riecker, 2013, p. 378). Moreover, France continued to participate in armament cooperation projects with allies as well as in NATO exercises (Pesme, 2010, pp. 47–48). Finally, was France also a member of the "Quad", a grouping with the United States, the United Kingdom, and Germany, which today continues to permit informal consultation especially for crisis management.

Over the two decades following the end of the Cold War, the role of France in NATO became increasingly less "special" in practice if not in discourse. De facto rapprochement started as early as 1991 with Mitterrand's decision to engage in the Gulf War alongside the United States. President Mitterrand committed 12,000 troops to the US-led operation (Prater, 1991, p. 442). France successfully tested a model where it delegated operational control while maintaining operational command. The experience also permitted building closer links between the French presidency and the US administration and between the two military communities. Therefore, the Gulf War was also an instance where French elites perceived they could gain strategic weight through enhanced cooperation with the United States (De Durand, 2010, p. 5). Following the

138 *France and its partners*

Gulf experience, Mitterrand supported the Alliance's 1992 strategic review and agreed to NATO's involvement in peacekeeping activities, to which it would provide support on a case-by-case basis (Riecker, 2013, p. 378). Mitterrand also negotiated in 1993 an observer status for French representatives in the Military Committee, in the context of the Balkan Wars (Ibid.).

Another turning point was indeed France's full participation in the NATO operations in Bosnia in 1995, just after the election of Jacques Chirac. According to Vaïsse, the experience convinced the newly elected Jacques Chirac that "the only way for France was to work in an Atlantic framework" (Vaïsse, 2009, p. 215). Indeed, as we have explained, the EU's defence institutions were still underdeveloped at the time, and France and Europe had to work with the United States to tackle crises in their immediate neighbourhood. In December 1995, Chirac announced France would participate in the meetings of the Council of Defence Ministers and be fully involved in the Military Committee, while intensifying working relations with the military structure, to the extent that they did not "encroach on [France's] sovereignty" (Millon, 1996). Overall, France joined every NATO committee except for the NATO Defence Planning Committee and the Nuclear Planning Group (Riecker, 2013, p. 379).

Despite no change in its formal status, France contributed to the operations in Kosovo (1999) and Afghanistan (2001–2012). While initially seeking to obtain a UN mandate for the operations in Kosovo, France did not oppose NATO's involvement and eventually took part in Operation Allied Force and "behaved as a reliable ally for NATO" (Tardy, 2000, p. 4). After the 9/11 terrorist attacks, Chirac was the first foreign leader to fly to the United States to meet with George W. Bush. France then deployed alongside the United States in Afghanistan, with a contingent that grew to 3,000 under the Sarkozy presidency (Auerswald and Saideman, 2014, pp. 105–107). This occurred in parallel to a strengthening of bilateral security links with the United States to tackle transnational terrorism (cf. next section). At the same time, in line with his opposition in 2003, Chirac refused an American plan for NATO be involved in a stabilisation in Iraq (Vaïsse and Sebag, 2009, p. 139).

Aside from military interventions, France was particularly involved in certain dossiers in the NATO Headquarters. Chirac supported NATO's "transformation" agenda agreed at the Prague summit in 2002 (Pesme, 2010, p. 48), that led to the setting up of NATO's Response Force (NRF) with a High Readiness Forces (HRF) headquarters. While Paris had originally opposed such a change in NATO's post-Cold-War role (Menon 1995, p. 24; Riecker, 2013), it then tried to ensure that the development of high readiness forces could also potentially benefit the EU (Pesme, 2010). France contributed substantially to the preparation of the NRF, and provided several multinational headquarters: the European Corps (Eurocorps), located in Strasbourg, received an HRF certification in 2002; the Joint Forces Air Component Command (JFACC) in Lyon was certified in November 2005; the Maritime Force HQ (FRMARFOR) in Toulon was certified in 2006; and the Rapid Reaction Corps HQ (CRR-FR) in Lille was certified in 2007 (Pesme, 2010, p. 50). In addition, France hosts a NATO Air Operations centre of excellence through its centre for analysis, simulation, and planning of air operations (CASPOA), accredited in 2008. France simultaneously increased its presence in NATO's military command. A special agreement was signed in 2004 to increase the number of French officers in NATO Command to 110, and the number of French military personnel reached 257 by 2009 across the whole of NATO (Cour des Comptes, 2012, p. 28). France's activism around the NRF and increased presence in the command and especially the Allied Command Transformation (ACT) can be understood as an attempt to influence the process and to exercise control over its own forces if they were to be deployed as part of NRF (Pesme, 2010). French forces were indeed deployed as part of the NRF in 2005, as part of two disaster relief operations in New Orleans and in Kashmir (Ibid., p. 50). By 2010, France was the largest contributor to the NATO Response Force (Riecker, 2013, p. 379).

The status quo of France's formal status became less and less tenable, from a practical and a strategic standpoint. In military interventions, France's absence from the integrated structures posed several constraints. To access information, France relied on "the narrowest of channels", either via its liaison officers in NATO Headquarters or, during the Balkans operations, through a planning cell located at the Supreme Headquarters Allied Powers Europe, SHAPE (Pesme, 2010, p. 53). Besides, it became increasingly absurd to not take part in the key strategic discussions at the NATO Defence Planning Committee, and to only be informed once decisions were made (Howorth, 2010, p. 16), especially considering the magnitude of France's de facto involvement in the Alliance. More generally, France had little say over NATO's profound evolution in a changing international context, due to its "aloofness" from key decision-making bodies (Bozo, 2010, p.178). "Reinforcing France's influence within NATO, especially in terms of the planning of operations to which it participates" thus appeared first on the list of goals they put forward for reintegration (Cour des Comptes, 2012, p. 29). Finally, it was thought that re-joining the Alliance fully would appease the doubts of other allies with regards to France's intentions. Indeed, NATO allies had repeatedly expressed concerns vis-à-vis France's insistence on developing EU defence institutions and capabilities. Playing a full part in NATO could thus be a way to "assuage" the Allies' possible "suspicions and distrust" (Riecker, 2013, p. 390; Ghez and Larrabee, 2009; Bozo, 2010, p. 179).

France in NATO since 2009: normalisation and reservations

France reintegrated all of NATO's integrated military structures – save the Nuclear Planning Group (see chapter 3) – in 2009. While the seeds had been sown already for a few years, reintegration could not take place under the Chirac presidency. Firstly, Chirac had tried to negotiate reintegration in 1995, but he had given up when he did not obtain what he demanded in exchange of France's normalisation: that the NATO Southern Command be offered to a French, Italian, or Spanish representative (Vaïsse, 2009, p. 215; Soutou, 2005, p. 112). Besides, reintegration was a debated subject, then, among the French elite. While the Ministry

140 *France and its partners*

of Defence was in favour for practical reasons, the Ministry for Foreign Affairs remained opposed, favouring instead cooperation within the EU and bilaterally with Germany (De Durand, 2010, p. 7). A generational change was in order. This occurred with the coming to power of Nicolas Sarkozy, a proclaimed Atlanticist who in 2007 inherited a situation where France was already strongly involved in NATO. The 2008 defence white paper clearly highlighted a contradiction between the proclaimed desire to have an "exceptional" role within NATO and the recognition of the Alliance's contribution to France's and European security (Pesme, 2010, p. 45; Premier Ministre, 2008). Because of this assessment, Sarkozy did not present the decision as ground-breaking at the 2009 Strasbourg-Kehl summit but talked of "renewal" (Pesme, 2010, p. 45). France then became one of the key contributors to the Alliance. First, France obtained the lead of the Allied Command Transformation as well as the joint allied command in Lisbon and the deputy command of the Joint Force Command (JFC) in Brunssum, alternating with Italy and the United Kingdom, respectively (Cour des Comptes, 2012, p. 33). Secondly, in 2012, France had around 900 personnel in NATO, most of them at Allied Command Operations, followed by ACT (Ibid., pp. 33–37). In 2010–2012, France contributed between 11% and 12% of NATO's total budget, behind the United States and Germany, which represents a share equivalent to that of the United Kingdom (Ibid., pp. 37–59). Of all French troops deployed in 2010, half were operating under NATO auspices, with another 20% taking part in UN operations, and less than 5% in EU missions (Pesme, 2010, p. 48). Since 2016, France has also held the position of deputy secretary general for defence.

Despite a much greater French involvement in NATO, which also translated into more positive policy discourses vis-à-vis the Alliance (Pannier and Schmitt, 2014), a form of French discomfort with NATO persisted. First, there was a feeling that France had gained little influence in the Alliance. A November 2012 report on reintegration, drafted by Hubert Védrine, approved of the reintegration into NATO, underlining that it allowed France to exert more influence on its partners (Védrine, 2012, p. 10). However, Riecker (2013, p. 381) reports that "the general impression among French officials was that reintegration has provided somewhat increased influence, but that such influence has its limits in an organisation so heavily dominated by the USA". Secondly, there was the question of NATO's out-of-area role. France's reluctance to have NATO engaged in the MENA region was noticeable during the Libya campaign in 2011 (Pannier, 2020). When plans for enforcing a no-fly zone and, soon after, a military intervention was under way, France's allies – especially the United Kingdom and the United States, but also Italy and Turkey – would only support the intervention if it occurred through NATO. But newly appointed Foreign Minister Alain Juppé affirmed on 3 March 2011: "I do not know how the public opinion in Arab countries would react if it saw NATO forces land on a territory of the southern Mediterranean. This could prove extremely counter-productive" (Nougayrède, 2011).

Juppé later commented the Atlantic Alliance was "not the appropriate organisation" to conduct an operation against the Gaddafi regime (Assemblée

Nationale, 2011). A compromise was finally reached with Paris: NATO would provide the military command, but the political leadership would be in the hand of an ad hoc creation, the Libya Contact Group. Besides, during the operation, the French gave NATO operational control but maintained command over their aircraft carrier, their submarines, helicopters and Special Forces (see chapter 5). Similarly, after Libya, despite the support for a NATO "360" approach (Ministère des Armées, 2019b), and lobbying for allies to care about the "Southern flank" and the threat of terrorism, French presidents have favoured coalitions or the EU, rather than NATO, as frameworks to act in Europe's southern neighbourhood. Illustratively, after the terrorist attacks in France in 2015, François Hollande called for allies' solidarity by invoking article 42.7 of the Lisbon Treaty, and not article 5 of the North Atlantic Treaty, as Washington had done after the 9/11 attacks.

Things did not become easier when the European and transatlantic security landscape evolved in the late 2010s. In response to Russia's annexation of Crimea, the destabilisation of eastern Ukraine, and maritime, air, and "hybrid" incursions in Europe, France took part in NATO's Enhanced Forward Presence operation as part of a UK-led battlegroup in Estonia in 2017 and 2019. Since the 2014 Wales NATO summit, held in the midst of the Ukraine crisis, France has been a key voice supporting increases in Europe's defence spending to reach 2% of GDP. Now, the Macron presidency brought a new set of challenges for Franco-NATO relations, in the context of the Trump and Erdogan presidencies in the United States and Turkey, respectively. The 2017 *Revue Stratégique* drafted at the onset of Macron's presidency highlighted NATO's ability to elaborate a balanced, deterrent and predictable approach in eastern Europe, and naval deployments in the south, and suggested that it remains the best tool for fostering human and technical interoperability among allies. However, the 2017 review also underlined that France's alliances had "changed" so that France "can no longer rely everywhere and forever with absolute certainty on our traditional partners" (Ministère des Armées, 2017, p. 6). Besides, President Macron from the outset advocated for a rapprochement with Russia, as he acknowledged the strategic deadlock in Europe and the growing role of Russia in areas of French interest, namely Syria, the Mediterranean Sea, and Africa. To the great displeasure of central and eastern European NATO members and partner countries, Macron declared he thought relations with Russia since the 1990s were based on "a succession of misunderstandings" (Macron, 2019), thus referring implicitly to the tensions surrounding NATO enlargement. He further suggested that relations with Russia had to be "rethought" in order to escape a status quo of sterile tensions and that that could be done by building a new confidence-building and security architecture in Europe. Finally, in November 2019, in an interview with *The Economist*, which soon became famous, Macron questioned the robustness of article V, and portrayed NATO as "brain dead" due to the lack of coordination and disruptive actions of Turkey and the US, notably in the context of the Syria civil war (*The Economist*, 2019).

142 *France and its partners*

France's bilateral relations with privileged partners

France's European defence effort and its complicated participation in NATO have since the 1990s been complemented with an investment in bilateral relationships with key partners Germany, the United Kingdom, and the United States. In the last years of the 2010s, we also see a diversification of partnerships in Europe and across the globe that reflect changes in European and global security dynamics.

Germany

The Franco-German relationship was institutionalised in 1963 with the signing of the Elysée Treaty of Friendship and Reconciliation. Due to strategic differences between France and Germany during the Cold War, the Elysée Treaty has always had more political significance than meaningful military content. Indeed, cooperation with Germany has always been seen as indissociable – and undissociated – from the project of European integration, including in defence. As Frédéric Mérand explains, the Elysée Treaty "provided for a modicum of military-to-military cooperation" and it is in the changed context of Soviet demise and German reunification that this provision was furthered in an additional protocol signed in 1988 (Mérand, 2008, p. 42). The protocol provided for the creation of a Franco-German Defence and Security Council under which a Franco-German Military Cooperation Group was created. Indeed, in the context of the German reunification, in 1989–1990 the French government was still worried about a German resurgence, not least due to its economic potential, and of the need to "anchor" it in the West (Menon, 1995, p. 22). In September 1990, at the Franco-German summit, Mitterrand announced the withdrawal of the 46,000 French troops from Germany within two years (Saunier and Vial, 2015, p. 454). Besides, the Treaty on Conventional Forces in Europe (CFE), signed in Paris in 1990, included a limit to the number of German troops (Saunier and Vial, 2015, p. 449). Shortly after, the 4,500-strong Franco-German Brigade was created in 1991 and turned into a European corps in 1992.

Cooperation problems abound, however, due to differences in strategic cultures and languages. Indeed, already in the early 1990s, it appeared that France and Germany's defence doctrines and military means had been growing increasingly apart, to the extent that "some [started] questioning the validity of the bilateral cooperation" (Sauder, 1996, p. 583). There was hope for a renewal of cooperation in the early 2000s. In 2002, Paris and Berlin signed an agreement for sharing spatial intelligence, based on both countries' possession of national satellite systems (Boyer and Le Gloannec, 2007, p. 2). During the 2003 crisis over the invasion of Iraq, the French President Chirac and the German Chancellor Schröder stood side by side, which permitted them to revive the partnership. But during the interventions in Lebanon and Afghanistan, while they both took part in the operations, France and Germany again adopted different approaches to the use of force. Throughout the Afghan campaign, casualty avoidance was the

Bundestag's top priority, to the extent that German troops could not engage in combat until 2009. Because of diverging security priorities and military practices, only elements of the control and command structure of the Franco-German Brigade were ever deployed (in Bosnia and in Afghanistan). Despite the French efforts to deploy the brigade in Africa, the German government has refused so far to engage the brigade in missions that could involve the use of force. The fact that Germany's defence budget, while having a bigger population and economy, remained smaller than France's and that the country still had not turned to fully professional armed forces contributed to a feeling of mismatch between the two partners. Even France's normalisation in NATO, which could have brought the two countries closer together, revealed their distinct approaches to the Alliance and to their roles within it, with France seeking political-military leadership and Germany adopting the posture of a reliable financial supporter to the organisation (Pannier and Schmitt, 2014, pp. 272–274).

To sum up, by the 2010s, it was clear that French and German defence policies were not converging. That said, there has been some development in German defence policy since 2014, which positively affects the Paris-Berlin partnership. First, the German strategic culture is slowly moving towards a more tolerant approach to external deployments and the use of force, notably as a result of the Bundeswehr's deployment in Afghanistan (Hilpert, 2014). If the institutional control mechanisms remain in place, the proliferation of terrorist attacks in Europe, the attitude of Russia to eastern Europe, the experience gained in Afghanistan, the "refugee crisis", the pressure of the allies, and Von der Leyen's arrival at the head of the German Ministry of Defence at the end of 2014 have all contributed to consolidating the "Munich Consensus" by which Germany intends to assume greater responsibility on the international scene. These ideas were endorsed in the 2016 German defence white paper. Proactivity on the Russian dossier, German decisions to contribute – by non-kinetic means – to multinational operations (EUTM Mali, Operation Inherent Resolve), and announcements of increases in the German defence budget are part of this logic. Reacting to France's call for solidarity and the invocation of article 42.7 following the terrorist attacks of 2015, Germany has been one of the main Western contributors to the UN mission in Mali, with 430 personnel, and helicopters and drones support supply convoys (International Institute for Strategic Studies, 2019).

To complete the revival of the Franco-German partnership, Emmanuel Macron and Angela Merkel signed in January 2019 the Aachen Treaty "on Franco-German cooperation and integration" (République Française et République Fédérale d'Allemagne, 2019). While not particularly focused on defence and security, the treaty provides for increased collaboration at the UN, including through the "twinning" of the two Security Council presidencies in 2019 and 2020 under the two-year mandate of Germany. Most notably, the treaty raises the need for agreement on the sensitive issue of arms exports. Article 4(3) states that "the two States will develop a common approach to arms exports with regard to joint projects".

144 *France and its partners*

The United Kingdom

Franco-British defence cooperation differs from Franco-German cooperation on almost all points of view: it is at the same time less political, less embedded in Europe and more operationally and industrially rich. Although their military relationship is old as it dates back to the Entente Cordiale of 1904 and even more to the seal of the trenches of the Great War, the UK-French defence relationship was only recently institutionalised with the Lancaster House Treaty of 2010. The logic behind that rapprochement is undisputable and differs significantly from Franco-German cooperation: the strategic proximity between the two countries is such that they are "condemned" to act as partners (Howorth, 2012, p. 5). It is indeed impossible to write about Franco-British cooperation without listing their common strategic characteristics: they are both members of the UN Security Council, maintain nuclear deterrence, have significant defence industries and significant budgets, notably in defence R&D, have global ambitions inherited from their colonial past, and expeditionary military cultures and capabilities.

While until the end of the 1980s their cooperation in military interventions was almost non-existent, the 1990s (Bosnia) and 2000s (Afghanistan) provided numerous occasions where France and the United Kingdom jointly intervened or contributed to the same missions. Illustratively, lessons learned in Afghanistan in the context of the "surge" was one of the areas in which French and British armies began cooperating in the late 2000s. The 2010 Lancaster House Treaty (Pannier, 2018b) thus built on this strategic and operational proximity, but went further than that, as they provided for the building of shared infrastructure for nuclear weapons stockpiling and safety, the creation of defence industrial "mutual dependences" (e.g., in the missile sector), and the creation of a non-permanent bilateral first-entry force. On multiple occasions, France and the United Kingdom have driven defence cooperation initiatives within the EU, for instance with the 1998 Saint Malo declaration. Twelve years later, after many disappointments vis-à-vis Europe's military capacities, and accounting for additional changes in the international system, the Lancaster House Treaty appeared as a "reversed Saint Malo" (Dumoulin, 2011, p. 663). Indeed, acting in a purely bilateral fashion also allowed France and the United Kingdom – in theory – to work around their different outlooks vis-à-vis the role of the EU and NATO in European security.

Since 2010, France and the United Kingdom have made progress in several areas of their cooperation. First, progress on the non-permanent bilateral force, the Combined Joint Expeditionary Force (CJEF), is underway, and it will be able to conduct high-intensity first-entry operations by the tenth anniversary of the treaty. Secondly, the two countries' missile industries are now integrated around the firm MBDA, which creates mutual dependences that bind the two countries in the production of guided weapon systems. Thirdly, Paris and London tested their solidarity in Libya in 2011, by conducting many joint operations, in the crises in the Sahel and the Baltic region where they have both acted in support of the other, and by jointly taking part in the US-led coalition efforts against ISIS in the Levant. Fourthly, we have addressed in chapter 3 the ambitious cooperation between the two countries on the testing and stewardship of nuclear weapons.

At the same time, several political factors have negatively affected the relationship, too. One structural factor has been the role of the United States in the UK defence strategy, which continues to affect the United Kingdom's ability to cooperate with other partners due to its ramification for the United Kingdom's intelligence, procurement, nuclear, and operational conduct. Other contextual factors have been the United Kingdom's strategic fatigue during and after the wars in Afghanistan and Iraq, as well as the financial crisis of 2008. These translated in less acceptability among the public and the establishment for military expeditions, as well as significant budget cuts from 2010 onwards. This occurred at a period in which France started to be heavily involved in Mali, the Central African Republic (CAR), and later Iraq/Syria, and in need of more political support – at least – from London.

If that was not enough, the 2016 Brexit vote has affected and will continue to affect France's ability to cooperate with the United Kingdom. Since 2016, successive British governments have been very weak, and the risks posed by Brexit to the United Kingdom's economy and even the political unity of the Kingdom have been repeatedly pointed. This obviously has weighed on Britain's relationship with the EU, and with France, including in defence. Paris and London assured that the bilateral partnership would be preserved and even strengthened, including in the fight against terrorism and in the cyber domain. Yet, there have been some disappointments too, already. The sector of combat aviation is another example of the negative short-term effects that uncertainty has had over the UK-French defence relationship. Given the strategic and symbolic importance of combat aircraft, the future combat air system (FCAS) became one of the flagship projects of Lancaster House. A feasibility study contract for the FCAS, involving Dassault and BAE, was created in 2014. The program was to be reconducted some time in 2017, leading to capacity by the 2030s. Yet, in January 2018, Dassault announced with Germany's Airbus that it was working on a manned version of a fighter jet as part of a bigger project of a "system of systems" that also included unmanned systems. For its part, the British government signed a 12-month *national* contract with BAE Systems to continue work on a future combat air system named Tempest and published a national strategy for the future of combat aviation that did not mention France even once (Ministry of Defence, 2018). The CEO of Dassault declared in the press that "British reasons" had caused cooperation to be put on hold, because "They [had] not managed to find the money, or [had] other priorities" due to the "strong turbulences" caused by Brexit (Tran, 2018).

Other European partners

France obviously cooperates closely with other European countries by virtue of their shared EU and/or NATO membership, and through bilateral or minilateral arrangements. In particular, France has a long tradition of cooperation with Benelux (Belgium, Netherlands, Luxemburg), Italy, and Spain. France and Italy

146 *France and its partners*

have historically cooperated in the naval and space domains, as well as operationally between their armies, in particular around their shared experiences in mountain areas. France and Italy announced in 2010, and confirmed in 2013, enhanced cooperation between their respective alpine brigades and the creation of an integrated non-permanent brigade command, which was deployed for the first time in Lebanon (FINUL) in 2015 (Ministère des Armées, 2010; Lagneau, 2015). Italy, like Germany, has its own space systems and exchanges information with France and collaborates with France on European systems (Premier Ministre, 2008, p. 128). Cooperation with Spain centres on the Mediterranean and north and western Africa and joint procurement in the airspace domain. There have also been collective endeavours. France cooperates with Spain, Germany, Belgium, and Luxembourg as part of the Strasbourg-based European corps "Eurocorps" established in 1993 (Premier Ministre, 1994, p. 32). Besides, due to their significant defence industrial bases, Italy and Spain, as well as Sweden, Germany, the United Kingdom, and France were signatories of the 2000 Letter of Intent aiming to bolster an integrated European defence industry.

The 2017 *Revue Stratégique* recognises the "specific capabilities" that other partners in eastern and northern Europe can contribute to France's operations (*Revue Stratégique*, 2017, p. 62) and help it meets its strategic objectives, especially in the fight against terrorism. Recent interventions in particular in the Sahel reminded the French that beyond the United Kingdom, Germany, and the United States, other European partners mattered operationally too, due to the support they bring to French forces on the ground. Spain, for instance, provided a third of the tactical airlift to French forces in the Sahel for Operation Barkhane (Pannier, 2018a, p. 3). Other links developed outside of the Sahel. For instance, a Finnish company became embedded in the French forces deployed with the United Nations Interim Force in Lebanon. Macron sought to build on these experiences and get Europeans involved operationally within a bottom-up logic and proposed the concept of European Intervention Initiative (EI2), taking place outside of the EU and NATO. The EI2 is a gathering of willing and able European nations to further their military interoperability and ability to conduct interventions. The project stems from a double assessment: first, that Europe needs to urgently improve its coordination in international crises and the interoperability of its forces, and second, that those countries most likely to deploy forces alongside France may or may not be members of the EU common defence policy (for example, the United Kingdom post-Brexit, or Denmark with its ESDP opt-out), or NATO.

The United States

Although it is different from the type of relationship that France can maintain with European partners such as Germany or the United Kingdom that are comparable in terms of economic and military weight, the relationship with Washington has provided structure for French strategic orientations. Paris and Washington can build on a century-old military relationship, forged in the First World War. Already well before that, France supported the United States in its War of Independence

France and its partners 147

against Britain. These factors explain why France is often referred to as the United States' "oldest ally". In spite of this historical foundation, it is fair to say that French governments have always struggled to balance between the need to work with Americans and the pursuit of national and European strategic autonomy. As Hubert Védrine, French minister for foreign affairs from 1997 to 2002, put it "squaring the circle" between being "a friend of the American nation, an ally of the United States but while not being aligned behind the American empire" has been a "permanent dilemma" for all French presidents (Védrine, 1996, p. 169; see also Pannier, 2017). A brief look at the past decades of Franco-US military links and crises indicate this constant state of flux: by and large, France was a "reluctant atlanticist" (Schmitt, 2017).

From its inception, NATO has been perceived as consisting mostly of the United States arm in Europe, rather than being seen as a potential alliance of equals. While French governments, as we have explained, have been uncomfortable with this European dependence, the 1994 defence white paper presented "the permanence of US commitment in favour of Europe's security and stability" as "necessary" (Premier Ministre, 1994, p. 31). Aside from the security and stability of Europe, that we explained earlier in this chapter, France developed operational ties with the United States from the 1990s onwards, starting with the Gulf War and continuing in Bosnia, Kosovo, and Afghanistan. At the same time, the 1990s–2000s were also the period of the United States' greatest relative power, with its accompanying unilateralism, which peaked with the doctrine of pre-emptive war and the invasion of Iraq in 2003. Yet, the 9/11 terrorist attacks also led to a France-US rapprochement in counter-terrorism, including through the creation of a secret international intelligence cell, "Alliance Base", in Paris from 2002 to 2010 (Priest, 2005; Servenay, 2010).

Overall, considering the sheer size of American power, its exceptional role as security guarantor in Europe, its leadership in coalition operations, and the fact that it has been driving the technological innovation race (communications, air, naval, space), France has tried hard to both work with the United States politically and strategically and to keep up militarily. Thus, during Sarkozy's presidency, on top of the return to NATO's integrated structures, there was a desire to solidify the links with the United States. However, Barack Obama arrived at the White House one year after the start of the Sarkozy presidency, and the two men did not enjoy a particularly good relationship. The United States, while providing support to French operations, has not been keen to get much more involved in support of "wars of choice" as illustrated in Libya in 2011. Obama later criticised his European partners, in particular France and Britain, for failing to deal with the deteriorating situation in Libya after the death of Gaddafi.

For Hollande, just like for Sarkozy, it was very important to work with the United States, especially in the context of the Syrian civil war after 2011, and the destabilisation of Mali and the Sahel in 2012–2013. Illustratively, in Mali, the United States Intelligence, Surveillance and Reconnaissance (ISR) system provided a third of the intelligence used in the French intervention (Chivvis, 2016, p. 119). Recognising the progress made in their bilateral cooperation,

148   *France and its partners*

Barack Obama and François Hollande affirmed in February 2014 that France and United States enjoy a "renewed alliance":

> A decade ago, few would have imagined our two countries working so closely together in so many ways. But in recent years our alliance has transformed. Since France's return to NATO's military command four years ago [...] we have expanded our cooperation across the board. [We] have been able to take our alliance to a new level because our interests and values are so closely aligned.
>
> (Hollande and Obama, 2014)

In the fight against ISIS from 2014 onwards, intelligence exchanges between France and the United States went to yet another level. In September 2014, France joined the US-led coalition against ISIS in Iraq, and later Syria. Increased cooperation on the ground between the United States and France has encouraged a greater (albeit still limited) institutionalisation of the partnership. After the 2015 terrorist attacks in France, Paris and Washington set up the "Lafayette Committee", which facilitated intelligence exchange in theatres of operation, and in a multilateral context, the "Five Eyes + France" format became increasingly used (Belin, 2018). Cooperation increased between the armed services, too. In 2015, the French and American armies signed a Strategic Vision Statement to increase cooperation between the armies around intelligence, logistics, and forecast (Armée de Terre, 2017). In November 2016, French and American defence representatives signed a Joint Statement of Intent to underline the importance and breadth of their cooperation and open it up to new areas, including space (Carter and Le Drian, 2016).

That being said, just as France and the United States were getting closer, French authorities perceived during the second term of the Obama presidency, and even more so during the Trump presidency, a weakening of the United States' global leadership, which has been seen as both a curse and a blessing for France's security interests and strategy. This started with the US decision to call off air strikes against Syria in response to the Al-Assad regime's use of chemical weapons in Summer 2013. To French policy-makers and analysts, this constituted a turning point in US foreign policy and opened the door to other countries crossing US so-called "red lines" without fear of being too bothered by Washington, like Russia in Ukraine from 2014 onwards. Macron saw this relative US decline, or at least partial withdrawal, and henceforth unreliability, as worrying for the world, but also as an opportunity for asserting French leadership in Europe and globally, in support of the multilateral, rules-based international order on the one hand, and of European strategic autonomy on the other. The French push for European defence from late 2016 onwards must thus also be understood in that context.

Partners in Africa

Cooperation with African countries is for the most part inherited from colonial times. Some of the "defence agreements" signed during decolonisation in the 1960s and 1970s (Dulait et al., 2006, p. 8), allowed France to intervene in those countries for evacuating French nationals, protecting official buildings and strategic infrastructure, and militarily assisting governments in cases of "major circumstances" (Lemayre, 2009), including through ensuring law enforcement. The bilateral agreement with Gabon, signed in 1960, illustratively specified that the Republic of Gabon could "with the agreement of the French republic, call on French armed forces for its internal and external defence" (Lemayre, 2009). At the time, the goal was to ensure that the partner's fragile government would be able to maintain its independence against external threats (Mitterrand, 1990), in the context of the global competition that characterised the Cold War (Dulait et al., 2006, p. 10). Aside from "defence agreements", technical agreements exist with 27 African countries. They permit the transit and stopover of French troops, the exchange of information, and the provision of military training and education and equipment, etc. (Lemayre, 2009). In certain cases, they allow France to maintain troops permanently stationed. In the early 2000s, there were 6,000 French forces in five countries, Djibouti, Senegal, Ivory Coast, Gabon, and Chad (Dulait et al., 2006, p. 7).

In 1990, Mitterrand had affirmed at the France-Africa summit in La Baule, that he intended to maintain the same policy and military support provided for in the bilateral defence agreements. By the next decade, the agreements were denounced as outdated and became increasingly criticised both in Africa and in France, not least due to the scandals surrounding the genocide in Rwanda in 1994 (De Rohan, 2011, p. 29). In the late 1990s, as part of a significant attempt at normalising France's relations with African partners, the Ministère de la Coopération (inherited from colonial times) was disbanded and fused with the Ministry of Foreign Affairs. France also launched the "RECAMP" program to reinforce African peacekeeping capabilities. A decade later, a report by French senators argued that it had now become "hardly conceivable" that France would today engage in law enforcement tasks in former colonies (Dulait et al., 2006, p. 9). Finally, the report suggested moving towards a multilateralisation of the French Africa policy, and a focus on the empowerment of partner countries, notably through military training.

Following the trend initiated in the late 1990s, Nicolas Sarkozy denounced the old bilateral agreements as "obsolete" (Lemayre, 2009). The president further tried to normalise French policy-making on Africa, for instance by integrating the "Africa cell" into the regular "diplomatic cell" of the Elysée, instead of it being separate as it had been until then (Leboeuf and Quénot-Suarez, 2015, pp. 9–10). Importantly, in 2008, he undertook a re-negotiation of bilateral defence agreements, and committed to (1) transparency, with the suppression of secret clauses allowing French interventions in partner countries, (2) a respect for partners' sovereignty and independence, (3) the objective of helping Africa to develop its collective security system, and (4) a multilateral approach engaging both the African Union and the European Union (Deflesselles, 2013, p. 9). Nonetheless, France has maintained pre-positioned ("*présence*") forces in Ivory Coast, Djibouti, Gabon, Senegal, and the UAE that facilitate – and thus to some extent also encourage – rapid military deployments. Interestingly, in 2013, France launched Operation

150 *France and its partners*

Serval in Mali (2013–2014) and Sangaris in the CAR (2013–2016), which both brought France back into its old posture of security guarantor in former colonies (France intervened at the request of the government in both cases). But there was also an opportunity to implement its newer approach combining local ownership and multilateralisation. In particular, Serval was replaced in 2014 with Operation Barkhane, located in and involving the armed forces of Mali, Burkina Faso, Niger, Chad, and Mauritania through the "G5 Sahel" and France actively pursued the support of European partners. Aline Leboeuf and Helene Quénot-Suarez argue that despite François Hollande's attempts (and Emmanuel Macron after him), the mix of normalisation of relations, empowerment of African partners, and maintenance of French influence appears impossible to reconcile (Leboeuf and Quénot-Suarez, 2015, p. 2).

Partners in Asia

Finally, we come to strategic partnerships with countries across the globe. The Asia-Pacific region is worth mentioning here. Due to its colonial past in that region, too, France maintains sovereign territories, including New Caledonia, Wallis and Futuna, and Polynesia. These provide bases for a permanent military presence, and, together with France's permanent seat at the UN, underpin France's strategic interests in the region. France indeed sees itself as "a power of the Indian ocean and of the Pacific" and therefore views French and regional security interests as inseparable (Ministère de la Défense, 2014, p. 2). France was mostly focused on relations with large Asian powers in the 1990s and signed bilateral strategic partnerships with Japan (1995), China (1997), and India (1998) and helped establish the Asia-Europe Meeting (ASEM) in 1996 (Lechervy, 2013; Ministère de la Défense, 2014, p. 3). The focus was then on matters of nuclear non-proliferation, counter-terrorism, the protection of French nationals, and humanitarian missions. Since the 1990s, France has also cooperated with other "Western" powers in the region, in particular through minilateral formats such as FRANZ, (with New Zealand, Australia) and the Quadrilateral Defence Coordination Group, with the same countries plus the United States.

From the 2000s onwards, the military assertion of China, growing interstate tensions, the economic rise of other Asian countries, and the ever-growing strategic importance of shipping routes have led to a renewed interest in the region and a desire to weigh on the strategic balance in Asia-Pacific and on maritime issues in particular (Lechervy, 2013; Ministère de la Défense, 2014, p. 3). As evidenced by the 2019 French defence strategy in the Indo-Pacific, the goal of preserving strategic stability in the Asia-Pacific region (rebranded Indo-Pacific to demonstrate the interlinking of the developments in both regions) became even more important amidst growing strategic competition between the United States and China, and Beijing's massive international investments through the Belt and Road Initiative (Ministère des Armées, 2019a). France thus signed bilateral "strategic partnerships" with Indonesia (2011), Australia (2012), Singapore (2012), and Vietnam (2013) (Ministère de la Défense, 2014, p. 3) and renewed its strategic dialogue

France and its partners 151

with South Korea in 2018 (Ministère de l'Europe et des Affaires Étrangères, 2018). Asia also became a prime target for French arms exports in the 2010s, in particular India and Australia (see chapter 4).

Conclusion

European security institutions and bilateral defence partnerships have evolved since the end of the Cold War to form a somewhat coherent set in France's defence strategy, despite some frustrations. Firstly, the EU has developed a speciality in civil-military missions in the 2000s but has significantly extended its scope over the past ten years. The creation of a common market in defence, and more recently the EDF and PESCO, all framed by the 2016 EU Global Strategy, have created opportunities for the EU to support member states' defence industries and help develop capabilities. Secondly, NATO has been maintained to keep the United States in Europe and to reinforce the Euro-Atlantic defence posture and the inter-operability of European and American armed forces. Since the mid-2010s, it has re-focused around its core tasks of collective defence, which is what successive French presidents have viewed as the Alliance's main role. Thirdly, bilateral or minilateral partnerships in Europe and across the globe fill a gap in the existing architecture. They provide support to France in military operations, including in the fight against terrorism, France's main battle over the last two decades. These arrangements endow France with responsibilities for its partners too, but they enhance its influence and its geographical reach – all significant gains for a middle power with a global role.

References

Armée de Terre (2017), "100 ans de coopération franco-américaine", 11 July. Available at: https://www.defense.gouv.fr/terre/actu-terre/100-ans-de-cooperation-franco-ameri caine (last access, 8 December 2019).
Assemblée Nationale (2011), "Compte rendu intégral, XIIIe legislature, Session ordinaire de 2010–2011", 22 March. Available at: http://www.assemblee-nationale.fr/13/cri /2010-2011/20110144.asp (last access, 13 December 2019).
Assembly of the Western European Union (1997), *Proceedings of the 43rd Session - First Part*, June.
Auerswald, D.P. and Saideman, S. (2014), *NATO in Afghanistan: Fighting Together, Fighting Alone*. Princeton: Princeton University Press.
Bagayoko-Penone, N. (2004), "L'opération Artémis, un tournant pour la politique européenne de sécurité et de défense?", *Afrique contemporaine*, 209/1, 101–116.
Belin, C. (2018), "L'excellente relation de défense franco-américaine, à l'épreuve des turbulences transatlantiques", *Institut Montaigne*, 11 July. Available at: https://www .institutmontaigne.org/blog/lexcellente-relation-de-defense-franco-americaine-lepreu ve-des-turbulences-transatlantiques (last access, 10 December 2019).
Black, I. (2003), "NATO Bid to Defuse EU Defence Row", *The Guardian*, 20 October.
Blair, T. and Chirac, J. (1998), "Joint declaration issued at the British-French Summit", *Saint Malo*, 3–4 December.

152 *France and its partners*

Boyer, Y. and Le Gloannec, A.-M. (2007), "La coopération franco-allemande en matière de défense: Jusqu'où l'Allemagne peut-elle aller?", *Note de la FRS*, Paris: Fondation pour la Recherche Stratégique.

Bozo, F. (2010) "Sarkozy's NATO Policy: Towards France's Atlantic Alignment?", *European Political Science*, 9/2, 176–188.

Carter, A. and Le Drian, J.-Y. (2016), "Joint Statement of Intent between the US and France", 28 November. Available at: https://dod.defense.gov/Portals/1/Documents/p ubs/Joint-Statement-of-Intent-between-the-US-and-France.pdf (last access 4 December 2019).

Charbonneau, B. (2008), "Dreams of Empire: France, Europe, and the New Interventionism in Africa", *Modern & Contemporary France*, 16/3, 279–295.

Charillon, F. and Ramel, F. (2010), "Action extérieure et défense: L'Influence française à Bruxelles", *Cahier de l'IRSEM No.1*, Paris: IRSEM.

Chivvis, C. (2016), *The French war on Al Qaida in Africa*. Cambridge: Cambridge University Press.

Colard, D. (2006), "Du couple franco-allemand au partenariat Paris-Berlin", Arès, 22/57, 37–45.

Cour des Comptes (2012), *La réintégration de la France dans le commandement intégré de l'OTAN: quel coût et quelles pistes d'économies possibles?*.

De Durand, E. (2010), "Entente or Oblivion: Prospects and Pitfalls of Franco-British Cooperation on Defence", Future Defence Review Working Paper No.8, London: Royal United Services Institute.

Deflesselles, B. (2013), "Avis fait au nom de la Commission de la Défense nationale et des forces armées sur le projet de loi autorisant la ratification du traité instituant un partenariat de défense entre la République Française et la République de Côte d'Ivoire", *Assemblée Nationale, Quatorzième legislature, No.931*, 16 April.

De Rohan, J. (2011), "La politique africaine de la France", Rapport d'information No.324 (2010–2011) fait au nom de la commission des affaires étrangères, 28 February.

Duke, S. and Vanhoonaker, S. (2016), "EU–NATO Relations Top-Down Strategic Paralysis, Bottom-Up Cooperation", in Chappell, L., Mawdsley, J. and Peter, P. (eds.), *The EU, Strategy and Security Policy: Regional and Strategic Challenges*. London: Routledge, 153–168.

Dulait, André et al. (2006), Rapport d'information fait au nom de la commission des Affaires étrangères, de la défense et des forces armées sur la gestion des crises en Afrique subsaharienne, Report No.450, Sénat, Session 2005–2006, 3 July.

Dumoulin, A. (2011), "PSDC: Le Jeu des Lettres et des 'Directoires'", *Politique Etrangère*, 2011/3, 661–671.

Duval, M. (1989), "The Prospects for Military Cooperation Outside Europe: A French View", in Boyer, Y., Lellouche, P. and Roper, J. (eds.), *Franco-British Defence Cooperation: A New Entente Cordiale?* London: Routledge, 67–83.

EU Council Secretariat (2009), "EU Military Operation in Eastern Chad and North Eastern Central African Republic (EUFOR Tchad/RCA)", *Factsheet*, 1 March. Available at: https://eeas.europa.eu/archives/csdp/missions-and-operations/eufor-tchad-rca/pdf /01032009_factsheet_eufor-tchad-rca_en.pdf (last access, 23 November 2019).

Federal Ministry of Defence (1994) *White Paper on the Security of the Federal Republic of Germany and the Situation and Future of the Bundeswehr*.

Gautier, L. (2009), *La défense de la France après la Guerre Froide: Politique Militaire et Forces Armées Depuis 1989*. Paris: Presses Universitaires de France.

Ghez, J. and Larrabee, F.S. (2009), "France and NATO", *Survival*, 51/2, 77–90.

Hilpert, C. (2014), *Strategic Cultural Change and the Challenge for Security Policy: Germany and the Bundeswehr's Deployment to Afghanistan*. Basingstoke: Palgrave McMillan.

Hollande, F. (2012), *Discours sur la défense nationale*. Paris, 11 March. Available at: https://www.dailymotion.com/video/xpe2fl

Howorth, J. (1997), "France", in Howorth, J. and Menon, A. (eds.), *The European Union and National Defence Policy*. London: Routledge, 23–48.

Howorth, J. (2010), "Sarkozy and the 'American Mirage' or Why Gaullist Continuity Will Overshadow Transcendence", *European Political Science*, 9/2, 199–212

Howorth, J. (2012), "European Security Institutions 1945–2010: The Weaknesses and Strengths of 'Brusselization'", in Biscop, S. and Whitman, R. (eds.), *The Routledge Handbook of European Security*. London: Routledge, 5–17.

International Institute for Strategic Studies (2019), *Military Balance 2019*. London: Routledge.

Irondelle, B. (2003), "Europeanization without the European Union? French Military Reforms 1991–1996", *Journal of European Public Policy*, 10/2, 208–226.

Lagneau, L. (2015), "Premier déploiement de l'état-major non permanent de la brigade franco-italienne", *Opex 360*, 23 October. Available at: http://www.opex360.com/2015 /10/23/premier-deploiement-de-letat-major-non-permanent-de-la-brigade-franco-italie nne/ (lass access, 4 December 2019).

Leboeuf, A. and Quénot-Suarez, H. (2015), *La Politique Africaine de la France sous François Hollande: Renouvellement et impensé stratégique*. Paris: IFRI.

Lechervy, C. (2013), "La France, l'Europe et l'Asie-Pacifique", *Lettre de l'IRSEM No. 2*, 2 April. Available at: https://www.defense.gouv.fr/english/irsem/publications/lettr e-de-l-irsem/les-lettres-de-l-irsem-2012-2013/2013-lettre-de-l-irsem/lettre-de-l-irse m-n-2-2013/dossier-strategique/la-france-l-europe-et-l-asie-pacifiqu (last access, 2 December 2019).

Lellouche, P. (2009), *L'allié indocile: La France et l'OTAN, de la Guerre Froide à l'Afghanistan*. Paris: Editions du Moment.

Lemayre, P. (2009), "France-Afrique: des accords militaires 'nouvelle génération'", *Le Monde Diplomatique, blog*, 11 June. Available at: https://blog.mondediplo.net/2009-06 -10-France-Afrique-accords-nouvelle-generation (last access, 2 December 2019).

Macron, E. (2017), "Initiative for Europe" (official translation), *Speech*. Paris, 26 September. Available at: https://www.diplomatie.gouv.fr/IMG/pdf/english_version_transcript_-_ initiative_for_europe_-_speech_by_the_president_of_the_french_republic_cle8de628 .pdf (last access, 14 January 2020).

Macron, E. (2019), "Discours du Président de la République à la conférence des des ambassadeurs et des ambassadrices", *Speech*. Paris, 27 August.

Menon, A. (1995), "From Independence to Cooperation: France, NATO and European Security", *International Affairs*, 71/1, 19-34.

Mérand, F. (2008), *European Defence Policy, beyond the Nation State*. Oxford: Oxford University Press.

Million, C. (1996), "France and the Renewal of the Atlantic Alliance", *NATO Review*, 3/44, 13–16.

Milzow, K. (2006), "Le discours politique et la sécurité en Europe: Blair, Chirac et Schröder et la politique européenne de sécurité et de défense (1998–2003)", *Relations Internationales*, 125/1, 83–95.

Ministère de l'Europe et des Affaires Étrangères (2018), "Déclaration conjointe - Sommet entre la France et la République de Corée", 15 October. Available at: https://www.dip

154 *France and its partners*

lomatie.gouv.fr/fr/dossiers-pays/coree-du-sud/evenements/article/declaration-conjointe -sommet-entre-la-france-et-la-republique-de-coree-du-15 (last access, 2 December 2019).

Ministère de la Défense (2014), *La France et la sécurité en Asie-Pacifique.*

Ministère des Armées (2010), "Sommet franco-italien: création d'une brigade alpine commune", 6 July. Available at: https://www.defense.gouv.fr/actualites/articles/so mmet-franco-italien-creation-d-une-brigade-alpine-commune (last access, 4 December 2019).

Ministère des Armées (2017), *Defence and National Security Strategic Review.*

Ministère des Armées (2019a), *La Stratégie de défense française en Indopacifique.*

Ministère des Armées (2019b), "L'OTAN", 15 July. Available at: https://www.defense.gouv. fr/english/dgris/international-action/l-otan-fr/l-otan (last access, 12 December 2019).

Ministry of Defence (1998), *Strategic Defence Review*, Cm 3999, July.

Ministry of Defence (2018), *Combat Air Strategy: An Ambitious Vision for the Future*, July.

Mitterrand, F. (1990), "Allocution sur la situation économique de l'Afrique, les possibilités d'aide des pays les plus riches et la position française en matière de coopération et d'aide financière", *La Baule*, 20 June.

Nougayrède, N. (2011), "Paris n'exclut pas une interdiction de survol de la Libye", *Le Monde*, 3 March.

Hollande, F. and Obama, B. (2014), "France and the US Enjoy a Renewed Alliance", *The Washington Post*, 10 February.

O'Donnell, C.M. (2011), "Britain's Coalition Government and EU Defence Cooperation: Undermining British Interests", *International Affairs*, 87/2, 419–433.

Pannier, A. (2017), "From one Exceptionalism to Another: France's Strategic Relations with the United States and the United Kingdom in the Post-Cold War Era", *Journal of Strategic Studies*, 40/4, 475–504.

Pannier, A. (2018a), "France's Defense Partnerships and the Dilemmas of Brexit", German Marshall Fund, Transatlantic Security Task Force, Policy Brief No.22.

Pannier, A. (2018b), "UK–French Defence and Security Cooperation", in Meijer, Hugo and Wyss, Marco (eds.), *The Handbook of European Defence Policies and Armed Forces*. Oxford: Oxford University Press, 424–439.

Pannier, A. (2020), *Rivals in Arms: The Rise of UK-France Defence Relations in the Twenty-First Century*. Montreal/Kingston: McGill-Queen's University Press.

Pannier, A. and Schmitt, O. (2014), "Institutionalised Cooperation and Policy Convergence in European Defence: Lessons from the Relations between France, Germany and the United Kingdom", *European Security*, 23/3, 270–289.

Pannier, A. and Schmitt, O. (2019), "To Fight Another Day: France between the Fight Against Terrorism and Future Warfare", *International Affairs*, 95/ 4, 897–916.

Pesme, F. (2010), "France's 'Return' to NATO: Implications for Its Defence Policy", *European Security*, 19/1, 45–60.

Prater, F. (1991), "La France et la crise du Golfe", *Politique Etrangère*, 56/2, 441–453.

Premier Ministre (1994), *Livre Blanc sur la Defence*. Paris: La Documentation Française.

Priest, D. (2005), "Help Form France in Key Covert Operations", *The Washington Post*, 3 July.

République française et République fédérale d'Allemagne (2019), *Traité sur la Coopération et l'Intégration Franco-allemandes.*

Riecker, P. (2013), "The French Return to NATO: Reintegration in Practice, not in Principle", *European Security*, 22/3, 376–394.

Sauder, A., (1996), "Les changements de la politique de défense française et la coopération franco-allemande", *Politique Etrangère*, 3, 583.

Saunier G. and P. Vial (2015), *La France et sa défense: Paroles Publiques d'un Président*. Paris: Nouveau Monde.

Schmitt, O. (2017), "The Reluctant Atlanticist: France's Security and Defence Policy in a Transatlantic Context", *Journal of Strategic Studies*, 40/4, 463–474.

Servenay, D. (2010), "Terrorisme: Pourquoi Alliance Base a fermé à Paris", *Rue89*, 24 May. Available at: http://rue89.nouvelobs.com/2010/05/24/terrorisme-fermeture-d alliance-base-a-paris-152349 (last access, 7 December 2019).

Soutou, G.-H. (2005), "Three Rifts, Two Reconciliations: Franco-American Relations during the Fifth Republic", in D. Andrews (ed.), *Atlantic Alliance under Stress: US-European Relations after Iraq*. Cambridge: Cambridge University Press, 102–127.

Tardy, T. (2000), "La France, l'Europe et la guerre du Kosovo", *Regards sur l'Actualité*, 257, 3–18.

The Economist (2019), "Emmanuel Macron in His Own Words (English)", 7 November.

Tran, P. (2018), "UK Was the One to Put the Brakes on Drone Demo Project, Industry Says", *Defense News*, 13 April. Available at: https://www.defensenews.com/global/ europe/2018/04/12/uk-was-the-one-to-put-the-brakes-on-drone-demo-project-industry -says (last access, 4 November 2019).

Vaïsse, M. (2009), *La puissance ou l'influence? La France dans le monde depuis 1958*. Paris: Fayard.

Vaïsse, M. and C. Sebag (2009), "France and NATO: An History", *Politique Etrangère*, 2009/5 série, 139–150.

Védrine, H. (1996), *Les Mondes de François Mitterrand*. Paris: Fayard.

Védrine, H. (2012), *Rapport pour le Président de la République Française sur les conséquences du retour de la France dans le commandement intégré de l'OTAN, sur l'avenir de la relation transatlantique et les perspectives de l'Europe de la défense*.

Waterfield, B. (2011), "'Big Five' tell Baroness Ashton to Bypass Britain over EU Military HQ", *The Daily Telegraph*, 8 September.

Conclusion

Three decades after the Fall of the Berlin Wall, assessing the scope, sources, and direction of changes in France's defence policy was a necessary exercise. It is even more the case when, despite France being at the forefront of Europe's external actions, the vast majority of publications about France's defence and foreign policies are unavailable to non-French-speaking readers. In this book, we have built on years of research on France, and on the many, little known scholarly works published in the French language, to provide a 360-degree appraisal of where France is coming from, and where it is going when it comes to its defence policy. Three decades after the Fall of the Wall, the changes have been deep, although continuities have been just as striking. And over the course of those decades, change has not been one-directional: some strands of defence policy have known a consistent, steady evolution towards the present state of affairs, while in other policy strands, adaptation has been more chaotic. Besides, some changes have been prompted by the evolution of the international security context, while others have come from the evolution of French society, or have been prompted by the vision and leadership of a single man, the president of the French Republic. In either case, what this book illustrates is that the ends of France's grand strategy, presented in the book's introduction, have remained, but the means to achieve them have evolved. Since the end of the Cold War, there has been an adaptation of the principles guiding France's actions to new realities, rather than a change of those principles. In this concluding chapter, we review the main lessons from this study about what kind of power France was and has become in the past 30 years, before assessing the opportunities and challenges that lie ahead as the 21st century continues to unfold.

Strategic changes and challenges since the end of the Cold War: a review

It is important to recall and summarise what have been the most significant shifts in international security and in Europe's security in particular over the past decades, to which France, like other countries, has had to adapt. The main initial shift following the Fall of the Berlin Wall was the disappearance of the Soviet threat to the east. This constituted both a change in terms of the immediate threat

Conclusion 157

to France's and her allies' territory and more generally a change in the structure of the international system. This prompted a reappraisal of the role of the armed forces for territorial defence, of the place of nuclear deterrence in nuclear-armed countries' strategies, and, for France, of the function of autonomy in a no-longer bipolar world order. With the disappearance of the Soviet threat, too, purely military tools lost centrality in democracies' defence strategies, which translated into lowering defence budgets. Concomitantly, the European security order, which had been locked in the East-West confrontation, unleashed new forms of intra-state, inter-ethnic violence in the Balkans, prompting Europeans to define their role in the region, their approach to crisis and conflict management, and the modalities of their collective engagement. Crises also erupted outside of Europe, and in particular in the Middle East, where the Gulf War marked the entrance into a new era of American domination of world affairs and of military interventions conducted by large, US-led coalitions. The Gulf War presented, too, a challenge in terms of the types of military equipment necessary for contemporary warfare, and of the training, doctrines, and interoperability needed for multinational interventions.

Soon after the end of the Cold War, too, transnational threats emerged and rapidly came to the fore, leading to a new conceptual and geographical definition of the notion of national security. Asymmetrical threats, and in particular those posed by transnational terrorism, came to hit at the heart of Western democracies, just like in many other parts of the world. The distinction between internal and external security challenges became increasingly blurred, both in terms of the Western countries' management of new threats on their own territory and in terms of the security, political, economic, and social environment in countries where terrorist threats emanated from. This forced a rethinking of the links between military force and non-kinetic action, and between national forces, military alliances and coalitions, and the role of international organisations endowed with broader mandates.

Both types of violence (intra-state, inter-ethnic conflicts and transnational terrorism), led to a multiplication of Western military interventions over the past three decades, particularly in what the French 2008 defence white paper described as the "arc of crises" spanning Sub-Saharan Africa, the Middle East and the Afghanistan/Pakistan zone. Large, US-led and multiorganisation coalition operations have been a continuous characteristic from the 1990s until today, as exemplified in Afghanistan, Libya, Iraq, and Syria. Despite the West's persistent technological domination, a constant adaptation of military equipment was necessary due to the diversity of theatres of deployment, the need to maintain a competitive edge, as well as an increasing casualty aversion among democracies – thus driving even more innovation. At the same time, while defence spending in Europe stagnated, the global arms trade grew sharply over the decades, with increased demand in the Middle East and Asia, and mounting competition, among producers, for export markets. In America and in Europe, this led to a greater dependence on exports for funding defence expenditures and forced the creation of large, integrated industrial groups and the diversification of their production and of their target markets. It also led to a technological levelling and a gradual

158   *Conclusion*

shrinking of the technological gap between the United States and Europe and their military adversaries. Finally, while the end of the Cold War initially decreased the centrality of nuclear weapons, the challenges posed by nuclear proliferation quickly came to the fore, from the 1990s onwards with the cases of Iraq, India, Iran, North Korea, Pakistan, as well as with the proliferation of dual vectors from Russia, the United States, and China.

The evolution of French defence policy since 1991 and the nature of French power

As the chapters in this book have explained, France has adapted to and tried to shape this ever-changing environment over the past decades. The main changes in French defence policy have arguably concerned nuclear deterrence capabilities and doctrines, and approaches to nuclear proliferation and arms control, reflecting the changing global strategic landscape; the role and structure of French armed forces, as a consequence of changing types and contexts of military interventions; and an update of France's alliances and partnerships, with the rise of the EU's Common Security and Defence Policy (CSDP), and NATO's post-Cold-War role. France's European and North American allies also adapted to this changing context. But what do the findings from the previous chapters reveal about the specific characteristics of France as a military power and how it translates into its defence policy? What is the "French touch" in defence, and how has it translated into the decisions made since 1991? How has France adapted its defence means to reach its persistent ends in an ever-changing environment?

A presidential power

Firstly, France is a presidential power. We have explained in this book that from the decision to use military force to undertaking organisational reforms and to defining nuclear doctrine and capabilities, the institutional setup of the Fifth Republic gives a lot of power to the president. For this very reason, since Charles De Gaulle and up to the post-Cold-War period and the present day, each president has left a singular mark on French defence policy, of which the subsequent presidents have been heirs. Even though several changes in the majority political party took place, no president unmade what his predecessors had undertaken, which explains a certain degree of consistency over the past three decades. Mitterrand, who was in charge during the transition period from the Cold War to its aftermath, was the president who decided that France would maintain nuclear deterrence in order to defend itself and maintain room for manoeuvre in the new international context. Although he had been initially skeptical about nuclear deterrence, he was very active in this domain over the terms of his presidency. Entering the 1990s, he was also the president of the Gulf War, who accepted the need to modernise the French armed forces and work within coalitions alongside the United States. Finally, he supervised the drafting of the 1994 white paper, which remained valid until it

Conclusion 159

was replaced only in 2008 and which recognised that in the new international context, France could do little on its own. Mitterrand was thus a strong defendant of a common European defence, whose bases were laid in the 1992 Maastricht Treaty. Then, Jacques Chirac is remembered as the president who ended conscription and professionalised the French armed forces. Using the leeway offered by French political institutions, he was able to impose his agenda and shaped this important reform. Chirac is also remembered for opposing the US-led invasion of Iraq in favour of diplomacy, multilateralism, and international law – but most importantly of France's autonomy of decision vis-à-vis allies, and in particular the United States. Building on an effort already undertaken by Chirac, Sarkozy was the president who brought France back into NATO's integrated military structures, conducted a liberally-inspired regime-change intervention in Libya, and undertook an important rapprochement with the United Kingdom and the United States. As the president during the financial crisis that started in 2008, Sarkozy was also the president of austerity measures, including a reform of the organisation of support in French military bases and of the structure of the armed forces. François Hollande, then, is remembered as the president of the French war against terrorism, both abroad, as exemplified by the military interventions in Mali, the Sahel, and Iraq/Syria, and at home, with the declaration of the *état d'urgence* and the deployment of troops on French territory with Operation Sentinelle. Hollande was also the president of massive arms exports that boosted the resources available for France's defence and came to underpin some of France's strategic partnerships. Finally, Macron in the first years of his mandate continued the fight against terrorism both at home and abroad and was able to seize the momentum of Brexit and the Trump presidency to push the decades-old French ambition of a more defence-active and strategically autonomous Europe.

France being a presidential power raises some questions with regards to state-society relations, as well as public oversight over defence policy. First, the decision in 1996 to move to an all-volunteer military force weakened the link between society and the armed forces, even though the social make-up of the armed forces came to be more representative of the French populations, with a rise in the share of women and of populations with an immigrant background. The link between society and the armed forces was renewed in the context of the terrorist attacks from 2015 onwards, with the deployment of military patrols in the framework of Sentinelle, and growing interest in military careers since the attacks. At the same time, France being a presidential power also means that there is little oversight from the parliament or civil society over defence policy, compared to other liberal democracies. Despite some public outrage over some covert military actions, such as the sinking of the *Rainbow Warrior*, or debatable weapons export contracts, defence has remained the *domaine réservé* of the French president. Criticisms and media revelations are watched cautiously. Illustratively, when a group of military officers wrote an anonymous op-ed against the Sarkozy reform, the president demanded that they be identified, while the journalists behind *Disclose*'s revelations about the use of French-made weapons against civilian targets in Yemen

160 *Conclusion*

were called in for questioning by the General Directorate for Internal Security (DGSI) and asked to reveal their sources. Despite this limited public scrutiny, the French population has, over the period studied, been largely supportive of the French armed forces, of the military interventions conducted, and of the maintenance and modernisation of the French nuclear arsenal.

A global power

The thematic analysis of the evolution of French defence policy that we have offered in this book shows how France has endeavoured to be a global power. By global power, we mean that it has both global ambitions and means it is a country with full-spectrum military capabilities, including nuclear weapons and satellites, and corresponding research, development, and production capacities; it is a country that maintains a capacity for military presence across the globe.

As we have explained in this book, France is a nuclear power whose capabilities have always been quite small compared to great powers, during the Cold War and today. Nonetheless, nuclear weapons provide France with "life insurance" and a seat at the very restricted table of nuclear-endowed states. For both of these reasons, while France re-scaled its capabilities and updated its doctrine in the post-Cold-War period, the maintenance of a nuclear deterrence has never seriously been questioned. Today, with nuclear proliferation and the future of arms control at the forefront of international security issues, it is less likely than ever to be the case. The French nuclear deterrent also underpins France's broad-ranging defence industrial power, as the development and maintenance of an independent nuclear deterrent has come together with means for autonomous research and manufacturing. Beyond deterrence, the provision of arms has been considered as one of the principles of national independence since the 1950s, and despite the geopolitical shifts of the 1990s and 2000s, the bases of the approach designed during the Cold War have remained: France continues to dedicate significant resources to the maintenance of high-end industrial activities and defence remains the first public investor in R&D, while the level of state participation in defence industries remains the highest in Europe. France's industrial strengths lie especially in the domains of aerospace, electronics, satellites, armoured vehicles, ships, submarines, and guided weapons.

The second element of France's global power is its extensive military presence, which for a large part results from its past colonial conquests. These continue to endow it with sovereign territories in the Caribbean, the Indian Ocean, the Pacific Ocean, and in South America, where "sovereignty" French military forces are located. Meanwhile, bilateral defence agreements with former colonies reflect France's commitment to the security and stability of West Africa in particular and allow it to maintain military bases and pre-positioned forces that facilitate rapid military deployments. As a consequence, France is the only European country that still deploys combat troops in Africa on a regular basis. Global territorial reach also means that France's direct security interests extend well beyond the territory of the metropolis and explain why the French aircraft carrier group regularly

Conclusion 161

sails the Indian and Pacific Oceans and the South China Sea, which distinguishes France from other European countries, save the United Kingdom. Concomitantly, France has developed since the 1990s an extensive network of strategic partnerships, of which the Middle East, Asia, and Oceania are an increasingly central part, as targets for arms exports but also in the more general context of the return of great power competition.

A constrained European power

Finally, and paradoxically, at the same time as it is a global power with a lot of political leeway domestically, France remains a medium-sized, European power that faces a lot of constraints when it comes to fulfilling its ambitious grand strategy. Throughout the past three decades, French ambitions on the global stage have remained intact. Yet, since the end of the Cold War, defence budgets in Europe have become increasingly constrained, while the demands on armed forces have diversified, and the costs of single equipment multiplied. France has not escaped this trend: in the 1990s, the end of conscription was costly, and the model envisaged for the new, professional armed forces was downsized after being acknowledged as unrealistic; in the 2000s, the financial crisis led to significant cuts in defence spending, in particular in equipment spending but also in civilian and military jobs. It was accompanied by the sale of the Defence Ministry's real estate in Paris, as well as a reform aimed at making savings on support costs by concentrating the logistics functions of regiments, air bases, and flotillas. Among other side effects, such as tensions between the head of state and military chiefs, these persistent constraints on national resources available for defence policy have increased the strategic importance of arms exports for France to fund the equipment of its own forces. It has also made French leaders increasingly aware of the need to work with allies both for arms procurement, for support during military deployments, and even on the maintenance and safety of nuclear weapons. The 2010 rapprochement with the United Kingdom, in particular, must be understood in this context.

That being said, cooperation with allies and especially European partners has always been much more than a way to make ends meet and has, consistently in the past three decades, been pursued as a political goal. French presidents have always supported the European project and showed great ambition for Europe in defence, often teaming up with Germany in their endeavour. In turn, the EU's defence policy – even though it has never met France's ambitions in scope – has since the early 2000s displayed a certain "French touch", whether it has been the overrepresentation of areas that are French strategic priorities (as reflected in the zones where EU military missions have been deployed) and of French troops in the contingents, or more recently with the appointment of a Frenchman as "Directorate-General for Defence Industry and Space" in the EU Commission. That being said, European defence has thus far been Paris' lost battle, again an indication of the limit of France's power. Indeed, it is the US-led NATO that, since the end of the Cold War, has received the most support from other European

162 *Conclusion*

states, and has successfully adapted to the post-Cold-War context to become the primary instrument not only for territorial defence but also for military operations outside of Europe. While France gradually normalised its role in NATO (except in the nuclear domain), it has been wary of enlarging the Alliance's mandate and membership, has persistently sought to continue enhancing the EU's role, and has developed other avenues for military cooperation with American and European partners, either bilaterally or minilaterally, as a way to pursue its goals.

The future of French defence policy

Significant overarching changes within the international system are ongoing, which will shape French defence policy in the new decade. The 2010s have brought internal and external challenges to Europe that are likely to persist. At the same time as the world is becoming again multipolar, the multilateral order is eroding, whether it is the global trade system, the UN-led collective security system, the European security order, the nuclear non-proliferation and arms control regimes – all of which are critical for France's prosperity and security. Among liberal democracies, nationalist and/or populist parties are pushing for refocusing politics onto the domestic front and fuel Euroscepticism, often with an exclusive understanding of national identity. This erodes the political cohesion among liberal democracies. The Brexit referendum campaign in the United Kingdom and the Trump administration in the United States are cases in point. Questions on the future of the relationship with the United States and with the United Kingdom, as well as NATO's role, will be at the forefront of strategic considerations in Paris. Similarly, the longer-term relationship between Europe and Russia still has to be defined, in a way that France – who has tended to pursue an approach open to dialogue – will be unable to achieve on its own.

In this context of an existential crisis for Europe and more generally for Western democracies, transnational and homegrown Islamist terrorism (but also, increasingly, far-right terrorism) are likely to remain persistent threats and the top priority for French governments in the coming years. Whether maintaining Sentinelle will be desirable, considering its financial cost, its limited strategic achievements, and its consequences on the morale of French troops, is debatable. Similarly, France's strategy in the Sahel may need to be rethought; as the local security situation worsens, the United States risks withdrawing its troops, European support remains limited, and the governance reforms of regional partners are making only slow, if any, progress.

Meanwhile, the continuous rise of China and the fast pace of technological advances in information and communication technologies pose challenges to the world order in terms of its rules (as individual freedoms are at stake), of its strategic stability (as the United States is preparing for "great power competition"), and of Europe's place in that coming order. From a military angle, we are witnessing the end of the hitherto undisputed Western air supremacy; cyberspace and space are now well established as military domains, and physical attacks against satellites are now possible. These recent technological changes, just like those that lie

Conclusion   163

ahead, will challenge France and her allies' ability to maintain a competitive edge and will require adaptations to existing international normative frameworks – or their creation. Cyberspace and space are neither civilian nor military domains, just like the climate and global commons, which, with the opening up of sea routes in the Arctic and the potential for climate-driven migrations, will become increasingly critical issues. The key for France will be to work with European partners to ensure that they do not collectively lag behind technologically, but also that they are key players in shaping the norms and rules that frame these domains.

Index

Note: page references in **bold** indicate tables; *italics* indicate figures; 'n' indicates chapter notes.

A400M aircraft 39, 49, 84, 96
Aachen Treaty 143
Aérospatiale 55, 85, 87
Afghanistan 17, 27, 28, 29, 37, 40, 91,
98, 99, 107, 117–120, 138, 142–143,
144, 145
Africa 6; military operations (1991–)
107–108, 123–126, **124**; partnerships in
134–135, 141, 143, 146, 148–150; *see*
also colonies, former; *specific countries*
Agence des Participations de l'État
(APE) 86
AI *see* artificial intelligence (AI)
Airbus **86**, 87, 88, 95–96, 145
air force: industry and procurement 84–87,
86, 92–94, 96–98, 100–101; military
operations (1991–) 116, 118–119, 121,
122–123; modernisation of 36, **36**, **39**,
47–49, 50; partnerships 145; soldiers 22
Albion Plateau 56, 57
Alcatel-Alstom 87
Algeria 4, 24, 55
Algerian War 13, 14, 16, 18, 19, 25, 36
allies/alliances *see* partners/partnerships
Anglo-French Defence Research Group 64
Anrig, C. 47–48
antimilitarism 20, 30n2
Antonov aircraft 98
APE *see Agence des Participations de*
l'État (APE)
Arab countries *see* Middle East; *specific*
countries
Arab Spring 120
"arc of crises" 38
armed forces 9, 33–51; within
contemporary French society 26–30;

first reforms 33–35, **34**; future of
49–51; modernisation of 44–49;
professionalisation of 34, 35–40, **36**, *38*,
39, 44; soldiers 22–26, *23*; stabilisation
of 40–43; *see also* air force; army;
cybersecurity; navy; space
Armoured Army Corps 36
arms industry *see* defence industry and
procurement
army: changes and structure of **36**, **39**,
44–46; military operations (1991–) 109,
122, 126
Arquus **86**, 92
artificial intelligence (AI) 48–49, 92
Ashton, Catherine 135
Asia-Pacific region 42, 150–151; *see also*
colonies, former; *specific countries*
Australia 100, 150
autonomy, strategic 4, 6–7, 9, 33, 55, 63,
67, 75, 81, 82, 85, 93, 108, 116, 133

Balkans 27, 33, 110–112, 115, 133, 134,
138, 139, 157
Balladur government 34
Baltics 126
Balzacq, Thierry 8
Belgium 95, 100, 135, 145–146
Bérégovoy government 34
Berlin Plus agreement 134
Blair government (UK) 133
Boeing 87
BPI France 87
Brazil 100
Brustlein, C. 56
Burkina Faso 150
Bush, George W., administration 71

166   Index

C-130 aircraft 98
Cameroon 6
Catholicism 18–19, 24, 26
CEA *see* Commission for Atomic Energy
 (*Commissariat à l'Énergie Atomique*,
 CEA)
CEMA *see* chief of the joint staff (*Chef
 d'État-Major des Armeés*, CEMA)
Central African Republic (CAR) 29,
 145, 150
Central Army Group (CENTAG) 5
Chad 6, 125, 149, 150
Charbonneau, Bruno 123
Charette, Hervé de 133
Charles de Gaulle aircraft carrier 47, 118,
 121, 127
Charlie Hebdo attacks 28, 126
chemical/biological warfare 42
Chequers Declaration 64–65
chief of the joint staff (*Chef d'État-Major
 des Armeés*, CEMA) 1, 17–18, 19, 34,
 42, 60, 62–63
China 42, 49, 54, 58, 69, 80, 82, 97, 99,
 113, 150, 162
Chirac presidency: and the armed forces
 34, 35, 36, 37, 44; defence institutions
 and civil-military relations 13; and
 French partnerships 133, 134, 138,
 139–140, 142; and French power 159;
 military operations (1991–) 110–111,
 114–115, 116, 118; nuclear deterrence
 57, 58, 61, 64–65, 66–67
Chocolate Summit 134
civil-military relations 1, 9, 13–30,
 113–114, 127, 159–160
climate change 163
Clinton administration 64, 114–115
coalition warfare 107–108, 113, 114–123
colonies, former 4, 6, 25, 123–126, **124**,
 148–150, 160–161
Combined Joint Expeditionary Force
 (CJEF) 144
Commission for Atomic Energy
 (*Commissariat à l'Énergie Atomique*,
 CEA) 55, 58, 62, 87
Comprehensive Nuclear Test Ban Treaty
 (CTBT) 54, 58, 69
Congo 134
conscription 13, 19–22, 24, 33, 34,
 35, 109; *see also* armed forces,
 professionalisation of
Cordesman, A.H. 109
Cornu, C. 95

COVID-19 pandemic 1, 43, 97, 127
Crimea 66, 101, 141
CSF 87
CTBT *see* Comprehensive Nuclear Test
 Ban Treaty (CTBT)
cybersecurity/cyberspace 42, 49–51, 93,
 98, 162–163

Daho, G. 18
Dassault 55, 85, 86, **86**, 87, 88, 145
DCN 87
DCNS 85
Defence and National Security Strategic
 Review (2017) 1–2
Defence and Security Council 15–16
defence industry and procurement 9,
 80–101; arms exports 81–85, 88–91,
 98–101, 157; budgets and spending 2,
 33, 35, 37–39, *38*, **39**, 41–43, 45–46, 51,
 81–84, *83*, 157, 161; Europeanisation
 of 93–98, *96*; and French power 160;
 grands programmes and technological
 innovation 90–93; nuclear deterrence
 55, 62, 65, 70–73; partnerships 134,
 135–136, 144, 146; structures and main
 producers 85–90, **86**
defence institutions 8, 13–30; decision-
 making within 13–19; *see also* armed
 forces; chief of the joint staff (*Chef
 d'État-Major des Armeés*, CEMA)
defence policy 1–10, 156–163; during the
 Cold War 3–7; evolution of 158–162;
 future of 162–163; strategic changes and
 challenges 157–158
Defence Space Strategy (2019) 49
defence technology and industrial
 base (DTIB) 81–82, 87, 89, 95,
 99, 101
DefInvest 86–87
De Gaulle presidency 3–5, 18, 20, 34, 36,
 64, 68, 85, 88, 137
democracy 2, 162
Desportes, General 73
DeVore, M. 108–109
Directorate General of Armaments
 (*Direction Générale de l'Armement*,
 DGA) 55, 58, 62, 84, 86, 87–90,
 99, 101
Disclose 101
diversity 13, 25–26
Djibouti 149
domestic security 46, 130
drones 46, 93, 98

DTIB *see* defence technology and industrial base (DTIB)
Dyson, T. 90

EDA *see* European Defence Agency (EDA)
EDC *see* European Defence Community (EDC)
Egypt 100
Elysée Treaty of Friendship and Reconciliation 142
"epic identity" 28–30
ESDI *see* European Security and Defence Identity (ESDI)
Estonia 91, 126, 141
Eurocorps 146
Europe: defence industry and procurement 80, 81, 85, 87, 91, 93–98, *96*, 100; and French power 161–162; nuclear deterrence 64–68, 72, 74–75; *see also* European Union (EU); *specific countries*
European aeronautic defence and space group (EADS) 87
European Defence Agency (EDA) 94, 102n3, 133
European Defence Community (EDC) 131
European Defence Fund (EDF) 97, 136
European Intervention Initiative (EI2) 146
European Security and Defence Identity (ESDI) 134
European Union (EU): Common Foreign and Security Policy (CFSP) 132; Common Security and Defence Policy (CSDP) 130, 131–136; Defence and Security Procurement Directive (Directive 2009/81/EC) 135–136; defence industry and procurement 95, 97–98, 101; France's role within 130, 131–137; and the French armed forces 42, 44; and French power 161–162; military operations (1991–) 125; nuclear deterrence 54, 66–68, 69, 74–75; Permanent Structured Cooperation (PESCO) 97–98, 136–137; *see also* Europe; *specific countries*
Euroscepticism 162

Faure, S. 90
Figaro, Le 18, 40
financial crisis (2008) 83, 84, 99, 135, 145, 161
Finland 146
Finnemore, M. 125

Fleurant, A.-E. 81
Foucault, M. 84
French Polynesia 55, 58, 69, 150
Futuna 150
Future Combat Air System (*Système de Combat Aérien du Futur*, FCAS/SCAF) 48, 145

Gabon 6, 149
Gallois, General Pierre-Marie 4
Gautier, L. 54, 59
gender *see* women
General Review of Public Policies (*Révision Générale des Politiques Publiques*, RGPP) 37, 39
Georgelin, J.-L. 60
Germany: defence industry and procurement 87, 90, 91, 94–96, 98, 99; and French armed forces 34, 48; military operations (1991–) 116, 117–118, 125, 126; nuclear deterrence 54, 57, 67–68, 69; partnership with 130, 133, 135, 136, 137, 140, 142–144, 146; reunification 7–8
Ghana 113
GIAT 87, 91
Girardet, Raoul 19
grand strategy 2–4, 8–9, 108, 127, 156, 161
Griffon 100
Groupe Surcouf 40
Guisnel, Jean 22, 38
Gulf War 17, 33–34, 47–48, 108–109, 137, 157

Hadès program 56–57
Helios satellite 49, 58
Hollande presidency: and the armed forces 40–41; defence industry and procurement 93, 101; defence institutions and civil-military relations 17; and French partnerships 136, 141, 147–148, 150; and French power 159; military operations (1991–) 118, 120, 122; nuclear deterrence 66, 71, 74
Houlahan, T. 109
Howorth, Jolyon 132
humanitarian activities 28, 112–113, 124, 132, 150

Implementation Force (IFOR) 111–112
independence *see* national independence
India 61, 68, 70, 71, 100, 113, 150

168   *Index*

Indochina War 85
Indonesia 150
institutions *see* defence institutions
International Campaign to Abolish Nuclear
  Weapons (ICAN) 54, 72, 74, 75
International Security Assistance Force
  (ISAF) 117–118
interventions *see* military operations:
  interventions
Iran 54, 61, 69
Iraq 28, 41, 68, 99, 108, 117, 122–123,
  135, 138, 142, 145, 147, 148, 159
ISAF *see* International Security Assistance
  Force (ISAF)
Islamic State/ISIS 28, 41, 122, 148
Israel 68, 113
Italy 85, 88, 94, 95–96, 116, 135, 145–146
Ivory Coast 6, 29, 125, 149

Japan 150
Jaurès, J. 21
Joana, Jean 89
Jobert, Michel 98
Joint Comprehensive Plan of Action
  (JCPOA, Iran nuclear deal) 54, 69
Joint Nuclear Commission (Franco-British
  Joint Commission on Nuclear Policy
  and Doctrine) 64, 65
Jospin government 36–37, 115–116, 117
Juppé, Alain 67, 76n3, 140
Jurgensen, C. 71

King, Anthony 33
Kosovo 91, 107, 114–117, 138
Kosovo Force (KFOR) 112
Krauss-Maffei (KMW) 102n1
Kuwait 100
Kyrgyzstan 119

Lafayette Committee 148
Lancaster House Treaty 65, 144, 145
Land Logistic Force 36
Laval, P.-F. 68
Lebanon 91, 113–114, 146
Leboeuf, Aline 150
Leclerc main battle tank (MBT) 91–92
Le Drian, J.-Y. 70
Lefebvre, Admiral 22
Lewis, J.G. 63
Libya 28, 40, 120–122, 140–141, 144,
  147, 159
Lithuania 126
Lockheed Martin 87

LPM *see* Military Programming Law (*Loi
  de Programmation Militaire*, LPM)
Luxembourg 135, 145, 146
Lyautey, General 18

M51 missiles 72–73
Macron presidency 1; and the armed
  forces 41, 43; defence industry and
  procurement 101; defence institutions
  and civil-military relations 19; and
  French partnerships 136, 141, 143,
  146, 148, 150; and French power 159;
  nuclear deterrence 67, 72, 75
Maghrebi heritage 25
Major government (UK) 64–65
Malaysia 100
Mali 107, 143, 145, 147, 149–150; Operation
  Serval 17, 29, 40–41, 108, 125, 150
Mallet, Jean-Claude 38
Matra 85, 87
Mauriac, François 7
Mauritania 150
McLeod, A. 116
MDBA **86**, 87, 96
media coverage 5, 27–30
Mediterranean region 121, 141, 146
Mérand, Frédéric 142
Merkel chancellorship 143
Middle East 69, 71, 98, 101, 108, 120,
  157; *see also specific countries*
military operations (1991–) 9, 107–127;
  Africa 123–126, **124**; coalition warfare
  107–108, 113, 114–123; Gulf War
  17, 33–34, 47–48, 108–109, 137, 157;
  interventions 6, 7, 16–17, 27–29, 30, 35,
  40, 48, 80, 107–108, 122, **124**, 125, 130,
  138–140, 144, 157–160; peacekeeping
  29, 108, 110–114, 132, 134, 138; political
  and diplomatic contingencies 126–127
Military Programming Law (*Loi de
  Programmation Militaire*, LPM): 1989
  34; 1997–2002 36–37; 2003–2008 37;
  2009-2014 37, 39, **39**; 2014–2019 41,
  73, 83–84; 2019–2025 43, 51, 72
Mirage aircraft 59, 100
Mitterrand presidency 7; and the armed
  forces 33, 34, 37; defence institutions
  and civil-military relations 16; and
  French partnerships 131, 132, 137,
  142, 149; and French power 158–159;
  military operations (1991–) 108–110,
  112; nuclear deterrence 56–58, 59,
  66–67, 73

national independence 63, 64, 81, 82, 85, 90, 94, 101, 130, 160
National Strategy for Cyber Defence (2018) 50
NATO (North Atlantic Treaty Organization): and defence industry and procurement 91; France's role within 3–4, 8, 130, 131–135, 137–141, 143, 147, 162; and the French armed forces 33, 37, 44; and French power 159, 162; High Readiness Force (HRF) 138; military operations (1991–) 107, 110, 114–118, 121, 126–127; and nuclear deterrence 56, 65–68, 75; Response Force (NRF) 138–139
Naval Group **86**, 88, 100
navy: changes and structures of 36, **36**, **39**, 46–47; industry and procurement 82, 85, **86**, 93, 100; military operations (1991–) 109, 120–121, 122, 126
Netherlands 95–96, 145
New Caledonia 150
New Public Management 37, 89
New Zealand 150
Nexter 86, **86**, 91, 92, 102n1
NH90 helicopters 95–96, 100
Niger 150
9/11 attacks 37, 38, 61, 71, 117, 138, 141, 147
Non-Proliferation Treaty (NPT) 54, 59, 68, 69, 70, 74
North Atlantic Treaty Organization *see* NATO
North Korea 42, 54, 61
nuclear deterrence 2, 4, 7, 9, 54–75, 157; alliance dimension 63–68; and the armed forces 33, **34**, 36, 42, 43, 47, 50; arms control and disarmament 70–72; changes to nuclear capabilities 57–59; decision-making 14–15, 30n1; defence industry and procurement 87, 88, 93, 94; doctrine 59–61; and French power 158, 160; institutions and decision-making powers 61–63; and military operations (1991–) 111; modernisation of 72–75; non-proliferation 68–69; origins of 55–57
Nuclear Planning Group (NPG) 65
nuclear submarines (SSBNs) 56, 57, 59, 63, 72–73
nuclear testing 54, 55, 57–58, 63–65, 67–71, 74, 75
Nuclear Weapons Council (*Conseil des Armements Nucléaires*) 62

Obama administration 74, 75, 147–148
O'Donnell, Clara 133
OOCAr *see Organisation Conjointe de Coopération en Matière d'Armement* (OOCAr)
Operation Artemis 134
Operation Barkhane 28, 29, 41, 91, 108, 150
Operation Chammal 122
Operation Inherent Resolve 122
Operation Sentinelle 30, 126, 162
Operation Serval 17, 29, 40–41, 108, 125, 150
operations *see* military operations (1991–)
Operation Unified Protector 121
Organisation Conjointe de Coopération en Matière d'Armement (OOCAr) 94–95

Pakistan 42, 70, 71, 112, 119
Parly, Florence 1, 22–23, 50, 101, 127
partners/partnerships 10, 130–151; bilateral relations 142–151; EU defence and strategic policy 130, 131–137; and French power 161; future of 163; NATO 130, 131–135, 137–141, 143, 147; *see also* coalition warfare
peace dividends 33
peacekeeping 29, 108, 110–114, 132, 134, 138
peacetime military justice 20
PESCO *see* European Union (EU), Permanent Structured Cooperation (PESCO)
Poland 135
policy *see* defence policy
Pompidou, Georges 5
Pouponneau, F. 69–70
Powell, Nathaniel 124–125
power 2, 10, 55, 73, 92, 100, 125–126, 127, 158–162
privatization 85–87, **86**
procurement *see* defence industry and procurement
Provincial Reconstruction Teams (PRTs) 118, 119
public relations *see* civil-military relations; media coverage

Qadhafi, Muammar 121
Qatar 100
Quéau, Y. 81
Quénot-Suarez, Helene 150
Quilès, P. 74

170 Index

Rafale aircraft 1, 39, 47, 48, 59, 61, 73, 93, 100
Rainbow Warrior 63
Rapid Action Force 36
Rapid Reaction Force (RRF) 111
Raytheon 87
R&D *see* research and development
Reagan administration 49
Reapers 98
Renault Trucks Defence 92, 102n2
republican mythology 20–21, 24
research and development (R&D) 82, 91, 92, 93, 97, 101
Research and Technology (R&T) 88, 89, 101
Riecker, P. 140
Rieker, Pernille 8
robots 93
Rocard, Michel 74
RRF *see* Rapid Reaction Force (RRF)
R&T *see* Research and Technology (R&T)
Russia 5, 7; and the French armed forces 41, 42; and French defence industry and procurement 82, 98–99, 101; and French military operations (1991–) 115–116, 126; and French partnerships 141, 143, 148; nuclear deterrence 54, 55, 57–58, 66, 69
Rwanda 28, 125

S3 missiles 56
Sadowa, Battle of 21
Safran (ex-Sagem) 85, **86**, 87, 88, 90
Sahel 107, 108, 126, 127, 146, 147, 162; Operation Barkhane 28, 29, 41, 91, 108, 150
Saint Malo declaration 133, 144
Sarkozy presidency: and the armed forces 37, 40; defence industry and procurement 96–97, 99, 101; and French partnerships 138, 140, 147, 149; and French power 159; military operations (1991–) 118–119; nuclear deterrence 57
satellites *see* space
Saudi Arabia 100–101, 108
Schröder chancellorship 142
Scorpion 45–46, 92–93
Senegal 125, 149
Sentinelle (operation) 30, 126, 162
SFOR *see* Stabilisation Force (SFOR)
Shurkin, Michael 107
Simulation program 57, 58
Singapore 100, 150

SLBMs *see* submarine launched ballistic missiles (SLBMs)
SNECMA 87
socialism 21
Société Nationale des Poudres et Explosifs (SNPE) 87
soldiers 22–28, *23*
Somalia 112–113
South Korea 151
Soutou, G.-H. 68
space 42, 49–51, 58, 162–163
Spain 48, 85, 91, 95, 100, 135, 145, 146
Special Forces (SF) 119, 122
SSBNs *see* nuclear submarines (SSBNs)
Stabilisation Force (SFOR) 111–112
Strategic Air Force 56, 63
Strategic Oceanic Force 63
Strategic Review of Defence and National Security (2017) 41–42
submarine launched ballistic missiles (SLBMs) 73
Suez crisis 137
Sweden 146
SYDEREC (*Système de Dernier Recours*) 63
Syria 28, 41, 42, 122–123, 141, 145, 147, 148

Taiwan 100
Tajikistan 119
Task Force La Fayette 120
technology 64–65, 80–81, 82, 90–93, 97, 157–158, 162
terrorism 14, 28, 35, 38, 41, 46, 60, 61, 72, 122, 126, 138, 141, 147, 148, 157, 159, 162
Tertrais, B. 63
Teutates program 65
Thales **86**, 88, 90, 92
Thiéblemont, André 111
Thomson-CSF 55, 85, 87, 99
threat perception 3, 33, **34**, 35, 41, 44, 71–73, 156–157, 162
Tiger helicopter 95, 98
Trump administration 69, 141, 148, 162
Tunisia 24
Turkey 141

Ukraine 41, 54, 71, 91, 98, 101, 141, 148
UN *see* United Nations (UN)
UNIFIL I and II *see* United Nations Interim Force in Lebanon I and II (UNIFIL I and II)

Index 171

UNITAF *see* United Task Force
  (UNITAF)
United Arab Emirates (UAE) 91, 100, 101,
  118, 149
United Kingdom: Brexit 136, 145, 162;
  defence industry and procurement 50,
  82, 84, 85, 88, 90, 91, 94–95, 96, 98,
  99; and French power 159, 161; military
  operations (1991–) 116, 121, 126;
  nuclear deterrence 54, 59, 64–67, 69, 73,
  74, 75; partnership with 133, 135, 136,
  137, 140, 144–145, 146
United Nations (UN) 54, 108–109
United Nations Interim Force in Lebanon I
  and II (UNIFIL I and II) 113–114
United Nations Operations in Somalia I
  and II (UNSOM I and II) 112
United Nations Protection Force
  (UNPROFOR) 110–112
United Nations Security Council (UNSC)
  115, 122
United States of America 8; defence
  industry and procurement 80–81, 82,
  85, 91, 97, 98–99, 100; and the French
  armed forces 44–45, 50; and French
  power 159, 162; and future French
  defence policy 162; military operations
  (1991–) 108, 114–121; nuclear
  deterrence 54, 55, 57–58, 64, 65, 68,
  69, 71, 73, 75; partnership with 135,
  137–138, 140, 146–148

United Task Force (UNITAF) 112
unmanned vehicles/systems 48, 92, 93,
  98, 145
UNSC *see* United Nations Security
  Council (UNSC)
UNSOM I and II *see* United National
  Operations in Somalia I and II (UNSOM
  I and II)

Védrine, Hubert 70, 115–116, 140, 147
Vietnam 150
Vigipirate plan 126
Villiers, General Pierre de 19

Wagner, A.R. 109
Wallis 150
Western European Armaments Group
  (WEAG) 94
Western European Union (WEU)
  131, 133
white papers: 1972 59, 60, 63–64; 1994
  34, 34–35, 49, 59, 60, 93–94, 132,
  133, 147, 158; 2008 37–40, 59, 60,
  93, 135, 140, 157; 2013 46, 59, 81;
  2017 59
women 13, 22–24, *23*

Yemen 100–101
Yost, D. 67

Zajec, Olivier 107